# A GUIDE TO LITERARY
# CRITICISM AND RESEARCH

# A GUIDE TO LITERARY CRITICISM AND RESEARCH
## Third Edition

**Bonnie Klomp Stevens**
*Augustana College*

**Larry L. Stewart**
*The College of Wooster*

**Harcourt Brace College Publishers**

Fort Worth   Philadelphia   San Diego   New York   Orlando   Austin   San Antonio
Toronto   Montreal   London   Sydney   Tokyo

| | |
|---|---|
| Publisher | Ted Buchholz |
| Editor in Chief | Christopher P. Klein |
| Executive Editor | Michael Rosenberg |
| Assistant Editor | Tina Winslow |
| Senior Project Editor | Angela Williams |
| Production Manager | Serena Barnett Manning |
| Senior Art Director | Don Fujimoto |

Requests for permission to make copies of any part of the work should be mailed to: Permissions Department, Harcourt Brace & Company, 6277 Sea Harbor Drive, Orlando, FL 32887-6777.

Portions of this work were published in previous editions.

*Address for Editorial Correspondence*
Harcourt Brace College Publishers, 301 Commerce Street, Suite 3700, Fort Worth, TX 76102

*Address for Orders*
Harcourt Brace & Company, 6277 Sea Harbor Drive, Orlando, FL 32887
1-800-782-4479, or 1-800-433-0001 (in Florida)

ISBN: 0-15-501987-2

Library of Congress Catalog Number: 95-80803

Printed in the United States of America

5 6 7 8 9 0 1 2 3 4   066   10 9 8 7 6 5 4 3 2 1

*For Carol Stewart and Dennis Stevens*

# PREFACE

Those familiar with earlier editions of *A Guide to Literary Criticism and Research* will find that this third edition features a number of significant changes and additions.

- In Part 1, "Critical Approaches to Literature," we have revised and, in some cases, substantially expanded and reorganized the discussions of the thirteen approaches considered. To make information easier to locate, we have increased the number of subheadings. We have also brought up to date the list of "Works Cited and Recommended" at the end of each section.
- In Part 2, we have added sample student paragraphs to Chapter 4 ("Elements of Critical Essays") to illustrate ways of approaching such tasks as introducing a thesis, summarizing and refuting another critic's argument, and concluding an essay.
- Also in Part 2, we have completely rewritten Chapter 5 ("Methods of Literary Research") to give much fuller treatment to the various electronic resources that have become increasingly important in literary research.
- In Appendix A ("Literary Research: Some Basic Resources"), we have added several new sources and brought all the listings up to date.
- In Appendix B ("Some Advice on Form"), we have made several changes, in response to changes in the fourth edition of the *MLA Handbook for Writers of Research Papers.*
- In Appendix C ("Some Guidelines on Documentation"), we have increased the number of sample citation entries to illustrate ways of documenting a wider variety of sources, including ones obtained through access to CD-ROM or online services.
- We have added a new appendix ("A Glossary of Critical Terms"), which includes definitions both of terms used in this book and of some others that students may encounter while reading contemporary criticism.

In making these changes and additions, we have been guided by reviewers' comments and by the suggestions of teachers and students who used the first two editions of the book. All of these comments and suggestions have, we think, helped us to more fully realize our original goal of preparing a concise but reasonably comprehensive guide.

Like the first two editions of *A Guide to Literary Criticism and Research,* this edition is based both on a recognition of a practical need felt in many literature courses and on a view of literary study. It attempts to meet the practical need by offering upper-level students a condensed but adequate guide to the range of modern literary criticism and to basic methods of research. In addition, we hope the book will give students a more comprehensive view of literary study by helping them to recognize criticism and research as two closely linked parts of a single process.

Our experience, shared by colleagues with whom we have spoken, is that even good students in well-designed literature programs frequently enter upper-level courses with only vague notions of the purpose and nature of literary criticism and little grounding in the writing of a thoroughly researched critical essay, a fact hardly surprising given the many demands on the curriculum in literature. Introductory courses perform an admirable service if they teach the fundamental skills necessary for a sensitive reading of drama, poetry, and prose fiction and if they acquaint students with a basic knowledge of literary history. Upper-level courses may consider in depth certain periods, genres, authors, or problems in literature, but they often leave discussion of critical approaches and detailed instruction in research to courses specifically devoted to those subjects, courses which, if taken at all, may come near the end of the student's undergraduate career or at the beginning of graduate study. Thus, at best, many students are unaware of the rich diversity of critical approaches and the various possibilities for intriguing research available to them; they are cut off from exciting recent developments in literary study. At worst, some students are unfamiliar with and suspicious of any critical approach except the formalist one favored in many introductory courses, and their only experience in research is a term paper in freshman composition.

This book is no panacea; it is not a substitute for courses in literary criticism and research or for years of study and reflection. However, the book does give students access to current literary criticism and scholarship, and it provides a context for their own reading and writing. Also, it should free teachers from spending inordinate amounts of time explaining the assumptions behind recent critical approaches and giving instruction in research techniques—instruction which, if repeated in every class calling for a critical research essay, will be redundant for some students though necessary for others.

By bringing together in one volume the information students need to read and write documented critical essays—information about critical approaches, about the composition of critical essays, about research methods, and about form and documentation—this book encourages an integrated understanding of literary study as a whole. It aims to show students that papers about literature, whether written by the professional critic or the beginning researcher, are attempts to share insights and perspectives—insights based on certain assumptions and methodologies, informed by solid research, and communicated clearly and with attention to the conventions of form and documentation. No other book, as far as we know, contains such information in a single volume or provides this integrated approach.

The goal of Part 1 is to familiarize students with the main contemporary approaches to literature. The premise is that all critical and scholarly approaches share a fundamental aim: to add to an understanding of literature by applying certain knowledge or insight. Thus, approaches are grouped accord-ing to the main source of the insights, the field or area from which they come. We begin with approaches that elicit insights from the study of literary works themselves. Formalist studies, for example, depend on a knowledge of literary elements such as character, plot, and image, and genre studes depend on a knowledge of particular literary forms. In each case, the knowledge has been derived from a study of literary works and is applied to literary works. Other studies, however, bring insight not simply from a study of literary texts but also from a body of knowledge concerning the history, composition, and develop-ment of literature. Studies in literary history and biography, even when not di-rected toward specific literary texts, are traditional approaches which add to the understanding of literature. Still other studies have as a main source of knowledge fields outside of literature. For instance, psychological studies obvi-ously depend on a knowledge of psychology, and feminist studies depend on new insights from a number of areas such as sociology, psychology, and his-tory. We believe our classification both reflects current critical practice and gives students a way to see relationships among approaches, but we stress that any classification is somewhat arbitrary and represents only one perspective. Few studies are purely of a single kind, and there is inevitably some overlap-ping from one approach to another.

Each chapter in Part 1 defines a particular approach and, through exam-ples, describes the main lines of its development. The discussions conclude with brief, representative lists of important works. Depending on the ap-proach, the lists include seminal works in the field, theoretical discussions, major critical applications, and periodicals in which students may find exam-ples of the approach. Throughout, we remind students of the obvious: that the reading of a dozen pages will not turn them into archetypal or structuralist or biographical critics. It should, however, give them the background to read criti-cal books and articles with a greater awareness of their particular assumptions and aims; and for students who become interested in specific approaches and are willing to do reading of the kind recommended, the book will provide a good start for their own writing.

One caution is necessary here. We do not, on the one hand, attempt to me-diate among critical approaches or, on the other, try to establish any one ap-proach as privileged. Clearly, certain approaches are incompatible with others, and the assumptions of one may contradict those of another. Therefore, we make no synthesis nor do we urge students to adopt some kind of integrated pluralism. Rather, we try to explain each approach in its own terms and to give students as clear and comprehensive a view of contemporary criticism as is possible within the limits of a short text.

Part 2, on elements of the critical essay, attempts to give students a sound basis for their own writing by describing features shared by most effective papers on literature, regardless of the specific approach. We begin with a brief discussion about arriving at and using an approach, then illustrate common organizational and structural elements of critical essays, and conclude with remarks on the language and style of critical writing. Certainly, no formula exists for the composition of a successful critical essay. However, by drawing examples from works of professional criticism and from several student essays, we try to show that most writers face common problems and that many use common techniques and strategies. Chapter 4 does not tell students what they should do but allows them to make decisions based on a recognition of the practice of professionals in the field. The chapter also points out the similarities of critical essays to kinds of essays with which they may be more familiar.

Chapter 5, on methods of literary research, emphasizes the nature and importance of literary research, stressing the interdependence of research and criticism and the ways in which each guides and informs the other. The explanation of research methods is organized around a simple but workable search strategy consisting of four stages—planning, preliminary reading, working with reference materials, and locating secondary sources. Throughout the chapter, we attempt to impress upon students the need for care and thoroughness while assuring them that research is not an impossibly difficult task.

Recognizing the unevenness of student preparation, we assume some of our readers know very little about reference tools and may never before have attempted an extensive library search, at least one on a literary subject. We have been guided by experiences with students such as the intelligent M.A. candidate who read literature with considerable insight but concluded that no criticism had ever been written about *The Seafarer* because she could find no references to that work in the *Reader's Guide*. Thus, we include quick definitions even of basic terms; and although we generally try to keep our explanations brief, we give fairly detailed directions about matters that often confuse inexperienced researchers (for example, using the *MLA Bibliography*). Since we assume many of our readers will be unfamiliar with specialized reference tools, we mention a number of these in our chapter and then give fuller descriptions in the annotated bibliography that follows.

Appendices B and C, addressed directly to the student, offer advice on basic but crucial and frequently troublesome matters of form and documentation. Appendix B, on form, does not attempt to cover all the grammatical and mechanical problems which may arise but concentrates instead on those likely to cause difficulty for competent writers facing for the first time the special challenges of writing critical research papers. Because problems with quotations are so common—and, often, so damaging to a paper's content, as well as to its style and correctness—the first and longest section of this chapter is devoted to discussing the art and mechanics of quotation. Matters such as tense, punctuating titles, and manuscript form are handled more briefly. Students who have problems with grammar and mechanics in general will need to supplement this appendix with a more comprehensive handbook.

Appendix C, on documentation, briefly explains the purpose, logic, and importance of documentation; defines and warns against plagiarism; outlines the basic formats of notes and bibliography entries; and gives examples of notes and entries for various kinds of works. Although we remind students to consult the *MLA Handbook* for further details, the appendix is added as a convenience and should answer many questions about documentation. The discussion on plagiarism is included at the suggestion of reviewers who commented, correctly we believe, that even fairly sophisticated students are sometimes uncertain when documentation is necessary.

Appendix D, "A Glossary of Critical Terms," was added because several colleagues and reviewers commented that many students are confused by the increasingly specialized vocabulary they encounter while reading criticism and would find a quick reference source helpful. The glossary does not attempt to define longstanding literary terms but instead focuses sharply on the language of contemporary criticism. Thus, *lexie* is included in the glossary, but *lyric* is not.

Individual instructors will doubtless find their own uses for *A Guide to Literary Criticism and Research*. We think it could appropriately be used as a primary text in seminars in criticism and research, as supplementary reading in intermediate- and upper-level literature courses, and as a reference book for students doing independent study. In some courses, professors might make the entire text required reading, while in others they might encourage students to read only those sections most relevant to their particular interests and problems; in some courses, professors might devote class time to a discussion of this text, while in others they might make students responsible for reading the text on their own and asking questions about any matters that remain unclear. However the text is used, we hope that its integrated approach will help students to understand literary study and to see the relationship of their own writing to that of critics and scholars in the field. Both in the subjects we have covered and in the style we have adopted, we have tried to make this text truly helpful to students at any level who are attempting literary scholarship for the first time.

A final note about the book's style and tone should be added. We have attempted to make the main chapters descriptive rather than prescriptive for several reasons. First, a prescriptive approach might well seem patronizing, especially to sophisticated students. Second, the descriptive approach best reflects our own view of literary study as a collegial activity and our desire for a book that will allow students to see themselves as partners in that activity. Finally, we do not believe there exists a single method of criticism, of writing, or of research; and, therefore, we do not wish to tell students what they should do but hope to give them a basis for making their own decisions. The best any of us can do is to understand current practices and successful strategies and then to determine our own procedures. On the other hand, the appendices on form and documentation are more directive and prescriptive in tone, simply because they deal largely with matters governed by accepted conventions or rules.

Several people at Harcourt Brace College Publishers have made invaluable contributions to this edition. We both feel very grateful for the support and guidance of Michael Rosenberg, executive editor; Tina Winslow, assistant editor for English; and Angela Williams, senior project editor. Serena Barnett Manning, production manager, and Don Fujimoto, senior art director, were also appreciated parts of the production team. We also thank the reviewers who helped us shape and revise this text: Edward M. Griffin, University of Minnesota; David Rota, University of Missouri–St. Louis; Nancy Cook, University of Montana; and Darryl L. Tippens, Abilene Christian University. In addition, a number of our colleagues have contributed to this book by reading portions of the manuscript and offering suggestions. Ann Smith, chief reference librarian at Augustana College, was especially generous with her time and expertise, helping to reshape the chapter on literary research and making important contributions to the appendices on resources and documentation. We are also particularly indebted to Lowell Coolidge, Thomas Falkner, and Constance Perry. All of these people added to the strengths of this book but must not be held responsible for its weaknesses.

And finally, we are grateful to our families for their generous encouragement and advice: Esther and Norman Anderson; Dennis, Sarah, and Rachel Stevens; Carol, Greg, and Laurel Stewart; and Ray and Hilda Stewart.

# CONTENTS

*Introduction*    *1*

## PART 1
## Critical Approaches to Literature    5

*Chapter 1*
### THE INSIGHT OF LITERATURE    9

Formalist Studies and the New Criticism    10
Genre Studies    19
Rhetorical Studies and Reader-Response Criticism    25
Structuralist and Deconstructionist Studies    33

*Chapter 2*
### THE INSIGHT OF LITERARY HISTORY    46

Historical Studies and the New Historicism    47
Biographical Studies    56
Studies of the Literary Tradition    61

*Chapter 3*
### THE INSIGHT OF OTHER FIELDS    67

Moral and Religious Studies    69
Sociological and Political Studies    74
Feminist Studies    82
Ethnic and Minority Studies    93
Archetypal Studies    100
Psychological Studies    106

## PART 2
## The Critical Essay    113

*Chapter 4*
### ELEMENTS OF CRITICAL ESSAYS    115

The Approach    115
Structure and Organization    119
The Language of Criticism    133

## *Chapter 5*
## METHODS OF LITERARY RESEARCH    138

Planning    139
Preliminary Reading    141
Working with Reference Materials and Electronic Resources    143
Locating Secondary Materials    153

## *Appendix A*
## LITERARY RESEARCH: SOME BASIC RESOURCES    157

Works on Literary Research    157
Literary Histories: General    158
Literary Histories: Specialized    159
Bibliographies of Bibliographies    159
Bibliographies    160
Serial Bibliographies    162
Other Helpful Books    163
Journals    165

## *Appendix B*
## SOME ADVICE ON FORM    167

Quotations    167
Titles    176
Authors' Names    179
Tense    179
First-Person Pronoun    180
Manuscript Form    180

## *Appendix C*
## SOME GUIDELINES ON DOCUMENTATION    182

Proper and Improper Uses of Sources: Plagiarism    182
The Mechanics of Documentation    186
The List of Works Cited    186
Parenthetical Documentation    190
Traditional Documentation    191

## *A Glossary of Critical Terms*    *195*

## *Index*    *201*

# A Guide to Literary Criticism and Research

# INTRODUCTION

Nearly forty years ago, a book on modern literary criticism began with the observation that criticism had become increasingly specialized, "partial and fragmentary" (Hyman viii). Today, there seems an even greater sense of literary scholarship as a specialized and fragmented activity, inaccessible not only to the general public but also to many serious students of literature. Much of the work found in scholarly journals and books appears at a far remove from what is done either in the classroom or in the reader's private encounter with a literary text. This book attempts to bridge the gap by supplying the materials necessary to understand current practices of literary criticism and research and by offering a reminder that even highly technical literary studies have their origin in an individual's questions about a work of art.

In a sense, then, the true subjects of this book are fascination, curiosity, the desire to know more, and the need to share experiences and thoughts with others. Surely, most of us at some time have read a book, or perhaps seen a play or film, and been moved to read it or see it again, to find out more about its ideas or techniques, to think out our own views and opinions of it, and to talk about it with others. Probably most of us have been, in class discussions, excited by an exchange of ideas but frustrated by the lack of time to formulate our own statements and perhaps feeling we do not know quite enough to say what we want. This book views literary criticism and research as arising from these same needs and frustrations and sees literary studies, even very specialized ones, as organized ways of expanding our knowledge and sharing our ideas about literature.

Criticism and research are interdependent aspects of a single process. Knowing more about a literary work calls for the application of certain insights and knowledge. Gaining that knowledge demands research or study, whether it be study of poetic techniques or of psychology or of historical events. Intrigued by Jonathan Swift's *Gulliver's Travels* and, perhaps, feeling that it shows something important about human frailties and pretensions, a reader may want to find out more about Swift and his ideas; or the reader might wish to discover if there were other, similar satires at the time and if they were concerned with the same issues. The reader might find it useful to explore satire as a form and to determine how it usually works. He or she might want to know more about politics and society at the time Swift was writing. The possibilities are nearly limitless; but they all demand study and thought, and they are all likely to result in a reader's seeing more in *Gulliver's Travels* and thereby enjoying and appreciating it more.

The kinds of questions a person wants to ask and the procedure used to answer the questions determine an individual's approach to literary study. This book classifies critical approaches according to the field or area from which the methods and insights of the approach come. The classification has the advantage of allowing the use of the most widely recognized labels for current approaches, and it also emphasizes the common pursuit of all approaches: to bring to bear insights from certain fields in order to understand literary works more fully. Looking at approaches according to the fields from which they draw information may also avoid the sometimes misleading distinction between scholarship and criticism. There seems to be no reason to speak of a study of literary history as scholarship and a rhetorical study as criticism. Both are attempts to gain the knowledge and insights needed for a better understanding of literature. The fields from which they draw their knowledge may differ but not their rigor or their objective.

Insights about literature may come from the study of language and literature itself, the traditional focus of English studies. Obviously, any student of literature must become well acquainted with the elements of literary works. Formalist criticism deals with the techniques and forms of the individual literary text, with the text as a unified entity that can be studied and analyzed in its own terms. Genre criticism, the study of types of literary works, gains information by considering works that have similar forms. Rhetorical criticism studies the way in which literary works affect readers and the techniques through which they accomplish their purposes. Structuralist studies use a knowledge of language and linguistics to describe the structures of literary works. All these ask the reader to know literature and language well in order to understand the individual work. They assume that the knowledge of one work is built on a knowledge of many others.

Literary history is a traditional area of study and is concerned with the origin and composition of literary works. Although the field could be divided in several ways, the following are in accord with contemporary critical practice: historical studies, those studies concerned with the intellectual and social context of the time at which the work was written; biographical studies, which deal with the creator of the work; and studies of the literary tradition, which are concerned with the literary context from which the work comes. These share the assumption that a knowledge of the factors surrounding a work's composition increases our understanding of the work itself. For example, we can more fully appreciate John Milton's "Lycidas" if we know about the events and ideas of the time, if we know more about Milton himself, and if we know about the tradition of the pastoral elegy and its uses up to the time Milton wrote.

Finally, insights about literature come from the special knowledge of other fields. As literature concerns the whole life of humanity, not simply a part, so literary studies draw on all those fields that can tell us more about ourselves. Traditionally, the areas to which literary critics have looked for new insights have been religion, sociology, psychology, political science, anthropology, and philosophy. Recently, feminist studies have added a new dimension to our thinking about literature and have caused us to reassess many of our attitudes and procedures, and studies of ethnic and minority literature have called our attention to issues of particular concern to various groups. Any list of extrinsic approaches, as these are sometimes called, is limited only by the number of fields of knowledge and the possibility of their contributing to literary understanding.

Readers should not be misled by the schematic nature of the list. There are few "pure" studies, that is, studies that take one and only one approach, and there probably should not be. Certainly, the person who wants to know more about a piece of literature should read widely and not be limited by the insights of a single approach. The concept of approaches can be helpful, however, in "placing" literary studies and recognizing what they are trying to accomplish. For example, it is sometimes dismaying to read three studies of Joseph Conrad's *Lord Jim* and to find one discussing Conrad's experiences as a sailor, another viewing Jim as a Christ figure, and a third tracing the archetypal pattern of Jim's descent to the depths. This seems proof that literary criticism is a hopelessly fragmented product of idiosyncratic writers who cannot even agree on their subject. Once we realize, however, that these critics are trying to increase understanding of the novel by applying knowledge gained from Conrad's life, from religion, and from myth, we can at least recognize their common goal.

The concept of approaches can also help the person beginning a literary study by providing a place to start and a sense of direction. To ask, in somewhat more precise and limited form, "What does sociology tell us about the events of this novel?" or "What are the techniques by which this play moves the audience?" is at least a starting point for shaping one's own perceptions about the work. Of course, these questions should arise from a studied response to the work. The events are intriguing and seem especially significant, or the play's effect is pronounced or, perhaps, ambiguous. Most studies do begin with a question about the text, and the knowledge of different approaches helps to shape the question more precisely and to find appropriate methods of pursuing the answer.

Once an answer is found, the impulse to communicate it almost inevitably follows. The second part of this text discusses the composition of critical essays and demonstrates the practice of successful scholars and critics. Although each study has its own special problems and challenges, it is likely to share certain goals not only with other critical essays but also with works of argumentation and exposition generally. To see the strategies used by professional writers to achieve these goals may be especially beneficial in one's own attempt to communicate effectively with readers.

Most critical essays are informed not only by the writer's own ideas but also by a knowledge of the ideas others have proposed. Knowing how to plan a research strategy, being aware of the appropriate reference materials, understanding how to locate the necessary sources, and simply having the skills to keep track of research are imperative for following through on any line of inquiry. Research supplies the content of literary studies. Learning its techniques is essential. The third section of this text guides the reader through the process of research.

Finally, the two appendices on form and documentation offer advice in areas governed by conventions and rules. Literary studies are formal presentations and are expected to follow formal conventions. Awkwardness, mechanical errors, and unconventional practices of documentation are sure ways to distract the reader and to inhibit the sharing of ideas. A third appendix provides a brief glossary of critical terms used in this book, along with some other terms students may encounter while reading contemporary criticism.

This book, then, attempts to allow its readers access to the world of contemporary literary scholarship by explaining the main approaches being used today, by showing how critics communicate their ideas, by outlining effective research strategies and listing important research sources, and by giving advice about the conventions of literary composition. Although not forgetting that a literary study begins with the reader's personal response to a work of art, the book attempts to provide the context or environment in which these responses can be developed and communicated. The book is an introduction. It does not attempt to be exhaustive or to mention all or even most of the important books and articles that exemplify various critical approaches. It will certainly not substitute for wide and sustained reading. However, it should give a starting point for those who are excited about literary study and ready to learn more about it.

## WORK CITED

Hyman, Stanley Edgar. *The Armed Vision: A Study in the Methods of Modern Literary Criticism.* New York: Random, 1955.

# PART 1

—

# Critical Approaches to Literature

Fredric Jameson begins his book *The Political Unconscious: Narrative as a Socially Symbolic Act* with the following paragraph:

> This book will argue the priority of the political interpretation of literary texts. It conceives of the political perspective not as some supplemental method, not as an optional auxiliary to other interpretive methods current today—the psychoanalytic or the myth-critical, the stylistic, the ethical, the structural—but rather as the absolute horizon of all reading and all interpretation. (17)

Most of the thirteen approaches that follow have had, at one time or another, such a claim of priority made on their behalf. These claims need to be taken seriously insofar as they represent considered statements of the significance of literature and of the methods most useful for drawing out and explaining that significance. That persons care deeply enough about literature and literary study to argue their convictions with rigor and passion is surely a sign of vitality in the field. Still, for the person pursuing literary study, to be faced with numerous approaches, each having at least some adherents who claim it as absolute, is a daunting experience and one that can lead to a desperate arbitrary selection of *an* approach or to an eclectic borrowing in hopes of forming a more or less coordinated pastiche.

There is no easy answer to this problem, but a few comments may give some background for thinking it through. First, every literary study takes an approach whether or not the writer is aware of doing so. An approach to literature is simply the method one uses to find answers to questions about literature, and each writer must decide what questions can legitimately be asked about literary texts and what method is likely to be effective in answering them. However much a person may wish to escape critical controversy or however little a person may know about traditional approaches, the very fact of asking and attempting to answer a question about a literary work means that the writer has, consciously or not, made decisions about approach. Innocent of theory, a person reading Milton's sonnets may wonder about Milton's religious beliefs and decide to research some aspects of his life. The question and the attempt to answer it may seem matters of interest and common sense, but some critics would dispute both the legitimacy of asking about a writer's beliefs and the possibility of answering literary questions through biographical study.

As this illustration suggests, disagreements about critical approaches center on the nature of the questions to ask about literary works, the best ways of finding answers, and the relationship between the two. Unfortunately, it is not always easy to determine precisely where disagreements occur or even if disagreements exist. For example, some people are likely to view the thirteen approaches discussed here simply as different perspectives, each valid in its own way and each contributing to a fuller understanding of a literary work. Others will find it difficult to accept the truth of more than a single approach. In fact, the real need seems to be a recognition that some differences among critical approaches reflect varying interests and emphases, whereas others result from fundamentally contradictory assumptions. Distinguishing the two is an important step in coming to grips with modern literary study.

To some extent, each approach discussed here reflects the special interests and backgrounds of those who use it. It is not surprising, for example, that the person who has studied psychology or who finds psychology especially helpful in dealing with the pressing concerns of life should use psychological insights when approaching literature. Such a person does not necessarily rule out the validity of other approaches but may only be saying that his or her own interests and knowledge give the approach priority. Wayne Booth speaks of the bitter controversies concerning R. S. Crane's Aristotelian criticism and of the need to read Crane's work as if "every statement, every word, was in effect surrounded with a special kind of quotation mark: *if* you want to work in this corner of the intellectual universe, *then* it becomes absurd for critic X, Y, or Z to do a, b, or c" (80). Some apparent disagreements about criticism come from the lack of such implied quotation marks, from not recognizing that a given writer is simply working in one corner of the intellectual universe. That a critic asks certain kinds of questions and uses a particular method does not restrict others from asking different questions and using different methods.

Other disagreements, however, are fundamental and irresolvable. Jameson, for example, in the opening quotation, does not say only that he prefers to ask political questions of literature; rather, he contends that meaningful questions about literature must ultimately be political. Obviously, this stance cannot be reconciled with, say, a claim for the absolute priority of formalist criticism. Nor is it possible to compromise by appealing to a middle ground or by stating that truth lies somewhere in between. Fundamental disagreements occur because of contradictory assumptions about literature and literary study or sometimes about life itself, and these assumptions need to be understood and finally accepted or rejected. This does not mean, of course, that one cannot learn from the insights of critics whose assumptions differ from one's own; it does suggest the need to recognize the assumptions on which a critical approach is based and the need to be clear about one's own assumptions.

Some assumptions are directly linked to one's larger understanding of the world. Simply put, any person who has a unified view of life will surely consider literature in light of this view. The person who believes, for example, the ultimate concern of life to be the moral behavior of human beings can hardly escape the belief that literature and literary study must contribute to an understanding of morality. Such a person might employ the insights of psychology, sociology, or historical study but would use and value these insofar as they furthered knowledge about the relationship of literature and morality. It is tempting to speak of such views as partial or narrow. In fact, however, critics who argue absolute positions frequently offer particularly comprehensive schemes, which may work out not only the relationship of literature to ultimate concerns in life but also the relationship of contributory approaches to what the critic sees as the main business of literary study.

Other critical disagreements are less directly related to larger concerns in life and are more specifically pointed toward what literary study can and should accomplish. During the last forty years, for example, questions about authorial intention have generated controversy and, at times, confusion. Some critics argue the importance of determining an author's intention or meaning; others argue the impossibility of ever knowing the intention of another human being; still others simply deny the necessity of such knowledge, arguing that literary study should consider only the words on the page, whether or not readers can know the motives behind them. Recently, attention has shifted from the author to the reader, causing a related debate. Here, the question is whether all readers will or should garner approximately the same meaning from a literary text. Those who argue for a text's univocal or single meaning contend that language as a tool of communication assumes common agreement between speaker and listener or writer and reader, that the restaurant patron who requests a hamburger with lettuce can assume he or she will not receive a hot dog with ketchup. Others, however, say the situation is far more complicated, that what a reader understands depends on a variety of factors in the individual's makeup, experience, background, and knowledge. These critics may cite the variety of interpretations of a given text as partial evidence for their views.

The point here is not to emphasize the fragmentation of literary study or, conversely, to celebrate its diversity but to indicate some of the inescapable issues involved in any approach to literature. The person who writes about literature divorces it from the concerns of life only at the risk of irrelevance. Similarly, the person unaware of the implications of a given approach or the assumptions behind it is likely to end in confusion and contradiction. The way a man or woman thinks and writes about literature results from a complex interplay between that person's values and attitudes and what the person comes to believe about the methods and limits of literary study. In that sense, an approach is not so much chosen as developed, developed out of the reading of literature and literary criticism and out of one's experiences and values in other areas of life.

Therefore, the approaches that follow are not models from which one is to make a choice for emulation. Neither are they individual parts which taken together make up the whole of literary criticism. Rather, they represent the main ways literary critics are thinking and writing about literature at present. The examples within each approach have in common assumptions about the value of using knowledge and insights derived from specific fields, but each example is also unique and individual in its particular combination of emphases and procedures. What the discussion of these approaches should offer is an increased ability to read contemporary criticism and a background for establishing and clarifying one's own assumptions.

## WORKS CITED

Booth, Wayne. *Critical Understanding: The Powers and Limits of Pluralism.* Chicago: Chicago UP, 1979.

Jameson, Fredric. *The Political Unconscious: Narrative as a Socially Symbolic Act.* Ithaca: Cornell UP, 1981.

# Chapter 1

## THE INSIGHT OF LITERATURE

The four approaches presented in this chapter—formalist, generic, rhetorical, and structuralist—have different emphases and histories, but they are related in their close attention to the formal elements of literary texts and in their assumption that the methodology of literary study must come from literature itself. Historically, formalism is especially well known for its close readings of literary works in order to describe how form produces or *is* meaning. However, genre criticism, in its attempt to recognize common properties among works, to classify works, and to interpret them in light of other texts of a similar kind, shares the need for a close analysis of form. Rhetorical criticism, in determining how a work affects its readers, calls for an equally rigorous scrutiny of the formal elements within a text. Structuralism, though seemingly the most divergent of the four, shares formalism's concern with the relationship of form or structure and meaning, genre criticism's interest in determining common properties or deep structures, and sometimes rhetorical criticism's concern with the relationship of text and reader and of the "contract" between the two.

More fundamental than the common attention to form, however, is the assumption that the principles of literary criticism should derive from the study of literature itself. In fact, these approaches are sometimes called *intrinsic* because they do not depend on an external field for their methodologies. That is, they are self-contained insofar as they apply insights, gained from a close reading of a literary work and principles developed from the study of other literature and language. Although individual critics may incorporate outside knowledge, none of these approaches in itself needs to rely on another field for its interpretation or description of a work. Even structuralism, whose methodology is often analogous to that of linguistics, treats literature as a system to be studied on its own terms.

Some critics contend that this concentration on the literary text in and for itself may lead to a narrowness of focus and divorce literary study from wider intellectual and cultural concerns. They warn against a criticism accessible only to a small group of specialists, a criticism that is no longer a broadly humane endeavor to bring to bear all the resources at the reader's command. Proponents reply that employing an appropriate methodology derived from the field itself is not narrow but simply the only way to achieve understanding in any area. Only through an intrinsic approach, they argue, can literary study become a true discipline with its own set of procedures and principles.

This definition of discipline is somewhat similar to that used in the sciences. For example, just as the discipline of biology is defined not only by what biologists study but also by the procedures they employ, so an intrinsic approach is defined not simply by its subject matter, literature, but by its methodology as well. A biologist studies plant and animal life, induces rules and principles, develops a vocabulary, and applies and modifies findings in the study of new, individual forms. Similarly, the intrinsic critic studies literary works, inductively determines literary principles, builds a vocabulary, and uses this knowledge in the interpretation and description of individual texts. Obviously, no single critic, as no one biologist, retraces the entire process; in fact, the development of a body of knowledge from which to draw is an important advantage of a discipline. The defining characteristic, though, is that the procedures or methodology comes from the study of its subject matter and is not imposed from the outside.

Although the appropriateness of this kind of discipline in a humane field is open to debate, there is little question that these four approaches have brought rigor to the reading of literature and have demonstrated the value of giving close attention to the form and structure of literary texts. Whether or not one is willing to accept all their implications, these approaches teach important lessons about possible questions one can ask about literature and ways of finding answers. They have developed methods of working with literature which have their own internal logic and consistency but which also can frequently be used in conjunction with other approaches.

## FORMALIST STUDIES AND THE NEW CRITICISM

Formalism is for many both the most familiar critical approach and the most elusive: It is difficult to isolate the distinctive features of *formalist criticism* because they seem to be shared by almost all sensible approaches to literature. One might say that formalist criticism is marked by close attention to the text and by a concern with the forms of literary works. Still, any fair-minded person would have to admit that most good critics, regardless of their approaches, read texts carefully and offer intelligent analyses of form. Formalism's truly distinctive characteristics, then, seem to be negative ones: a hostility to biographical and historical evidence and to any other information that invites the reader to look beyond the text itself and, perhaps as a consequence, an inability to go beyond formal analysis and discuss a literary work's broader significance or its relation to life. One may, however, be able to understand more fully the unique characteristics and contributions of formalist criticism if one begins with some of the more theoretical works of the most well-known and influential modern formalist critics, those who became known as the New Critics. These works reveal that formalism involves not only an approach to criticism but also a theory of literature, a theory that informs and sets apart the work done by many formalist critics.

## Form versus Meaning

Although no two critics share exactly the same assumptions and approaches, it seems fair to say that, in general, the New Criticism begins with a distinctive view of the nature and origin of literary works. The literary work is seen as unique both because of the particular way in which it is created and because of the particular sort of insights it offers. Presumably, most writers—scientists, historians, or philosophers, for example—are almost exclusively concerned with meaning or content. When they write, their overwhelming desire is to communicate ideas. Such writers will almost inevitably pay some attention to style and form, looking for the words that will most precisely express their ideas, for a form that their readers can understand, and perhaps for graceful and eloquent language. Still, form is always subordinate to meaning and is seen primarily as a vehicle for ideas. The poet, the dramatist, and the novelist, in contrast, are from the beginning intensely concerned with both meaning and form. They do indeed have ideas they want to express, but they also have forms they want to achieve—perhaps something so concretely defined as a sonnet, perhaps some new idea of form involving a certain pattern of sounds, a certain dramatic structure, a certain interplay of characters and incidents. Thus, as John Crowe Ransom says in *The New Criticism*, the literary artist who attempts to satisfy the demands of both meaning and form has chosen to "try to do not one hard thing but two hard things at once." The poet, for example, finds that "the composition of the poem is an operation in which the argument fights to displace the meter, and the meter fights to displace the argument" (295).

In the final chapter of *The New Criticism*, Ransom uses an analogy to argue that this battle between meaning and form does not merely blur or water down the statement a literary work makes; rather, it can be a truly creative process that transforms and enriches both form and meaning. He describes the poet's task as similar to that of a servant whose mistress tells him to look through one hundred apples and find the twelve "biggest and reddest" ones to display in a bowl. In his search, he finds that he must reject some solidly red apples because they are not big enough and some very big apples because they are not red enough; in effect, he must make constant compromises in order to find apples that come close to meeting both of the standards that his mistress has set. Still, the mistress may find that the twelve apples her servant eventually presents to her make a display lovelier than the one she originally had in mind:

> She will not secure the perfection of her object in one aspect if she is also trying to secure its perfection in another aspect. . . . But she may find an unexpected compensation. In regretting the loss of certain nearly solid-red apples which are denied to her because they are little, she may observe that the selected apples exhibit color-markings much more various, unpredictable, and interesting. She finds pleasure in studying their markings, whereas she would have obtained the color-value of her solid-red apples at a glance. (297)

Similarly, Ransom says, the meaning of a poem, because it has been shaped by meter, may be richer and more fascinating than the meaning the poet originally had in mind: In searching for a rhyming word or a word to fit the meter, the poet may have discovered new subtleties of meaning. Thus, the need to adapt meaning to form is not an unfortunate necessity but an immensely valuable part of the creative process. And although Ransom does not carry the analogy quite this far, one might say that the inevitable variations in the sizes of the twelve apples also make the display more interesting; similarly, variations in meter forced by the need to accommodate meaning make the sound of the finished poem more interesting and beautiful than an absolutely regular meter could. The poet begins with an intended meaning and an intended form but is forced to modify each in order to retain some of the other, and it is these modifications—these "indeterminate elements," as Ransom calls them—that enable the poem to transcend the poet's original intentions and give to literature much of its unique value and fascination (295-301).

## Literature and the Creative Process

Thus, for Ransom and most of the other New Critics, a literary work is truly autonomous, the outgrowth of a particular creative process rather than the product of an artist and an age, and it is most accurately regarded as an independent object, not as a manifestation of something else. Speculating about a poet's intentions, for example, is both futile and beside the point: Even if one could somehow determine what the poet's original intentions were, one could not be sure that those intentions are perfectly preserved in the final poem—indeed, one can be fairly sure that they are not. New Critics also typically reject the notion that a work of literature is an expression of a historical or sociological trend or of the author's psychological state: A literary work is shaped by the struggle between meaning and form, not by the struggle between agrarianism and commercialism, between bourgeoisie and proletariat, or between id and ego. The New Critics are not so unreasonable as to claim that history, sociology, and biography have no influence on literature. Cleanth Brooks and Robert Penn Warren, for example, concede in *Understanding Poetry* that a poet's "ideas are conditioned by his time" and that "the imagination is not completely free; it is conditioned . . . by the experience of the poet" (516-517). Still, because the literary work also has an independent existence, information about anything outside the work itself is not likely to be very enlightening—it may set some limits to interpretation, but it cannot say what the work is—and it may well be distracting or misleading.

## Focusing Criticism on the Work Itself

Although other sorts of evidence need not be completely disregarded, therefore, the critic's attention must always be focused primarily on the work itself; the New Critics reject approaches that invite the critic to focus on anything else. Allen Tate, for example, argues in his essay "The Present Function of Criticism" that "the historical approach to criticism, insofar as it has attempted to be a scientific method, has undermined the significance of the material which it proposes to study. On principle the sociological and historical scholar must not permit himself to see in the arts meanings that his method does not assume" (198). Ransom is skeptical of I. A. Richards's psychological approach to criticism, finding his analyses of individual poems far more valuable: It is as an "astute reader," Ransom declares, that Richards makes "his most incontestable contribution to poetic discussion," for he "looks much more closely at the objective poem than his theories require him to do"(45). In an influential essay entitled "The Affective Fallacy," W. K. Wimsatt attacks critical approaches that stress either the author's biography or the reader's response. The eventual outcome of either approach, he says, "is that the poem itself, as an object of specifically critical judgment, tends to disappear" (Wimsatt and Beardsley 21). In other words, most critical approaches tempt the reader to lose sight of the distinctive challenges and understanding that literature offers and to become entangled in secondary or even unrelated matters.

The New Critic resists such temptations and instead rigorously examines the work itself, paying particular attention to the relationship between form and meaning. "What is the primary office of criticism?" Allen Tate asks. "Is it to expound and elucidate, with as little distortion as possible, the knowledge of life contained by the novel or the poem or the play?" (42). Tate's definition points both to the New Critics' emphasis on painstaking explication and to their concern with what is "contained by" the literary work, not with anything outside it. Cleanth Brooks, similarly, in the preface to *The Well Wrought Urn*, declared that criticism must begin "by making the closest possible examination of what the poem says as a poem" (vii); he is, he says, "primarily concerned with the *poem* and only incidentally with the *poet* who produced the work or with the various kinds of *readers* who have responded to it" (ix).

## FORMALIST APPROACH TO POETRY

In *Understanding Poetry*, a widely used textbook by Brooks and Warren, an analysis of the short poem by W. B. Yeats that follows illustrates some of the distinctive characteristics of this approach.

# A Deep-Sworn Vow

Others because you did not keep
That deep-sworn vow have been friends of mine;
Yet always when I look death in the face,
When I clamber to the heights of sleep,
Or when I grow excited with wine,
Suddenly I meet your face.

Many readers would immediately respond to this poem by observing that it must be about Maud Gonne, Yeats's lost love; many would promptly plunge into comments about Yeats's love life or Irish politics—or perhaps into another poem, satisfied that they have understood this one adequately. Brooks and Warren, however, have other ideas of what the poem is "about." Almost coyly, they do not mention Gonne; the poem's theme, they say, "is the lasting impression made by a love affair which has been broken off, apparently long ago, and which has been superseded by other relationships" (160). They then devote several pages to analyzing the poem, commenting on its structure and tone and paying particular attention to the ways in which irregularities in meter underscore the particular emotions and effects the poem communicates—from the "calm, unexcited statement" of the opening lines to the "rapid, casual, even careless excitement" of the fifth line and the "reserved and solemn statement" of the last. It is only some twenty pages later, and in another context, that Brooks and Warren admit to knowing that the woman addressed in the poem is Maud Gonne, and they immediately declare that this "autobiographical identification is not *necessarily* important. We are concerned with the fact that the speaker of the poem, whether historical or fictional, is expressing an attitude through his particular use of language" (160-164, 183). Some readers might find Brooks and Warren's analysis of the poem's meter overingenious or even tedious; others might argue that some attention to Yeats's biography can only enrich appreciation of the poem and is indeed necessary to any complete analysis. Still, it seems hard to deny that the analysis of the poem's meter helps to illuminate the way the poem works and to forestall oversimplifications about its meaning; and it also seems hard to deny that with many readers, undue or premature interest in biography or other matters too often cuts short an exacting study of the work itself.

An essay from Brooks's *The Well Wrought Urn* provides further examples of formalist assumptions and methods. "The Language of Poetry" is both an explication of John Donne's "The Canonization" and a defense of the kind of poetry it represents, poetry that achieves its meaning through paradox. It may seem to some readers that Donne has chosen an unnecessarily and ostentatiously complicated way of expressing a relatively simple idea—that lovers who renounce the world for love actually find the world in each other. Brooks argues, however, that Donne could not have expressed the same meaning through a straightforward, unironic form: The precision and complexity of Donne's ideas are dependent on his particular use of language and metaphor. Donne's comparison of the lovers to a phoenix, for example, is not a casual poetic commonplace: This image absorbs earlier images in the poem, suggesting both the unity the lovers achieve and the nature of their love, which includes sexual consummation but is not exhausted by it. "The Canonization," Brooks says, is an example of a poem in which "the truth which the poet utters can be approached only in terms of paradox," (1) and the reader can understand that paradox only by paying the closest possible attention to the words of the poem itself and by recognizing to what extent the poem's meaning is determined by its form.

**FORMALIST APPROACH TO OTHER LITERARY FORMS**

Formalist criticism is most often associated with the close, penetrating analysis of poetry, but many formalist critics have directed their attention to other kinds of literature as well. Maynard Mack's "The World of *Hamlet*" shows how the same methods used to analyze a short poem may profitably be used to study longer works. In seeking to explain Hamlet's dilemma and motivations, Mack looks not to Freudian psychology or to the conventions of the revenge tragedy but to the words and images of the play itself. He finds there recurrent terms such as *seems, assumes, apparition,* and *put on;* patterns of imagery involving clothes, disease, poison, painting, and acting; and three central "attributes" or themes—mysteriousness, the difference between appearance and reality, and mortality. Mack concludes that the reader can best understand Hamlet's problem by realizing that he is required to act in "a certain kind of world" (518), a mysterious world where things are not what they seem and where human failure, corruption, and loss are everywhere evident. Hamlet delays because he cannot act until he understands and accepts his world and can therefore define his own role in it.

Mark Schorer calls for a formalist approach to the study of fiction, arguing that one cannot adequately understand works of fiction without recognizing the importance of technique. In fiction as well as in poetry, Schorer maintains, technique is not "merely a means to organizing material which is 'given'"; rather, "technique is the only means [the writer] has of discovering, exploring, developing his subject, of conveying its meaning, and, finally, of evaluating it." Schorer supports his thesis by examining a number of novels whose success or failure depends, in his estimation, on the author's mastery of technique. Thus, Schorer argues that *Moll Flanders* fails as literature because Daniel Defoe "had no adequate resources of technique to separate himself from his material, thereby to discover and to define the meanings of his material": Defoe's point of view is "indistinguishable" from Moll's, and the reader comes to see the absurdity of her character and the crassness of her morality "in spite of Defoe, not because of him." In *Wuthering Heights,* in contrast, Emily Brontë's technique— specifically, her use of Lockwood and Nellie as narrators—almost forces her to take a more objective view of her characters. Although Brontë probably began with the idea that Heathcliff and Catherine's love shows true "moral magnificence," her narrative techniques "compel the novelist to see what her unmoral passion come to . . . a devastating spectacle of human waste." *Wuthering Heights,* Schorer says, shows how "a certain body of materials, a girl's romantic daydreams, have, through the most conventional devices of fiction, been pushed beyond their inception in fancy to their meanings, their conception as a written book" (67-87).

## Criticisms of the Formalist Approach

Schorer's analysis of *Wuthering Heights* may indicate why some have accused formalist critics in general, and the New Critics in particular, of arrogance, of dogmatism, and even of a sort of mysticism. In order to prove his point about the importance of technique, Schorer speculates about Brontë's creative process (and thereby, very possibly, is guilty of the intentional fallacy): He assumes that Brontë began with a naive view of her characters and was somehow forced by her choice of narrative form to achieve a more adequate view. It would seem just as plausible to assume that Brontë began with a firm understanding of her characters' imperfections and deliberately chose a narrative form that would help her make those imperfections clear to the reader. If so, then form is clearly subordinate to meaning in literature, just as it is in other sorts of writing, a tool the writer consciously manipulates and not a force in shaping meaning; and if form is no more than a vehicle for meaning in literature, other formalist assumptions about the unique nature of literature and the unique sort of study it demands also come into question. R. S. Crane, for example, criticizes Brooks for seeing irony and paradox as the distinctive characteristics of poetry. In the first place, Crane argues, one can find the sort of irony Brooks sees as the essence of poetry in many philosophical and historical works, and even in some scientific formulae. Furthermore, Crane thinks that the New Critics' concern with "a universal poetic 'structure'" leads them to ignore distinctions among different kinds of poems. Poems should be regarded, Crane says, as "instances of one or another poetic kind, differentiated not by any necessity of the linguistic instrument but primarily by the nature of the poet's conception . . . of a particular form to be achieved"; the poet's decisions about such matters as action, character, and diction will depend primarily on considerations of genre (96, 102–105; see also the discussion of Crane and the Chicago school in the section titled "Genre Studies" later in this chapter).

Others have challenged the New Critics' view of a literary work as an autonomous object that is not to be interpreted and evaluated either in the context of the author's life or in the context of the reader's own ideas and beliefs. E. D. Hirsch, Jr., for example, challenges the view that one should not look beyond the text itself when interpreting a literary work. A literary text is not just a "piece of language" to be examined in isolation, Hirsch says. Rather, it "represents the determinate verbal meaning of an author," and the interpreter's task is to discover that meaning by using all the information available. Several different interpretations might be consistent with a given literary text; in order to prove that one interpretation is more probable than another, the reader must attempt to "verify" it with "extrinsic data," to show that it is consistent with "the author's typical outlook, the typical associations and expectations which form in part the context of his utterance" (476–478). Gerald Graff has different reasons for objecting to the idea that one can or should judge a literary work without reference to anything "outside" it. Critics such as Brooks, Graff says, try to maintain their view of the autonomy of literary works by arguing that the reader should judge them solely on the basis of their "dramatic propriety" or internal consistency—one does not ask whether one agrees with a speech a character makes or with a statement in a poem, but whether the speech is consistent with the character or the statement with the rest of the poem. But in fact, Graff argues, one's ideas about consistency itself are derived from knowledge of people, experiences, and ideas outside the work, making it impossible to judge a literary work without in some sense considering things external to it (94–102). Another critic, David Daiches, argues that many formalists overemphasize form and therefore misjudge both individual literary works and the true value of literature itself. Because these critics value paradox and complexity of expression so highly, Daiches says, they "discourse brilliantly about John Donne and other poets who, like Donne, deliberately use paradox as an essential part of their technique—and considerably less brilliantly about most other poets." More important, Daiches says, such critics come to "regard subtlety or complexity of arrangement as itself a criterion of literary worth. But pattern in literature is a means to an end, not an end in itself, and the neatest or subtlest arrangement of ideas or images is merely a parlor game unless that arrangement is placed at the service of some insight." The analysis of literature must be based on a recognition of literature's true value—which lies, according to Daiches, not in the form of a literary work but in the ideas it communicates: "In the last analysis, literature is valuable as a kind of knowledge—a unique kind of knowledge about man" (80–85).

Defenders of formalist criticism do, of course, have answers to these and other charges, arguing that their approach makes adequate provisions for the consideration of genre and "extrinsic data," that other approaches are too likely to degenerate into impressionism and irrelevance, and that a primary interest in form need not preclude full appreciation of literature's intellectual and moral significance. And even those who find fault with the New Critics and other formalists do not, as a rule, reject the approach entirely. True, some attacks have been extremely harsh—Grant Webster, for example, declares that in recent years, "Formalist values have come to seem totally irrelevant to almost everyone" (203). Most critiques, however, have been more measured, calling for a change in emphasis or a broader view while still recognizing the formalists' many contributions to the study of literature. As R. V. Young points out, even those who reject the New Critics' ideas and methods owe them a substantial debt:

> It is not too much to say that the activities of the New Critics and their followers staked out the literary field and defined the university environment in which the revisionists now operate. If the movement known as New Criticism had never occurred, it is improbable that the position and activities of literary scholars would be of much significance in the contemporary university. (38)

A number of works would be helpful to those interested in learning more about this approach to criticism. Most were published during the decades of New Criticism's greatest influence, the 1930s, 1940s, and 1950s. In addition to *Understanding Poetry*, Brooks and Warren have published *Understanding Fiction*, and Brooks and Robert Heilman have published *Understanding Drama*. Al these textbooks provide readers with practical advice and with many models of formalist analysis. Brooks's *The Well Wrought Urn* contains ten analyses, mostly of short poems, and an essay titled "The Heresy of Paraphrase" that explains some fundamental assumptions of formalist criticism; many consider the essays in this volume to be among the most brilliant and influential commentaries formalist critics have offered. Other important formalist critics are R. P. Blackmur, Wimsatt, and, of course, Ransom. Although not a statement of formalist theory, William Empson's *Seven Types of Ambiguity* has had a great influence on many formalist critics, and his commentaries on poems show the rigor and creativity often associated with formalism. Journals such as *The Kenyon Review, The Sewanee Review,* and *The Explicator* have long been associated with formalist criticism. A list of other important works follows.

## WORKS CITED AND RECOMMENDED

Blackmur, R. P. *Language as Gesture: Essay in Poetry*. New York: Harcourt, 1935.
Brooks, Cleanth. *The Well Wrought Urn*. London: Methuen, 1947.
Brooks, Cleanth, and Robert Heilman. *Understanding Drama*. New York: Holt, 1945.
Brooks, Cleanth, and Robert Penn Warren. *Understanding Fiction*. New York: Appleton, 1943.
———. *Understanding Poetry*. 1938. 3rd ed. New York: Holt, 1960.
Crane, R. S., ed. *Critics and Criticism: Ancient and Modern*. Chicago: Chicago UP, 1952.
Daiches, David. *A Study of Literature for Readers and Critics*. Ithaca: Cornell UP, 1948.
Empson, William. *Seven Types of Ambiguity*. Edinburgh: New Directions, 1930.
Graff, Gerald. *Poetic Statement and Critical Dogma*. Chicago: Chicago UP, 1970.
Hirsch, E. D., Jr. "Objective Interpretation." *PMLA* 75 (1960): 463-479.
Lentricchia, Frank. *After the New Criticism*. Chicago: Chicago UP, 1980.
Mack, Maynard. "The World of *Hamlet.*" *Yale Review* 41 (1952): 502-523.
Norris, Christopher. "Pope among the Formalists: Textual Politics and 'The Rape of the Lock.'" *Post-Structuralist Readings of English Poetry*. Ed. R. Machin and C. Norris. Cambridge: Cambridge UP, 1987. 134-161.
Ransom, John Crowe. *The New Criticism*. Norfolk: New Directions, 1941.
———. *Principles of Literary Criticism*. New York: Harcourt, 1925.
Schorer, Mark. "Technique as Discovery." *Hudson Review* 1 (1948): 67-87.
Schwartz, Sanford. "Conclusion: The New Criticism and Beyond." *The Matrix of Modernism: Pound, Eliot, and Early Twentieth Century Thought*. Princeton: Princeton UP, 1985. 209-215.
Siebers, Tobin. "The Ethics of Autonomy: Biography and the New Criticism." *The Ethics of Criticism*. Ithaca: Cornell UP, 1988. 44-68.
Stallman, Robert W., ed. *Critiques and Essays in Criticism, 1920-1948*. New York: Ronald, 1949.
Tate, Allen. *Essays of Four Decades*. New York: Morrow, 1970.
Webster, Grant. *The Republic of Letters: A History of Postwar American Literary Opinion*. Baltimore: Johns Hopkins UP, 1979.
Willingham, J. R. "The New Criticism: Then and Now." *Contemporary Literary Theory*. Ed. G. Douglas Atkins and Laura Morrow. Amherst: Massachusetts UP, 1989. 24-41.
Wimsatt, W. K., and M. C. Beardsley. *The Verbal Icon*. Lexington: Kentucky UP, 1954.
Wimsatt, W. K., and Cleanth Brooks. *Literary Criticism: A Short History*. New York: Knopf, 1957.
Young, R. V. "The Old New Criticism and Its Critics." *First Things* (Aug.-Sept. 1993): 38-44.

## GENRE STUDIES

The term *genre*, a French word meaning kind or type, is familiar to nearly all students of literature. Most have participated in genre courses, and all have used genre classifications simply by speaking of drama, poetry, satire, or the novel. As pervasive as is the concept of genre, however, its use is frequently confusing. Genre sometimes refers to such inclusive literary types as drama, epic, or lyric poetry and at other times to specific forms such as the sonnet, the ballad, or the sestina. Since genres are defined according to different methods of classification, *King Lear* and *As You Like It* may be considered members of a single genre, drama, or as members of different genres, tragedy and comedy, respectively. *Pride and Prejudice* may be grouped with *As You Like It* as a comedy or apart from it as a prose fiction. Even given a single genre, one may question the significance of recognizing *Othello* and *Death of a Salesman* as dramas or two fourteen-line poems as sonnets. However, precisely such questions and confusion can make genre studies exciting. Insofar as studies of genre attempt to understand a literary work through its relationship to other works with similar characteristics, the task of the critic is to determine which relationships are significant and likely to increase understanding.

### Aristotle's Groundwork

Aristotle's *Poetics* was among the earliest discussions of literary genre and is one to which most modern critics are indebted. Viewing poetic art as an imitation or representation of reality, Aristotle classified literary works according to the means, the objects, and the manner of the imitation. By means, Aristotle referred to the medium of the artwork, whether it communicated through words or music, prose or verse. By objects, he referred to the situations or characters that were being imitated; and these could be represented as "better than or worse than or like the norm." By manner, he referred to what might be called point of view. He mentioned three manners: An imitation might be narrated in the voice of a character, it might be narrated in the author's own voice, or it might be acted or dramatized. A consideration of all these possibilities was necessary to determine the kind or type of any work. For example, comic and tragic drama shared the same manner: Both were acted rather than narrated. However, the two had different means and objects. The comedy of Aristotle's time was unlikely to use the iambic meter that was a staple of tragedy; and in the drama with which Aristotle was familiar, comedy represented characters as worse than the norm and tragedy as better.

These classifications allowed for a number of distinctions among kinds of literature, but for Aristotle their significance was in their relationship to the function or purpose of the work of art. Aristotle seems to have believed that literary kinds had their own inherent forms or their own natures and that each literary kind developed toward the full potential of its nature. Tragedy, for instance, had undergone numerous changes until it had become the kind of drama Aristotle knew and defined in one of the most famous statements in literary criticism:

> Tragedy is, then, an imitation of a noble and complete action, having the proper magnitude; it employs language that has been artistically enhanced by each of the kinds of linguistic adornment, applied separately in the various parts of the play; it is presented in dramatic, not narrative form, and achieves through the representation of pitiable and fearful incidents, the catharsis of such pitiable and fearful emotions.

The definition clearly indicates the objects (noble actions of great magnitude), the means (artistically enhanced language), and the manner (dramatic, not narrative form). More important for Aristotle, however, was the function of tragedy, to which manner, means, and objects contributed. That function was the catharsis or purgation of pity and fear. It is not necessary to follow the many arguments over the precise meaning of catharsis to recognize that for Aristotle the elements within a literary work were significant only insofar as they allowed the work to achieve its purpose.

# The Chicago School

Among twentieth-century critics most concerned with genre have been those associated with the "Chicago school" of criticism, so named because many early practitioners were affiliated with the University of Chicago. These critics are sometimes called neo-Aristotelian because of their shared interest in the implication of Aristotle's poetic theory. Although the Chicago school is composed of highly individualistic critics, not followers of a rigid doctrine, R. S. Crane, in the introduction to his *Critics and Criticism* in 1953, articulated what has come to be considered a central premise of the school's understanding of genre study. Harkening back to Aristotle, Crane argued for the need to determine the kind of artistic object an author intended before considering other elements of the work. As Crane put it, "to what extent, and with what degree of artistic compulsion, any of the particular things the writer has done at the various levels of his writing, down to the details of his imagery and language, can be seen to follow from the special requirements or opportunities which the kind of whole he is making presents to him" (16).

Elder Olson, one of the early members of the Chicago school, in *Tragedy and the Theory of Drama*, discusses *King Lear* by considering it from the perspective of the dramatist who "wants to make a tragedy" (198). That is, Olson begins with the kind of work the author intends and then attempts to account for elements within it by determining their contribution to a whole work of that kind. For instance, in looking at the character of Lear, Olson asks, "If the play is to be made tragic, what must the character of Lear be made to be?" (200). He answers by recognizing that an audience must be made to feel pity for a tragic character and, therefore, that the character must be noble, although not perfect, and that his misfortune must be, in some sense, undeserved. Lear, in Olson's view, has been made that kind of tragic character. Too old to rule and without a male heir, Lear attempts to fulfill his kingly responsibility by dividing his kingdom among his daughters, thus preventing future wars. He asks from his daughters only what any feudal lord might expect—a pledge of fealty. Cordelia, of course, refuses and is banished. Although some readers see Lear as egomaniacal for his insistence on a pledge of complete and ever-lasting love and Cordelia as stubborn or perverse for her unequivocal refusal, Olson believes the tragedy ensues from the confusion of feudal loyalty with family love. Lear insists on the pledge in order to ensure harmony within the divided kingdom; Cordelia refuses in the belief that love cannot be contracted or limited.

In this reading, Olson moves from considering tragedy in general to an analysis of specific elements in Shakespearean tragedy. Olson shows Lear's confusion to be akin to that of other characters in Shakespeare's works. Lear, like the protagonists in *Hamlet, Macbeth, Coriolanus,* and *Othello*, is a charac-ter "of conspicuous virtues and abilities, who has distinguished himself through them in one sphere [and] is thrown suddenly into a sphere of action in which to exercise them—and he must exercise them—is to invoke catastro-phe" (202). In this case, Lear "is thrown into a domestic sphere where the laws of feudality do not operate" (203). Thus, Olson argues, in Shakespearean tragedy, character and situation are developed in a specific way in order to at-tain the end of any tragedy, the evocation of pity and fear.

As Olson goes beyond Aristotle to define a specific kind of post-Aris-totelian tragedy, Sheldon Sacks, in *Fiction and the Shape of Belief*, works with a form unknown to Aristotle, the prose fiction. Sacks distinguishes among three types of prose fiction: satires, like Jonathan Swift's *Gulliver's Travels*, which ridicule specific persons, traits, or institutions; apologues, like Samuel Johnson's *Rasselas*, which exemplify "formulable" statements or truths; and represented actions, works we usually think of as novels or short stories, which introduce characters in "unstable relationships," complicate these relationships, and finally resolve themselves by the "removal of the complicated instability" (15). Each of these types has its own end and is organized to achieve that end. To confuse these types, Sacks believes, is often to misunderstand literary works. For example, those who consider the Houyhnhnms in *Gulliver's Trav-els* as examples of Swift's ideal for humanity are reading the satire as if it was an apologue, in which characters and traits are selected in order to exemplify given truths. Instead, Sacks argues, Swift, as the writer of a satire, would select characteristics that best allow him to ridicule the object of satire, whether or not he regards those characteristics as admirable. The extreme rationality of the Houyhnhnms may be used to satirize irrational behavior in the English without making a case for the desirability of the Houyhnhnms' behavior. Simi-larly, to argue about Gulliver's character and to assume consistency in that character is to read the satire as a represented action, a novel. Like Olson, Sacks begins with a work's kind or genre and then explains its internal elements in this light.

## Structuralism and Genre

Whereas the Chicago critics, although with wide individual variations, focus on how the aim of a literary type determines a work's individual parts, many structuralist critics are especially concerned with the way in which expectations about a genre govern the reading of a work. As Jonathan Culler says in *Structuralist Poetics: Structuralism, Linguistics and the Study of Literature*, a genre "serves as a norm or expectation to guide the reader in his encounter with the text" (136); or to use another of Culler's formulations, genres constitute a "contract" between writer and reader. A person has different expectations of a tragedy and a comedy or of a lyric poem and a newspaper account and, thus, reads them differently. In a comedy, the reader may laugh at villainous characters, knowing they will be overturned by the play's end; in a tragedy, even at the height of a hero's glory, the reader may look for signs of the inevitable downfall. Structuralist studies are considered more fully later in this chapter, but their contribution to an understanding of genre justifies the inclusion of at least one example here.

Tzvetan Todorov, in *The Poetics of Prose*, attempts to identify the generic contracts of several kinds of detective fiction. The classic detective story, what Todorov calls the "whodunit," is characterized by a lack of physical action and an emphasis on the intellectual process. The whodunit contains two stories: the story of the crime, which may have occurred before the beginning of the book and which is given little space; and the story of the investigation, which makes up the bulk of the book. The reader comes to the whodunit not expecting the thrill or suspense of watching a crime unfold but anticipating the opportunity to work through clues, conflicting evidence, and misrepresentations in order to arrive at the solution. On the other hand, Todorov points to what he calls the "thriller," a genre that reverses the expectations of the whodunit. The thriller is the story of the events of a crime as they take place, and physical action is emphasized. The reader attends to the text not out of curiosity about the solution of the crime but out of suspense about the fate of the characters.

## Archetypes and Genre

A third approach to genre, that of Northrop Frye, is discussed at length in the section titled "Archetypal Studies" in Chapter 3. Many view Frye's mythoi of comedy, romance, tragedy, and irony as genres, and certainly these allow us to see both similarities and differences among various literary works. However, in *Anatomy of Criticism: Four Essays*, Frye reserves the term *genre* for distinctions based on what he calls the "radical of presentation"—that is, the relationship between artist and audience in the presentation of a work (246-247). Frye sees four relationships and, thus, four major genres: epos, in which the poet speaks or recites to an audience; drama, in which the artist's words are enacted by hypothetical characters before an audience; lyric, in which the audience seems to be overhearing a poetic speaker who does not direct the work to them; and fiction, in which the artist writes to a reading audience. Frye recognizes, of course, that the day of the oral epic is over, that drama can be printed and read, and that novels can conceivably be acted, but his classifications are based on the "ideal" presentation of a given text.

## Significant Patterns and Genre

Although the works of the Chicago critics, structuralists, and archetypal critics represent approaches to literature that have fairly clear methodologies and assumptions, other studies of genre rest on less explicit assumptions. Frequently, these studies simply recognize common elements in a number of literary works, elements that seem significant enough to justify using them as a basis for classification and discussion. For example, the Gothic novel or romance has long been considered a distinct fictional type or genre, early examples of which include Horace Walpole's *Castle of Otranto* (1764), Ann Radcliffe's *The Mysteries of Udolpho* (1794), and Gregory Lewis's *The Monk* (1797). These novels of mystery, terror, and the supernatural were often set in gloomy medieval castles with hidden rooms, labyrinthine passageways, and dungeons. Most frequently, a young and vulnerable woman was subject and victim for the horrors evoked.

Critics have begun to examine a number of twentieth-century works with elements similar or analogous to the eighteenth- and nineteenth-century Gothic novels. For example, Irving Malin, in *New American Gothic*, discusses how elements of the traditional Gothic function in works of Truman Capote, Carson McCullers, Flannery O'Connor, John Hawkes, James Purdy, and J. D. Salinger. Malin believes three images form the earlier Gothic—the haunted castle, the voyage into the forest, and the reflection of distorted reality—form a psychological pattern in the works of these contemporary novelists, with "the castle as the outpost of authoritarianism; the voyage as the flight from such authoritarianism into new directions of strength or love; the reflection as the two-sidedness of motives, the 'falseness' of human nature" (79).

Although the meaning of this pattern can be debated, the recognition of these similarities does give fresh insights to the books. The rooms and houses in the contemporary works are not usually described as Gothic castles, but frequent images of imprisonment and confinement lead the reader to view the contemporary protagonists as no less entrapped than their Gothic predecessors. Similarly, although these fictions may not contain the supernatural element of a pool or mirror that distorts the world in its bizarre reflection, characters themselves may become grotesque reflections of reality. For instance, in Flannery O'Connor's "Wise Blood," a prostitute, Mrs. Watts, sees herself as "Momma" and is, in Malin's words, "an inverse reflection of the main character's self-righteous mother" (146). Seeing these common elements allows not simply a method of classification but also the possibility of gaining new and valuable ways of looking at the texts.

# Why Study Genre?

That possibility of discovering new perspectives is ultimately the reason for studies of genre. What Todorov says of a specific work and a specific genre in *The Fantastic: A Structural Approach to a Literary Genre* probably applies to all texts considered in light of their genre: "To study Balzac's *The Magic Skin* in the context of the fantastic as a genre is quite different from studying this book in and of itself, or in the canon of Balzac's work, or in that of contemporary literature" (3). The study of genre at its best pushes readers to see literary works differently and to become aware of important elements and meanings that might otherwise go unnoticed.

These new insights are only increased if we recognize that works need not be thought to "belong" to a single genre. In *The Genres of Gulliver's Travels*, Frederik Smith has brought together a collection of critical essays viewing Swift's text from the perspective of eight different genres. The collection makes a strong case not simply for Swift's method of a "deliberate mingling of genres" (19), but for the values of different readings with different conventions in mind. Viewing *Gulliver's Travels* as a children's book pushes us to see certain elements; reading it as a political satire or a philosophical treatise causes us to see others. The point is that genre critics do not insist that texts are written according to a formula but recognize that our reading takes place within a context of other texts with similar conventions.

Aristotle's *Poetics* remains the starting point for questions of genre. René Wellek and Austin Warren's *Theory of Literature* devotes a clear and helpful chapter to the discussion of genre, and Paul Hernadi's *Beyond Genre: New Directions in Literary Classification* is a comprehensive discussion of recent genre theory. Hirsch gives a chapter to "The Concept of Genre" in *Validity in Interpretation*. These and other important studies are included in the following list.

## WORKS CITED AND RECOMMENDED

Booth, Wayne. *The Rhetoric of Fiction*. Chicago: Chicago UP, 1961.

Crane, R. S. *Critics and Criticism*. Chicago: Chicago UP, 1953.

Culler, Jonathan. *Structuralist Poetics: Structuralism, Linguistics and the Study of Literature*. Ithaca: Cornell UP, 1975.

Derrida, Jacques. "The Law of Genre." *Acts of Literature*. Ed. Derek Attridge. New York and London: Routledge, 1992. 221–252.

Frye, Northrop. *Anatomy of Criticism: Four Essays*. Princeton: Princeton UP, 1957.

Hernadi, Paul. *Beyond Genre: New Directions in Literary Classification*. Ithaca: Cornell UP, 1972.

Hirsch, E. D., Jr. *Validity in Interpretation*. New Haven: Yale UP, 1967.

Malin, Irving. *New American Gothic*. Carbondale: Southern Illinois UP, 1962.

Olson, Elder. *Tragedy and the Theory of Drama*. Detroit: Wayne State UP, 1961.

Sacks, Sheldon. *Fiction and the Shape of Belief*. Berkeley: California UP, 1964.

Smith, Frederick N., ed. *The Genres of Gulliver's Travels*. Newark: U of Delaware P, 1990.

Todorov, Tzvetan. *The Fantastic: A Structural Approach to a Literary Genre.* Ithaca: Cornell UP, 1975.

———. *The Poetics of Prose.* Ithaca: Cornell UP, 1977.

Wellek, René, and Austin Warren. *Theory of Literature.* New York: Harcourt, 1956.

## RHETORICAL STUDIES AND READER-RESPONSE CRITICISM

Rhetoric is commonly defined as the art of using words to move an audience and is frequently associated with speech and oratory or with nonfiction prose. However, the rhetorical study of poetry and fiction has a long tradition, dating back at least as far as the Roman poet Horace, who described as the aim of the poet "to inform or delight." As simple and commonsensical as the formulation seems, it assumes literary works to have certain purposes relative to their audience, an assumption central to rhetorical criticism. M. H. Abrams uses the term *pragmatic* to emphasize that such criticism "looks at the work of art chiefly as a means to an end, an instrument for getting something done" (15). The purpose of literary works and the way they move an audience to achieve their purpose are the chief concerns of rhetorical studies.

### Early Approaches: Sidney and Johnson

Historically, rhetorical or pragmatic criticism, which according to Abrams "characterized by far the greatest part of criticism from the time of Horace through the eighteenth century" (217), has been especially concerned with moral instruction. For example, Sir Philip Sidney, in his *An Apology for Poetry* written in the early 1580s, combines the views of Aristotle and Horace in defining the nature and purpose of literature: "Poetry therefore is an art of imitation, for as Aristotle termeth it in his word *Mimesis,* that is to say, a representing, counterfeiting or feigning forth—to speak metaphorically, a speaking picture: with this end, to teach and delight." As Abrams notes, the emphasis here is on teaching: Poetry "imitates only as a means to the proximate end of pleasing, and pleases, it turns out, only as a means to the ultimate end of teaching" (14). What poetry should teach, argues Sidney, is virtue and nobility, "the . . . end of all earthly learning being virtuous action."

To show how literature teaches virtue, Sidney compares the poet to the philosopher and the historian. The philosopher may give moral precepts, but these are frequently so "abstract and general, that happy is the man who may understand." The historian, on the other hand, lacks the precepts and is tied "to the particular truth of things and not to the general reason of things." The poet has the advantage on both. Unlike philosophy, according to Sidney, literature is specific and concrete; it is able to present detailed and compelling pictures rather than general rules. Unlike history, literature is able to imitate not simply what is but also what should be. That is, not being bound to a recitation of facts, literature may get at the essence of a situation.

This view may be more clearly illustrated in the work of Samuel Johnson, the eighteenth-century poet and critic. In the tale *Rasselas*, Johnson's character Imlac says,"The business of a poet . . . is to examine, not the individual, but the species; to remark general properties and large appearances; he does not number the streaks of the tulip. . . ."The belief in literature's concern with the essential is central to Johnson's and Sidney's rhetorical conceptions. If literature is to speak meaningfully to an audience, it must deal with a situation relevant to the audience; the particular must be shown to be representative or universal. For example, in *The Rambler*, number 60, Johnson suggests biography to be "useful" because "there is such a uniformity in the state of man . . . that there is scarce any possibility of good or ill, but is common to human kind."The criterion of the pragmatic or useful is found throughout Johnson's writing. In deploring some aspects of eighteenth-century romances, for instance, he warns of the need to "distinguish those parts of nature, which are most proper for imitation. . . .If the world be promiscuously described, I cannot see of what use it can be to read the account" (*The Rambler*, number 4).

## Contemporary Approaches

Although contemporary rhetorical criticism does not necessarily share Johnson's or Sidney's views on morality, it retains an interest in the relationship between the literary work and the audience, in the way words are used to move a reader or a listener. Wayne Booth, in the preface to *The Rhetoric of Fiction*, calls his study a pursuit of "the author's means of controlling his reader." For example, in an extended analysis of Jane Austen's *Emma*, Booth attempts to determine how Austen keeps readers sympathetic toward the main character when Emma's faults are so potentially damaging. Booth focuses particularly on point of view, noting that most of the novel is seen through Emma's eyes, ensuring that the reader "shall travel with Emma rather than stand against her."A reader, Booth states, tends "to hope for good fortune for the character with whom he travels, quite independently of the qualities revealed" (245–246). Austen must also withhold inside views of certain other characters. Were the novel to move within the mind of Jane Fairfax, a deserving character who suffers as the result of Emma's insensitive actions, the reader's sympathy for Emma would surely be destroyed. Throughout the discussion, Booth demonstrates a complex of techniques that controls the reader's response. Of course, other critical methods might examine these same techniques; a formalist study, for instance, would probably consider point of view. However, treating these techniques as strategies designed, either consciously or unconsciously, to govern the reader makes for a rhetorical study.

Although the audience has always been crucial to rhetorical criticism, traditionally the focus of criticism has been on the author and the work. What is the author's purpose, and what techniques are used to accomplish it? The audience has been less examined than assumed. Recently, however, attention has shifted to the reader and to the act of reading itself, an orientation sometimes called *reader-response* criticism. This turn toward an interest in the reader, although usually seen as a product of the 1970s and 1980s, dates back at least to the work of Louise Rosenblatt, who, in the late 1930s, recognized the active and creative nature of the reader and suggested that "the literary experience must be phrased as a transaction between the reader and the text" (*Literature as Exploration* 34-35). Rosenblatt anticipated the emphasis of more recent reader-response critics in her call to "place in the center of our attention the actual process of literary re-creation" and in her belief that "our concern should be with the relation between readers and texts" (282).

## Fish: Affective Stylistics

Among those who look most closely at the reading of texts is Stanley Fish. For example, in "Literature in the Reader: Affective Stylistics," Fish argues for a view of reading as a process and for a method that continually questions what happens in a reader's mind during the process. As Fish states it, the method "involves an analysis of the developing responses of the reader in relation to the words as they succeed one another in time" (*Self-Consuming Artifacts* 387-388). Taking a line from *Paradise Lost*, in which the fallen angels find themselves cast out from paradise—"Nor did they not perceive the evil plight"—Fish examines the reader's expectations and responses word by word. The first word, *Nor,* causes the reader to expect a subject and verb following, an expectation affirmed by the auxiliary *did* and the pronoun *they.* The expectation is frustrated, though, when the reader next encounters not a verb but a second negative, *not.* The negative causes the reader to pause and upsets the expected logic. The reader may then either reread or continue searching for the expected verb. "In either case," Fish contends, "the syntactical uncertainty remains unresolved." Fish sees the most important effect of the line to be "the suspension of the reader between the alternatives its syntax momentarily offers" (387), the difficulty of determining during the reading process whether or not the fallen angels did perceive. Fish goes on to suggest that, in effect, the angels did and did not perceive their plight: They physically saw the situation, but they did not recognize its full moral significance. The point, however, is not so much a final interpretation as an attempt to describe what happens within the reader during the act of reading. Meaning, for Fish, is "an event, something that is happening between the words and the reader's mind" (389).

Thus, in Fish's terms, literature is an experience, and readings are descriptions of the nature of that experience. *The Living Temple: George Herbert and Catechizing* contains a telling example of the difference between Fish's interest in reader response and the formalist critic's concern with form. Fish discusses Herbert's "Church Monuments," a poem dealing with the mortality and decay of all earthly things as the speaker views crumbling monuments and recognizes his own flesh as merely the glass "which holds the dust / That measures all our time." Fish quotes from an analysis of the poem's techniques by Joseph Summers: "the dissolution of the body and the monuments is paralleled by the dissolution of the sentences and stanza. . . .The sentences sift down through the rhyme scheme skeleton of the stanza like the sand through the glass and the glass itself has already begun to crumble" (134–135). The analysis is clearly formalist in its depiction of the relation between meaning and structure, and Fish recognizes it as "an authoritative description of what is happening in the poem." His question, though, is what is happening in and to the reader. What he discovers as he traces the encounter of a reader with the words on the page is nothing less than a "dissolution, or falling away, of the perceptual framework a reader brings with him to the poem and indeed to life" (165). That is, as readers "experience" the poem, they find their own assumptions and characteristic ways of viewing the world changed.

## Iser: The Implied Reader

Fish's affective stylistics is only one of several important contemporary *reader-response* theories. Another is derived from phenomenology, a philosophical approach to the study of consciousness and immediate experience. A phenomenological approach to literature developed by the Polish critic Roman Ingarden sees a literary work as an intended act of the consciousness of an author, which is then reexperienced or realized in the consciousness of a reader. To explain this, Wolfgang Iser, in *The Implied Reader: Patterns of Communication in Prose Fiction from Bunyan to Beckett,* speaks of "two poles" of a literary work—the artistic, which "refers to the text created by the author," and the aesthetic, which refers to the "realization accomplished by the reader" (274). The patterns and situations of a literary text supply the materials and determine the boundaries for the creative act of reading. The text must, in Iser's words, "engage the reader's imagination in the task of working things out for himself" (275). A text may supply too much, leaving too little work for the reader, and thus become boring; on the other hand, a work may be too open with few guidelines for the reader and thus result in confusion and "overstrain." However, the text which successfully guides the reader through the working out of things should ultimately result in the reader's self-discovery.

Iser's discussion of Henry Fielding's *Tom Jones* provides an example of the approach. Iser begins with the dialogue between narrator and reader in volume 5, book 1, of the novel, a dialogue in which the narrator speaks of the importance of contrast in demonstrating the beauty and excellence of any phenomenon. For Iser, this principle of contrast is crucial to the reader's participation, for "the reader must provide the link" between contrasting phenomena if the novel is to be understood (48). For instance, relatively late in the novel, Tom is discovered to be the kept man of the promiscuous Lady Bellaston. What are readers to make of this seamy revelation? Iser believes creative readers, guided by the narrator's statements about contrast, will bring to bear earlier and contrasting scenes as they read of the rendezvous with Lady Bellaston. The immediately preceding scene, for example, reminds us of Tom at his most compassionate and best, as he meets with an impoverished highwayman whose life he had once saved. The reader, guided by the novel, creatively links the various scenes and perspectives to come finally to a fuller understanding of Tom's character and, perhaps, of human nature in general.

## Holland: Transactive Reading

It may be helpful to think of reader-response criticism as having two poles or two contrasting emphases: the one stressing the means by which the text controls or guides the reader and the other emphasizing the way in which the individual reader creates or recreates the text. Iser's work, to some extent, illustrates the first insofar as it argues that the text guides the reader and determines the boundaries for the reading. Norman Holland, on the other hand, using the insights of psychology, stresses the reader's role in the transaction with the text, arguing that the reader is not constrained in the way Iser suggests and that the reader does far more than to fill in textual gaps.

In "The Miller's Wife and the Professors: Questions about the Transactive Theory of Reading," Holland puts forth what he calls a feedback model of his transactive theory of reading, a model somewhat similar to those explaining perception in cognitive psychology. Essentially, the model suggests that in reading the reader brings her or his individual identity to the work, an identity constructed from all the reader's experiences in the world, including everything from unconscious fantasies and needs to hypotheses and expectations of texts. This identity sends forth hypotheses and the text returns answers, which may then become incorporated in the individual's identity. Thus, the model is a loop with the reader in some sense constructing the text but with the text also acting on the reader.

For example, a student schooled in formalist criticism is likely, when reading a poem, to have certain expectations or hypotheses about the unity of poems or the likelihood of ironies and, thus, reads the poem in light of those hypotheses. The hypotheses are, in a sense, tested against the poem, and an answer is returned; a reading is made. In all likelihood, the student will discover within the poem unities or ironies of the kind she hypothesizes; she will find what she is looking for. However, the poem may resist these expectations, and the student does not find what she expects. New hypotheses may need to be attempted, and the student's identity will be subtly changed. Thus, the model demonstrates both how the reader constructs the text (in this case, by reading in light of expectations of unity) and how the text acts on the reader (by confirming or resisting those expectations).

This example may be too simple, however, because identity consists of far more than simply a set of hypotheses about literary texts. An identity is made up of one's total experience. As Holland says, "We are the history of what we have experienced" (435). For instance, the person whose experiences have led to deep concerns about fears of failure may read in light of hypotheses concerning failure and inadequacy. Holland believes that person will employ strategies of reading (for example, strategies of formalism) to produce a reading in accord with those concerns. As Holland states, "The transactive theory of reading models this process as a person, with a certain identity, *using* (as an artist or craftsman uses) the poem and the various codes, strategies, and settings to achieve a reading that *feels right*" (432).

## Other Rhetorical Approaches

Other critical approaches sometimes associated with the reader-response criticism are treated elsewhere in this book. Archetypal studies, for instance, focus on the reader insofar as they are concerned with the universal patterns to which all humans respond. Also, as the discussion of Holland may suggest, psychological criticism has come to emphasize the role of the reader. The work of Harold Bloom and other works of Holland are discussed in the section on psychological studies in Chapter 3. However, two other rhetorical approaches should be mentioned here, although both can also legitimately be considered as varieties of historical study.

### HISTORY AND RHETORIC

The first is the study of rhetoric itself, particularly the theory and application of rhetoric at a given time. Of special interest to students of sixteenth- and seventeenth-century literature is Sister Miriam Joseph's *Rhetoric in Shakespeare's Time: Literary Theory of Renaissance Europe*, an attempt "to present in organized detail essentially complete the general theory of composition current during the Renaissance" (ix). The book is organized according to sixteenth-century rhetorical theory and includes definitions and illustrations from works on grammar, rhetoric, and logic of that time. For example, "Logos: The Types of Invention" is divided into eleven topics: testimony, definition, division, subject and adjuncts, contraries and contradictions, similarity and dissimilarity, comparison, cause and effect, notation and conjugates, genesis or composition, and analysis or reading. Within these topics are subdivisions. The reader finds, for instance, that "Tudor rhetoricians treat eleven figures based on contraries and contradictions," including such figures as litotes, synoeciosis, paradox, antiphrasis, and antanagoge. The last, "a figure whereby something spoken unfavorably is in a measure counteracted, though not denied, by the addition of something favorable," is illustrated from George Puttenham's *The Arte of English Poesie* (1589): "Many are the paines and perils to be past, / But great is the gaine and glorie at the last." To be aware of what writers of the sixteenth and seventeenth centuries learned about communication is likely to give a fuller understanding of their methods of communicating to an audience.

### RECEPTION STUDIES

A second and very traditional kind of rhetorical study is the reception study, which documents the response to authors or works in their own or subsequent times. A representative example is W. Powell Jones's "The Contemporary Reception of Gray's *Odes.*" Like many such studies, this article depends heavily on newspaper and magazine reviews and on personal letters as it attempts "to present all possible evidence which will tend to show how [Thomas Gray's] *Odes* were received by the public at the time of their appearance and shortly afterward" (62). Jones concludes that the *Odes* were well known and widely discussed but thought to be obscure, a charge that both annoyed and amused Gray. Although such knowledge may not substantially alter a reader's understanding of a literary work, it can supply information about the literary climate and the reading public of a given time.

Recently, new theories of reception criticism have emerged. Hans Robert Jauss, in "Literary History as a Challenge to Literary Theory," writes of the "horizon" of a reading public—that is, expectations developed "from a previous understanding of the genre, from the form and theme of already familiar works, and from the contrast between poetic and practical language" (15). These horizons of expectations may change from one generation of readers to another. For instance, Jauss notes the 1857 publication of two works, Gustave Flaubert's *Madame Bovary* and Ernest Feydeau's *Fanny*. Although the two novels are similar in their handling of adultery and jealousy, they have had very different receptions. Feydeau's book was enormously successful at publication, with thirteen editions in one year, but is now nearly forgotten. *Madame Bovary*, on the other hand, was popular with only a "small circle of knowledgeable readers" but is now considered a masterpiece. Jauss accounts for *Madame Bovary*'s initial lack of popularity by the expectations of its readers. They did not understand Flaubert's method of "impersonal telling" and saw the narrator as a "story-telling machine." However, the novel eventually fashioned a new set of expectations, a new horizon, in knowledgeable readers. As Jauss puts it, "the group of readers who were formed by this book sanctioned the new canon of expectations, which made the weaknesses of Feydeau—his flowery style, his modish effects, his lyrical confessional clichés—unbearable" (22).

## Rhetorical Study: An Overview

Rhetorical study as defined here includes an especially wide range of specific methods and concerns. The traditional contemporary reception study may seem far removed from reader-response criticism or even from traditional rhetorical analysis. However, all these approaches share an interest in the relationship between the literary text and its reader, between what is being communicated and how it is being received. Whether the emphasis is on the strategies of a text, the mind of an individual reader, or the reaction of a larger audience, each approach recognizes that literary works do not exist in a vacuum but have meaning through interaction with readers.

Along with works already mentioned, persons interested in rhetorical criticism should be aware of the importance of Aristotle's *Rhetoric*, which is available in a number of good editions. Also helpful are Edward P. J. Corbett's *Rhetorical Analysis of Literary Works* and Kenneth Burke's *A Rhetoric of Motives,* a complex but rewarding presentation of Burke's rhetorical theory. As mentioned, Louise Rosenblatt's *Literature as Exploration* is a pioneering work in reader-response criticism; her theories are elaborated in her later book *The Reader, the Text, the Poem.* Jane Tompkins's *Reader-Response Criticism: From Formalism to Post-Structuralism* and Susan Sulieman and Inge Crossman's *The Reader in the Text: Essays on Audience and Interpretation* both contain excellent cross sections of essays on reader response.

## WORKS CITED AND RECOMMENDED

Abrams, M. H. *The Mirror and the Lamp: Romantic Theory and the Critical Tradition.* New York: Norton, 1953.

Bleich, David. *Reading and Feelings: An Introduction to Subjective Criticism.* Urbana: NCTE, 1975.

Booth, Wayne. *A Rhetoric of Irony.* Chicago: Chicago UP, 1974.

———. *The Rhetoric of Motives.* New York: Prentice, 1950.

Corbett, Edward P. J. *Rhetorical Analysis of Literary Works.* New York: Oxford UP, 1969.

Fish, Stanley. *The Living Temple: George Herbert and Catechizing.* Berkeley: California UP, 1978.

———. *Self-Consuming Artifacts: The Experience of Seventeenth-Century Literature.* Berkeley: California UP, 1972.

———. *Surprised by Sin: The Reader in "Paradise Lost."* New York: Macmillan, 1967.

Foss, Sonja K., Karen A. Foss, and Robert Trapp. *Contemporary Perspectives on Rhetoric.* Prospect Heights: Waveland, 1985.

Holland, Norman. "The Miller's Wife and the Professors: Questions about the Transactive Theory of Reading." *New Literary History* 17 (1986): 423–447.

Iser, Wolfgang. *The Implied Reader: Patterns of Communication in Prose Fiction from Bunyan to Beckett.* Baltimore: Johns Hopkins UP, 1974.

Jauss, Hans Robert. "History of Art and Pragmatic History." *New Perspectives in German Literary Criticism.* Eds. Richard Amacher and Victor Lange. Princeton: Princeton UP, 1979.

———. "Literary History as a Challenge to Literary Theory." *New Directions in Literary History.* Ed. Ralph Cohen. Baltimore: Johns Hopkins UP, 1974. 11–41.

Jones, W. Powell. "The Contemporary Reception of Gray's *Odes.*" *Modern Philology* 28 (1930): 61–82.

Joseph, Sister Miriam. *Rhetoric in Shakespeare's Time: Literary Theory of Renaissance Europe.* New York: Harcourt, 1962.

Rosenblatt, Louise. *Literature as Exploration.* New York: MLA, 1938.

———. *The Reader, the Text, the Poem.* Carbondale: Southern Illinois UP, 1978.

———. "The Transactional Theory: Against Dualism." *College English* 55 (1993): 377–386.

Sulieman, Susan R., and Inge Crossman, eds. *The Reader in the Text: Essays on Audience and Interpretation.* Princeton: Princeton UP, 1980.

Tompkins, Jane, ed. *Reader-Response Criticism: From Formalism to Post-Structuralism.* Baltimore: Johns Hopkins UP, 1980.

# STRUCTURALIST AND DECONSTRUCTIONIST STUDIES

## Structuralism

Structuralist criticism shares with formalism a close attention to the literary text and an attempt to account for its features. Yet, although formal analysis has become central to the classroom study of literature, structuralism seems never to have been as widely disseminated or understood. Perhaps the most important reason for misunderstandings about structuralist studies comes from a confusion about their purpose, a purpose Jonathan Culler defines as the development of "a poetics which would stand to literature as linguistics stands to language and which therefore would not seek to explain what individual works mean but would attempt to make explicit the system of figures and conventions that *enable* works to have the forms and meanings they do" (foreword to Gerard Genette's *Narrative Discourse* 8). That is, structuralist studies do not necessarily attempt to give interpretations of literary works but to examine the structures underlying these works.

### THE LINGUISTIC BACKGROUND

As Culler's statement suggests, the methodology and much of the vocabulary of structuralism derive from linguistics, particularly from the insights of the Swiss linguist Ferdinand de Saussure, whose lectures at the University of Geneva were published posthumously as *Cours de Linguistique Générale* and later translated as *Course in General Linguistics.* Among elements necessary for an understanding of Saussure's structural linguistics is, first, the distinction between what Saussure calls *langue*, the system of convention and rules that govern language, and *parole*, the individual utterances of a language. That is, all speakers recognize their own capability to make grammatical statements they have never seen or heard before. To explain this ability, linguists assume a knowledge, intuitive or otherwise, of principles or rules concerning word order, tense, and other grammatical and syntactical elements. These principles are the *langue*, which leads the speaker to structure individual statements, the *parole*, in certain ways. In literary studies, texts are treated as examples of *parole*; the task of the structuralist is to determine the principles that govern their formation.

A second key element for Saussure concerns the relationship between language and what language refers to. Traditionally, words were viewed as standing in a one-to-one relationship to objects in the world. The word *tree*, for instance, stood for a certain kind of plant with a trunk and branches. Saussure believed the case to be more complicated and used three terms to explain it— the signifier, the signified, and the sign. The signifier is what Saussure calls a "sound-image," for example, the sound combination *trë*. The signified is a concept, in this case the concept of a kind of plant. The sign, *tree*, is a combination of the signifier and the signified, the sound-image and the concept. The person seeing the word *tree* has in mind both the sound and the concept.

These distinctions lead to two insights fundamental to structuralism. One is a recognition of language as arbitrary; it is cultural, not inborn. For the French speaker, the sign *tree* would not signify the concept of a certain type of plant nor would a statement such as "I planted a tree" be generated according to the conventions of the French language (*langue*). The second, related insight is that meaning depends on relationships within the language. Once these relationships, or the structure of the language, are changed, meaning changes. Obviously, the two structures "the dog bit the man" and "the man bit the dog" are considerably different although only the relationship of the signs has changed.

Saussure realized these insights were significant to more than the study of language, and in fact, he anticipated a science based on them: "A science that studies the life of signs within society is conceivable; it would be a part of social psychology and consequently of general psychology. I shall call it *semiology* (from Greek semeion, 'sign'). Semiology would show what constitutes signs, what laws govern them" (16). Whether a science of semiology yet exists is debatable, but in literary study as well as in other areas, much of the critical activity of the last twenty-five years has been an attempt to lay the groundwork for it.

## PROPP AND RUSSIAN FORMALISM

To make these ideas more specific, it may help to consider the work of a precursor of modern structuralism, the Russian formalist Vladimir Propp. Propp, attempting to classify one hundred Russian fairy tales, found among them certain common elements. He noticed, for example, seven recurring categories of characters: the villain, the donor or provider, the helper, the sought-for person and her father, the dispatcher, the hero, and the false hero. The term *character*, however, may be misleading since the categories refer to certain roles rather than to individuals who take these roles. Propp uses the phrase "spheres of action" to emphasize that these are concerned with actions that are performed and not simply with the personages who act. In somewhat the same way that many different words can serve, for instance, as adjectives in a sentence, many different individual characters can perform acts of villainy or acts of help. Conversely, just as a single word can sometimes function as different parts of speech, a single character can serve in several spheres of action—for example, as donor at one point and helper at another. The concept of spheres of action, and such related terms as *actant* and *actantial* role, encourage the critic to look not at specific characters or personages but at the underlying structure of actions.

Propp also noted among the fairy tales specific elements he called *functions*—defining function as "an act of a character, defined from the point of view of its significance for the course of the action" (21). Propp discovered thirty-one such functions. Although no tale included all thirty-one, the functions each tale did have always followed the same sequence. This led Propp to believe that just as language has certain conventions that determine sequence (for instance, article-adjective-noun, "the green tree," but never a sequence of noun-adjective-article, "tree green the"), so the folktale has conventions that determine order. As Propp concluded, "all fairy tales are of one type in regard to their structure" (23). The following are the first seven of Propp's functions:

1. One of the members of a family absents him- or herself from home— absentation.
2. An interdiction is addressed to the hero or heroine—interdiction.
3. The interdiction is violated—violation.
4. The villain makes an attempt at reconnaissance—reconnaissance.
5. The villain receives information about his or her victim—delivery.
6. The villain attempts to deceive the victim in order to take possession of the victim or of his or her belongings—trickery.
7. The victim submits to deception and thereby unwittingly helps his or her enemy—complicity.

Although Propp's analysis is more complex, a simplified examination may indicate something of the nature of structural analysis. The well-known fairy tale "Little Red Ridinghood" begins with Red Ridinghood absenting herself from the house to take a basket of food to her grandmother. In some versions, her mother explicitly makes an interdiction, commanding her daughter to go straight to grandmother's house without going astray or talking to strangers. Of course, Red Ridinghood immediately violates the interdiction, in some versions by forsaking the straight path to grandmother's and in other simply by talking to the villainous wolf. The wolf's attempt at reconnaissance is successful; Red Ridinghood gives him the necessary information about her destination. The wolf arrives first at grandmother's house and deceives the woman by speaking in a high-pitched voice in imitation of Red Ridinghood. Grandmother unwittingly helps the wolf by inviting him in and explaining how to unlatch the door. The tale, then, has in sequence the functions of absentation, interdiction, violation, reconnaissance, delivery, trickery, and complicity. The eighth of Propp's functions—the villain causes harm or injury to a member of the family—is about to be enacted. The point here is not to arrive at a new interpretation of the tale but to see the structure underneath it. The tale can be viewed as an individual utterance of the *parole*, which is governed by conventions of the *langue*.

## CALLOUD AND LEXIES

A difficulty in structural analysis is determining the significant elements. Some structuralists use the term *lexie* to designate these basic elements, a lexie being, in Jonathan Culler's words, "a minimal unit of reading, a stretch of text which is isolated as having a specific effect or function different from that of neighboring stretches of text. It could thus be anything from a single word to a brief series of sentences" (*Structuralist Poetics* 202). For example, in *Structural Analysis of Narrative*, Jean Calloud analyzes the temptation scene in Matthew 4:1-11 and defines as lexies both sentences and parts of sentences. The first six lexies follow:

**Lexie 1:** Then Jesus was led by the Spirit out into the wilderness to be tempted by the devil.

**Lexie 2:** He fasted for forty days and forty nights, after which he was (very) hungry.

**Lexie 3:** And the tempter came and said to him . . .

**Lexie 4:** If you are the Son of God, tell these stones to turn into loaves.

**Lexie 5:** But he replied: Scripture says . . .

**Lexie 6:** Man does not live by bread alone but on every word that comes from the mouth of God.

Although it is not possible to account fully for these lexies in a brief discussion, the nature of the analysis can be seen by considering lexie 5 and asking why it consists only of part of a sentence. Lexies, according to Calloud, are composed of actors and processes, with processes further divided into two classes on the basis of the kind of verb used. In Calloud's procedure, derived in part from the work of A. J. Greimas, all verbs are reduced to those of "doing" and those of "being" or "having"; processes related to "doing" are spoken of as *functions*, whereas those having to do with "being" or "having" are referred to as *qualifications*. Thus, the predicate of "the professor lectured to her class" would be a function; the predicate of "the professor was very articulate" or "the professor had a Ph.D." would be a qualification. Further, functions are grouped into several categories, usually paired sets of actions: arrival vs. departure or departure vs. return; conjunction vs. disjunction; mandating vs. acceptance or vs. refusal; confrontation; domination vs. submission; communication vs. reception; and attribution vs. deprivation. Calloud describes the third of these functions, mandating vs. acceptance or vs. refusal, as one in which "an action is explicitly or implicitly proposed to an actor who accepts it or refuses it" (17). Lexie 5, then, has an actor, "he" (Jesus), and a process, in this case the function of refusal. In lexie 4, the devil has mandated Jesus to turn stones into bread. In lexie 5, Jesus refuses by appealing to a prior mandate, the scriptural contract between himself and God. If lexie 5 was shortened to include only "But he replied," its function of refusal would not be clear; on the other hand, if the whole sentence, including the scriptural quotation, was treated as a single lexie, several different processes would have to be considered.

## BARTHES AND CODES

Perhaps the fullest discussion of lexies and how they operate is Roland Barthes's *S/Z*, an analysis of Honoré de Balzac's short story "Sarrasine." Barthes divides the story into 561 lexies and suggests they can function on five levels. The description of these levels, or *codes* as they are usually called, is sometimes confusing, but Culler in *Structuralist Poetics* offers the following definitions: the proairetic code, which relates to plot and actions; the hermeneutic code, which concerns the "puzzle" of the narrative, the questions it raises and eventually answers; the referential code, which contains allusions to cultural values and background, including proverbs, stereotyped knowledge, and scientific facts; the semic code, which presents material relating to characters; and the symbolic code, which includes thematic elements.

A simplified illustration using a passage from William Faulkner's "A Rose for Emily" may help to show how these codes operate within a text. The passage recounts an incident in which the protagonist, Emily, is buying a poison, which the reader later realizes is used to kill her lover, who planned to desert her:

> "I want some poison," she said to the druggist. She was over thirty then, still a slight woman, though thinner than usual, with cold, haughty black eyes in a face the flesh of which was strained across the temples and about the eye-sockets as you imagine a lighthouse-keeper's face to look. "I want poison," she said.
>> "Yes, Miss Emily. What kind? For rats and such? I'd recom—"
>> "I want the best you have. I don't care what kind."

It is not necessary to divide the passage into lexies to see how some of the codes function. For example, much of the passage clearly works on the proairetic level, giving signs about plot. The climax of the short story occurs when, after Miss Emily's death, the townspeople find the bones of Emily's dead lover in the upstairs bedroom. The buying of poison is a plot incident which leads to that climatic scene. However, until the final scene, readers do not know what happened to the lover; thus, the passage also operates on the hermeneutic level. Why Emily purchases the poison, why she wants the "best" or strongest, and why she refuses to divulge her reason for the purchase are questions the narrative answers only later. Her refusal may also provide semic information. Throughout the story, readers are made aware of Miss Emily's sense of privacy. She answers only those questions which suit her purposes to answer. Certainly, the statements about age and appearance are part of the semic code. However, the description of her being "over thirty" may also be part of the referential code, especially if the reader has cultural stereotypes about unmarried middle-aged women in that society. If the theme of the story concerns an attempt to hold on to a dead past, a past that appears both more dignified and more destructive, both richer and more vicious, than the present, then surely much of the passage operates on the symbolic level. Miss Emily cannot let her lover go, but she can keep him only by killing him.

## PARADIGMATIC AND SYNTAGMATIC ELEMENTS

The preceding discussion calls for another distinction crucial to structuralist criticism, the distinction between paradigmatic and syntagmatic relations. Once again, the terms come from Saussure's linguistics, which stresses the importance of the syntagmatic element of language. Briefly, the syntagmatic is concerned with the linear aspect of language, the positioning of words in a given sequence and in a certain relation to other words. The paradigmatic refers to the vertical aspect of language, the many words that could fit a given slot in the sequence. Barthes illustrates the distinction through the example of a menu. To consider, for instance, all entrées or all salads on the menu is to read it paradigmatically. Steak, chicken, lamb, or pork chops could each fit the entrée slot in a meal. On the other hand, considering the menu in sequence, from appetizer to dessert, is syntagmatic.

As the discussion of "A Rose of Emily" may show, proairetic and hermeneutic codes are largely syntagmatic, whereas semic and symbolic codes have more paradigmatic features. Clearly, sequence is important to plot. Emily must buy the poison and then use it before her lover can be found dead. Plot is linear or syntagmatic: $X$ buys poison; $X$ gives poison to $Y$; $Y$ is found dead. Similarly, on the hermeneutic level, the question of the poison's purchase must be raised before it can be answered. If the sequence was reversed, if the lover's remains were discovered before the reader knew about the poison, different questions would be asked: Who murdered the lover? Or how was the lover killed? Character and theme are not bound to sequence in the same way. The character Emily is more than the $X$ of the plot diagram because of descriptions and characterizations that have occurred throughout the story; these are cumulative and do not necessarily depend on the order in which they are given. The reader can pick out all the descriptions associated with Emily to come to an understanding of her character. In the same way, thematic elements are found throughout the story and combine to provide a sense of theme.

## CONVENTIONS GOVERNING POETRY

The examples so far probably indicate the emphasis structuralist criticism has placed on narrative, possibly because narrative sequence seems analogous to the sequence of a sentence. However, as Culler points out, poetry, even if not narrative, also operates according to certain conventions which govern the reader's understanding of a text. That is, readers come to a poem with different assumptions and read it differently from the way they would a newspaper article or a political speech or a prose essay. Culler notes four conventions, or rules, that shape the assumptions of competent readers: the conventions of significance, of metaphorical coherence, of poetic tradition, and of thematic unity. To illustrate these, he uses William Blake's "Ah, Sun-flower":

Ah, Sun-flower, weary of time,
Who countest the steps of the Sun,
Seeking after that sweet golden clime,
Where the traveller's journey is done;

Where the Youth pined away with desire,
And the pale Virgin shrouded in snow
Arise from their graves, and aspire
Where my Sun-flower wishes to go.

According to the rule of significance, readers assume a poem will express "a significant attitude to some problem concerning man and/or his relationship to the universe" (115). Thus, readers immediately know not to treat the sunflower here as they might treat a reference to a flower in a garden catalogue. The sunflower "weary of time" is likely to represent a statement about human weariness or the human condition. The convention of metaphorical coherence concerns the assumption that a poem will cohere or make sense both on a literal and on a metaphoric level. Readers recognize the literal way in which a sunflower turns toward the sun and also the figurative statement about human aspiration. The convention of poetic tradition allows readers to assume allusions used in other poetry and justifies, for instance, an equating of sunset and death, a time-honored poetic figure. Perhaps the most significant of the conventions, that of thematic unity, pushes the reader to view the poem as an integrated whole to which all elements contribute. The theme is a product of all parts of the poem.

## Deconstruction

The assumptions underlying structuralism's examination of the conventions of literary discourse have been challenged by a mode of criticism usually spoken of as post-structuralism or *deconstruction*. The names suggest two important aspects of the approach. On the one hand, it is an outgrowth of structuralism and uses structural analysis to probe the deep patterns of a work. On the other hand, it rejects many of the most basic premises of structuralism and is concerned not with demonstrating how the structures of a work signify but with revealing the inadequacy of these structures. As Steven Lynn puts it, "If structuralism shows how the conventions of a text work, then post-structuralism, in a sense, points out how they fail" (263).

Ross Murfin suggests what such a statement may mean on the simplest level by pointing to the common experience of being nearly convinced by a particular reading of a text while at the same time recognizing that evidence within the text might also support an opposite reading. To want to make the point "that texts can be used to support seemingly irreconcilable positions," Murfin argues, ". . . is to feel the deconstructive itch" (199). That is, deconstruction shows the inadequacy of structures or conventions by pointing to those places where the structures convey or signify opposing meaning. In M. H. Abrams's definition, deconstructionists suppose that "the meaning of any text remains radically 'open' to contradictory readings" (203).

### DERRIDA AND *DIFFÉRANCE*

The theory that leads to this understanding of openness and opposition within texts is based on the work of the French writer Jacques Derrida in such studies as *Of Grammatology, Speech and Phenomena*, and *Writing and Difference*. Derrida's thought, grounded in the philosophy of Friedrich Nietzsche and Martin

Heidegger, is especially resistant to brief explanation. Indeed, many critics refuse, in Lynn's words, "to risk the spectacle of defining deconstruction" (263). However, it is important to recognize that Derrida's theory of deconstruction results in large part from a certain understanding of the nature of language, from a belief that ultimately language cannot have a single decidable meaning or set of meanings. A brief example of one aspect of Derrida's work may be illustrative.

Derrida begins, as structuralists began, with Saussure's linguistic concept of the signifier, the signified, and the sign and, more particularly, with Saussure's understanding of the "linguistic identity" of the sign. What is a sign? To use our earlier example, what characterizes the identity of the sign *tree*? Saussure argues that the sign's identity is not in the sign itself but in its relationship to other signs and that relationship is one of difference. That is, a sign's identity is not to be found in some intrinsic property of its own but in its difference from all other signs. For example, the identity of the sign *tree* is in its difference from other signs, from *free* or *bree* or *street*. As Saussure says, "Everything . . . boils down to this: in language there are only differences" (120).

For Derrida, this recognition of language as composed only of differences leads him to understand language (as well as texts and systems generally) as always indeterminate, as having no fixed meaning. Derrida arrives at this conclusion by reasoning (in a far richer way than can be suggested here) that insofar as words or signs have meaning only in their difference from other signs, their meaning is open to all possible oppositions. The meaning of *tree* is that it is not *free*, that is not *bree*, that it is not *street*, that it is not *bird*, and so on. To write about this point, Derrida coins the term *différance*. To explain this concept, Jane Tompkins, using her own illustrations, suggests that one does not hear the difference between the *t* and *f* in *tree* and *free*; what one hears is the *t* and *f*. One does not hear difference; one hears sounds. However, *différance* "is that which allows us to think in terms of contrast/comparative relationships. It is the very possibility of thinking relationally and, therefore, it couldn't itself ever appear. It is what enables other things to appear" (741).

It may seem a long way from what might appear to be abstract linguistic theorizing to the discussion of literary texts. Yet, these kinds of understandings, which call our premises concerning language into question, are the fundamental assumptions underlying deconstructionist thought. Texts are language, and in language there is only difference. For Derrida, there is nothing outside of language, nothing to which signs refer. Therefore, texts, being composed of signs, are not stable or fixed but are always open and indeterminate. Each word has identity in terms of all the words it is not and is understood in relation to all other words.

Derrida views deconstruction not as a critical method but as a way of reading, and there is considerable argument concerning the validity of using deconstruction as an approach to literature. Jane Tompkins flatly states that "you can't apply post-structuralism to literary texts" (746). However, since deconstructionist thought is pervasive in current critical discussion and has come to be used as a method of analysis, it seems important to consider its application and, to some extent, note the relationship of application to theory.

## TEXTUAL OPPOSITIONS

As might be expected, most deconstructionist readings focus on oppositions within a text, particularly oppositions that seem dichotomous or hierarchical. That is, since Derrida understands a sign to have identity in terms of what it is not, it seems natural to note such oppositions as masculine/feminine, presence/absence, awake/asleep, bright/dim, and so on. Deconstructionists note that these opposing pairs generally suggest a hierarchy; as Murfin says, "they contain one term that our culture views as being superior and one term viewed as negative or inferior" (200). The recognition of these hierarchical oppositions allows Steven Lynn to formulate a three-step process for a deconstructionist reading, a process based on Jonathan Culler's statement that "to deconstruct a discourse is to show how it undermines the philosophy it asserts, or the hierarchical oppositions on which it relies" (*On Deconstruction* 86):

> First, a deconstructive reading must note which member of an opposition in a text appears to be privileged or dominant (writers versus editors, error versus correctness, men versus women, etc.); second, the reading shows how this hierarchy can be reversed within the text, how the apparent hierarchy is arbitrary or illusory; finally, a deconstructive reading places both structures in question, making the text ultimately ambiguous. For students to deconstruct a text, they need to locate an opposition, determine which member is privileged, then reverse and undermine the hierarchy. (263)

Although Lynn's description is an especially helpful one, it should be noted that many deconstructionists would probably question his emphasis on the agency of the critic, arguing that the reversal and undermining are not so much the function of the critic as they are part of the nature of language itself. In the words of J. Hillis Miller, "Deconstruction is not a dismantling of the structure of text but a demonstration that it has already dismantled itself" (19).

## ATKINS: AN EXAMPLE

One can see how this demonstration works within Lynn's three-part outline by considering G. Douglas Atkins's discussion of John Dryden's *Religio Laici* in Atkins's book *Reading Deconstruction: Deconstructive Reading. Religio Laici* or *A Layman's Faith* was written in 1682, before Dryden's conversion to Roman Catholicism, and is usually read as an argument both against deism and for the sufficiency of Scripture in the understanding of religion. The poem seems clearly to argue against the Roman Catholic position of the need for scriptural interpretation by the Church and against the Puritan belief in inward light. The Scripture, Dryden's poem states, "speaks itself, and what it does contain, / In all things needful to be known, is plain." Biblical Scripture is accessible to the layperson because of the plain clarity of the language, a clarity that Dryden hopes to emulate in his poem. As he says in the preface to *Religio Laici*, "The expressions of a poem, designed purely for instruction, ought to be plain and natural. . . . The florid, elevated and figurative way is for the passions." This desire is stated in *Religio Laici*: "This unpolished, rugged verse, I chose / As fittest for discourse and nearest prose." Thus, an opposition or hierarchy is demonstrated; in this case, the opposition is between the plain and the figurative with the plain being privileged.

Atkins argues, though, that the poem undermines its own hierarchy. When the question of the nature of Christ is raised, the poem, in Atkins's view, shifts its ground and moves to a different and figurative argument. That is, the poem indicates a dilemma: "We hold, and say, we prove from Scripture plain / That Christ is GOD; the bold Socinian / From the same Scripture urges he's but MAN." The argument that Scripture is clear and sufficient to answer important religious questions seems not to hold; and the poem moves to new ground, stating "That many have been saved, and many may, / Who never heard this question brought in play" and portraying an "unlettered Christian . . . who plods on to Heaven." By this shift, says Atkins, "from the particular question posed to the quite different and broader claim that a limited core of belief is essential for salvation, Dryden reveals that for him Scripture alone is not able, after all, to settle all necessary questions . . ." (99). The hierarchy is undermined or, to shift the metaphor, reversed. If the poem must turn to the figurative to make its case, the "inferior" term is now privileged.

Another example from Atkins's reading may clarify the oppositional nature of the plain and the figurative and show how that opposition leads to indeterminacy. Atkins considers a question in the poem concerning the ability of humans to understand God: "How can the less the greater comprehend? / Or finite reason reach infinity? / For what could fathom God were more than He." Atkins suggests that the first two lines have both literal and figurative meanings. If the lines are understood figuratively as rhetorical questions, then they are not asking for a response but are asserting that humans "cannot comprehend God and that it is, in fact, foolhardy even to ask the question since 'finite Reason' obviously cannot 'reach Infinity.'" However, Atkins argues, "the literal meaning of the lines insists on an answer, one that would deny the assertion of the figurative, describing the ways in which man can come to comprehend God" (101). For Atkins, the entire poem is at issue in these two lines, for they lead to two "entirely incompatible readings," the one that humans cannot come to comprehend God and the other that humans, through the mediation of Scripture, can do so. Both terms of the opposition are held up to question, and the poem is seen to have deconstructed itself, "for what the text describes differs from, indeed wars with, what it declares. . . . [T]he poem contains mutually exclusive meanings" (103).

## BELSEY'S APPROACH

Because individual critics differ in the practice of deconstruction and in their reliance on Derrida's concepts and vocabulary, it is worth not only considering another example of deconstructionist criticism but also noting a differently phrased definition of the practice. Catherine Belsey, in *Critical Practice,* explains deconstruction in this way:

> The object of deconstructing the text is to examine the process of its produc-
> tion—not the private experience of the individual author, but the mode of
> production, the materials and their arrangement in the work. The aim is to lo-
> cate the point of contradiction within the text, the point at which it trans-
> gresses the limits within which it is constructed, breaks free of the constraints
> imposed by its own realistic form. (104)

Thus, deconstruction for Belsey is especially concerned with gaps, indeterminacies, open spaces, and incoherences, those places where a text violates its
own conventions or its contract with the reader. It is at such places that she
sees the text deconstructing.

In a discussion of Arthur Conan Doyle's Sherlock Holmes stories, Belsey
begins by exploring what she calls the codes of realism within the stories and
the ideology these codes reflect. Above all, Doyle's works attempt to establish
an illusion of reality and plausibility in which an initial mystery or enigma is
explained through logic and science. They purport to reveal all and to demonstrate the ability of reason to account for any apparent mystery. Ideologically,
Belsey suggests, the stories "reflect the widespread optimism characteristic of
their period concerning the comprehensive power of positivist science" (112).
That is, the structures of the stories—a narrative that moves from enigma to solution, a main character who acts on logical premises, and a plot that is resolved through scientific deduction—all depend on a belief in the efficacy of
science and human reason.

However, Belsey finds several areas in which the stories are particularly
reticent and in which the usual disclosures and revelations are strangely absent. One of these is the area of male-female relationships and especially female sexuality. In "Charles Augustus Milverton," for example, Holmes becomes
engaged to a housemaid in order to gain needed information, but once the information is obtained the woman is never again mentioned. In the same story,
Holmes's client is a Lady Eva Blackwell, whose "imprudent" letters to a young
man have been discovered by a blackmailer. Although important to the plot,
Lady Eva never appears in the story, and the contents of the letters are never
revealed. In "The Crooked Man," the husband of a Mrs. Barclay "is found dead
on the day of her meeting with her lover of many years before." Mrs. Barclay,
however, becomes insane and can never indicate the nature of her relationship
with the lover or the husband. Belsey accumulates an impressive number of
"shadowy, mysterious and often silent women" (115), whose roles seem at
odds with the conventions of the stories.

By recognizing elements that contradict the assumptions of Doyle's fictions, Belsey has begun the act of deconstruction. Stories that seemed unified
and coherent are found to have gaps and aspects that do not fit. The significance of this for Belsey is in revealing the limits of "ideological representation."
In this case, the stories cannot reflect both prevailing attitudes toward human
sexuality and a belief in the need for scientific scrutiny of all facets of life.
There is an opposition between full and open scrutiny on the one hand and
reticence toward certain aspects of life on the other. The apparently privileged

concept of scientific scrutiny is undermined by the workings of the text. In Belsey's words, the Sherlock Holmes stories "are compelled to manifest the inadequacy of a bourgeois scientificity which, working within the constraints of ideology, is thus unable to challenge it" (116). Like many deconstructionist readings, Belsey's examines the ideological basis of literary structures and focuses on those places where the structures break down, where they deny the values they appear to profess.

As this chapter has probably demonstrated, neither structuralism nor deconstruction is a single, easily definable approach, but both are terms denoting a variety of practices and assumptions. For students interested in structuralism, Jonathan Culler's *Structuralist Poetics* is an invaluable introduction. Also helpful are Robert Scholes's *Structuralism in Literature: An Introduction* and Terrence Hawkes's *Structuralism and Semiotics*. Important critiques of structuralist theory and practice include Fredric Jameson's *The Prison-House of Language* and Frank Lentricchia's *After the New Criticism*. Obviously central to an understanding of deconstruction is the work of Jacques Derrida, and a valuable introduction to Derrida and his use of Saussure is Jane Tompkins's "A Short Course in Post-Structuralism." Culler's *On Deconstruction: Theory and Criticism after Structuralism*, Christopher Norris's *Deconstruction, Theory and Practice*, and Vincent Leitch's *Deconstructive Criticism: An Advanced Introduction* are all helpful.

## WORKS CITED AND RECOMMENDED

Abrams, M. H. *A Glossary of Literary Terms.* New York: Holt, 1988.

Atkins, G. Douglas. *Reading Deconstruction: Deconstructive Reading.* Lexington: Kentucky UP, 1983.

Barthes, Roland. *A Barthes Reader.* Ed. Susan Sontag. New York: Hill, 1982.

———. *The Pleasure of the Text.* Trans. Richard Miller. New York: Hill, 1975.

———. *S/Z.* Trans. Richard Miller. London: Cape, 1975.

Belsey, Catherine. *Critical Practice.* London: Methuen, 1980.

Berman, Art. *From the New Criticism to Deconstruction.* Urbana and Chicago: U of Illinois P, 1988.

Best, Steven, and Douglas Kellner, eds. *Postmodern Theory: Critical Interrogations.* New York: Guilford, 1991.

Calloud, Jean. *Structural Analysis of Narrative.* Philadelphia: Fortress, 1976.

Chatman, Seymour. *Approaches to Poetics.* New York: Columbia UP, 1973.

Culler, Jonathan. *On Deconstruction: Theory and Criticism after Structuralism.* Ithaca: Cornell UP, 1982.

———. *Structuralist Poetics.* Ithaca: Cornell UP, 1975.

Derrida, Jacques. *Of Grammatology.* Trans. Gayatri Spivak. Baltimore: Johns Hopkins UP, 1976.

———. *Speech and Phenomena.* Trans. David Allison. Evanston: Northwestern UP, 1973.

———. *Writing and Difference.* Trans. Allan Bass. Chicago: Chicago UP, 1980.

Dreyfus, Hubert L., and Paul Rabinow. *Michel Foucault: Beyond Structuralism and Hermeneutics*. Chicago: Chicago UP, 1982.

Foucault, Michel. *The Archaeology of Knowledge*. Trans. A. M. Sheridan Smith. New York: Harper, 1972.

Genette, Gerard. *Narrative Discourse: An Essay in Method*. Ithaca: Cornell UP, 1980.

Hartman, Geoffrey H., and J. Hillis Miller, eds. *Deconstruction and Criticism*. New Haven: Yale UP, 1980.

Hawkes, Terence. *Structuralism and Semiotics*. Berkeley: California UP, 1977.

Jameson, Fredric. *The Prison-House of Language*. Princeton: Princeton UP, 1972.

Lane, Michael. *Introduction to Structuralism*. New York: Harper, 1970.

Leitch, Vincent. *Deconstructive Criticism: An Advanced Introduction*. New York: Columbia UP, 1983.

Lentricchia, Frank. *After the New Criticism*. Chicago: Chicago UP, 1980.

Lynn, Steven. "A Passage into Critical Theory." *College English* 52 (1990): 258–271.

Macksey, Richard, and Eugenio Donato. *The Structuralist Controversy*. Baltimore: Johns Hopkins UP, 1970.

Miller, J. Hillis. *Fiction and Repetition: Seven English Novels*. Cambridge: Harvard UP, 1982.

Murfin, Ross C. *Heart of Darkness: A Case Study in Contemporary Criticism*. New York: St. Martin's, 1989.

Norris, Christopher, ed. *Deconstruction and the Interests of Theory*. Norman and London: U of Oklahoma P, 1989.

——. *Deconstruction, Theory and Practice*. London: Methuen, 1982.

Propp, Vladimir. *Morphology of the Folktale*. Austin: Texas UP, 1968.

Robey, David. *Structuralism: A Introduction*. Oxford: Clarendon, 1973.

Saussure, Ferdinand de. *Course in General Linguistics*. New York: Philosophical, 1959.

Scholes, Robert. *Structuralism in Literature: An Introduction*. New Haven: Yale UP, 1974.

Todorov, Tzvetan. *The Fantastic: A Structural Approach to a Literary Genre*. Cleveland: Case Western Reserve UP, 1973.

——. *The Poetics of Prose*. Ithaca: Cornell UP, 1977.

Tompkins, Jane. "A Short Course in Post-Structuralism." *College English* 50 (1988): 733–747.

# Chapter 2

# THE INSIGHT OF LITERARY HISTORY

Studies in literary history consider elements that contribute to the composition of literary works at a given time—such elements as the facts of an author's life, the culture and ideas of the time when a work was written, and the possible influences of previous literary works. Insofar as these studies depend on a knowledge of biography, of intellectual and social history, and of the tradition of literature at the time, they appear to be extrinsic, calling for the critic to go outside literature itself for knowledge and insights that can be applied to literature. However, literary historians argue that such knowledge is indispensable to an understanding of literary texts, that in fact the meaning of any work is inextricably bound to its nature as a statement from and of the past.

Two reservations about literary historical approaches are sometimes voiced, both concerning the relationship of literature and history. The first arises from a fear that literary history may make literature an adjunct to history and literary texts simply another set of facts on which historians ply their trade. Literary study, in this view, runs the danger of becoming a branch of history and losing its autonomy as a discipline in its own right. Even so eminent a literary scholar as Robert Spiller has written of the literary historian as "a historian among other historians—political, economic, intellectual, cultural, etc.—and his function is to write the history of man as revealed in literature . . ." (43). Of course, Spiller believes literature to be far more than simply subject matter for a certain kind of historian. Still, the statement suggests why some critics fear literary history as the imposition of a foreign discipline on the field of literature.

Related to this is a concern about the value and relevance of historical knowledge when applied to literature. Some see literary historical studies as peripheral to the main goal of literary criticism: the explanation and elucidation of a given work. In this view, literary history focuses on background rather than on the essentials of a work, and the literary text may be lost in accounts of the life and times of its author, examinations of intellectual and social forces behind it, and attempts to locate it within a literary tradition. Although insights about history may be interesting and, at times, even illuminating, they are not central to literary study and may distract attention from significant features of the text themselves.

These reservations are important because they force a consideration of basic assumptions underlying literary historical criticism, particularly assumptions about the nature of literature. The literary historian is likely to argue that the "pastness" of a work of art is part of its essential nature and therefore any reading that ignores this historical element is incomplete. As Lionel Trilling put it, "the literary work is ineluctably an historical fact, and . . . its historicity is a fact in our aesthetic experience" (179). The words, phrasings, ideas, and structures of literary works are products of a specific time, place, and person; and readers respond in light of these facts. Great literature may be said to transcend time insofar as it speaks to readers at many different historical moments, but it also exists within time, both the time of its composition and the time of its reading.

If the nature of literary texts is historical, then their investigation demands a procedure that takes the historical into account, a procedure designed to explain their time-bound elements. In that sense, literary history is a discipline derived from the nature of literature itself and focused on essential characteristics of literary texts. The work of the literary historian is the centrally literary task of elucidating a text by examining its significant elements, in this case, historical elements. Like other literary scholars, the literary historian attempts to illuminate works of literature and increase the readers' understanding of them.

Of course, not all studies in literary history consider a single text, nor is there any one agreed-upon manner of proceeding. Some studies establish facts of history upon which other studies build, and different critics emphasize various historical aspects. The three sections presented in this chapter define and illustrate three literary historical approaches, each with its own emphasis. The first, "Historical Studies and the New Historicism," considers approaches that examine the social, intellectual, and institutional elements behind and within literary works. The second, "Biographical Studies," discusses approaches concerned with the relationship of the author to the text. The third, "Studies of the Literary Tradition," looks at approaches that investigate the historical relationship of literary works to each other. Although each of the three focuses on different aspect of literary experience, they share a common goal: an increased understanding and appreciation of literary works through the study of their historical contexts.

## HISTORICAL STUDIES AND THE NEW HISTORICISM

Notwithstanding the wide influence of formalist criticism, perhaps no approach to literature is as diverse and pervasive as the historical. College courses are frequently organized chronologically, works and authors are categorized by period, and histories of literature abound. The belief that history matters, that the time and conditions of a work's origin are important, may be debated, but it remains implicit in the way most of us think and talk about literature. The attempt to account for literary works in terms of the circumstances of their time and place has come to seem a natural part of literary study.

The formative historical elements of literature have been variously defined and classified. The French scholar Hippolyte Taine, whose *Histoire de la littérature anglaise* was first published in 1863 and translated as *History of English Literature* in 1871 by H. Van Laun, argued that literary works were shaped by three factors: race, by which he referred to "the innate and hereditary dispositions" of various peoples; surroundings or milieu, including climate, geography, and other conditions that mold attitudes and customs; and epochs, large expanses of time, like the Middle Ages or the classical age, in which "a certain dominant idea has had sway" (23–25). Thus, John Milton's work was finally explained by his "place between the epoch of unselfish dreaming and the epoch of practical action" (277)—that is, between what Taine saw as the poetic genius of the Renaissance and the more austere and logical neoclassical age. Similarly, the Reformation could take place only in a climate that produced in the Germanic people a "militant attitude" caused by "mud, rain, snow, a profusion of unpleasing and gloomy sights, the want of lively and delicate excitements of the senses" (242).

More recently, in an MLA pamphlet entitled *The Aims and Methods of Modern Scholarship in Languages and Literature*, Spiller suggests a different list of "factors which contribute to the existence of literary works": ideas, culture, institutions, tradition and myth, and biography. That is, literary works are shaped by the great ideas of their time, whether these be religious, political, scientific, or psychological; and they are also influenced by their culture, the "habits, norms, values, roles, etc." of their time and place; and in addition, institutions such as the political party, the church, the military, and the school all contribute to literature (43–55). This section deals with these three areas; studies of myth, tradition, and biography are discussed in separate sections later in this chapter and in Chapter 3.

## The History of Ideas

Studies of ideas, like other historical studies, exist on a continuum, ranging from those that primarily investigate the history of certain ideas themselves to those that apply knowledge of a historical idea to the interpretation of a specific literary text. The former are sometimes more nearly historical or philosophical than literary studies, but they are important insofar as they document the context from which literary works come.

### LOVEJOY: CHAIN OF BEING

A landmark in the study of ideas is Arthur O. Lovejoy's *The Great Chain of Being: A Study of the History of an Idea*, a work that traces the idea of a chain of being from its genesis in ancient Greek philosophy into the nineteenth century. Although containing many complexities, the term *great chain of being* implies a hierarchical universe in which all creatures are linked in a continuous chain from high to low, or as Lovejoy quotes from Alexander Pope's *Essay on Man:*

Vast chain of being! which from God began,
Nature's aethereal, human, angel, man,

Beast, bird, fish, insect, what no eye can see,
No glass can reach; from Infinite to thee,
From thee to nothing. . . .

Although Lovejoy's study does not interpret specific literary works, it provides a knowledge of the ideas *underlying* many works. If, as Lovejoy argues, the great chain of being has been throughout much of Western history "the most widely familiar conception of the general *scheme* of things, the constitutive pattern of the universe" (vii), it has surely shaped literary texts and been reflected in them

## TILLYARD: IDEAS OF THE TIME

While Lovejoy traces the idea of the chain of being throughout Western thought, E. M. W. Tillyard in *The Elizabethan World Picture* is more specific, looking at the idea in relationship to sixteenth-century English literature. His attempt is to "expound the most ordinary beliefs about the constitution of the world as pictured in the Elizabethan age" (viii). The need, Tillyard believes, is to articulate the commonplace understandings of the time, ideas so fundamental they are assumed rather than made explicit in literature. A knowledge of these ideas leads to many new insights. Even so minor an instance as a reference in Shakespeare's *Antony and Cleopatra* to Antony as "dolphin-like" becomes richer upon recognizing that on the chain of being the dolphin was "king of the fish" (35).

More significant are the implications of Tillyard's discussion of the human being's place on the chain, midway between the angels and the beasts. Whereas the sixteenth century saw humans as allied to beasts through sensual desire, it also viewed them as linked to the angels through the mind, the highest faculties of which were the understanding and the will. Insofar as it was the task of the understanding to sift evidence and to gather wisdom and the job of the will to make decisions on the basis of the evidence, Tillyard believes these two faculties to have been at the center of Elizabethan ethics, according to which the human being has the duty to gain knowledge and to act rightly in light of that knowledge. Tillyard assumes that a people's ethical principles are crucial to literature, and he sees it as no "accident that of the heroes in Shakespeare's four tragic masterpieces two, Othello and Lear, are defective in understanding and two, Hamlet and Macbeth, in will" (72). Othello and Lear are misguided and do not determine the truth; Hamlet and Macbeth understand but do not act correctly according to their knowledge.

## MONK: HISTORICAL IDEAS AND A SINGLE TEXT

Whereas Lovejoy traces the history of the idea of the chain of being and Tillyard focuses on the idea in relation to the literature of a specific time, Samuel Holt Monk applies a knowledge of this and other historical ideas to the interpretation of a single literary text, Jonathan Swift's *Gulliver's Travels*. In "The Pride of Lemuel Gulliver," the question before Monk is whether to read the book as a diatribe against humanity. Of course, by the end of the book, the narrator, Gulliver, has come to prefer the company of horses to that of humans since horses remind him of the purely rational, stoic Houyhnhnms, but does Swift advocate his character's misanthropy? Are readers to conclude that Gulliver is correct?

To answer these questions, Monk considers eighteenth-century ideas of Christianity, humanism, Cartesian rationalism, stoicism, and the chain of being. He begins by noting Swift's opposition to optimistic Enlightenment ideas about human rationality, ideas propounded in part by the French philosopher René Descartes. Monk argues that Swift as a Christian humanist would believe "that man's fallen nature could never transcend its own limitations" even as he would value "those moral and spiritual qualities which distinguish men from beasts" (51). Thus, Gulliver's misanthropy is based on a delusion about human potential, one that does not recognize humanity's middle place on the chain of being. The Houyhnhnms, whom Gulliver embraces, are not fit or possible models for men and women. Their pure rationality is beyond the human condition, and their stoicism is inhuman, as Monk demonstrates by quoting Swift's *Thoughts on Various Subjects:* "The Stoical Scheme of supplying our Wants, by lopping off our Desires, is like cutting off our Feet when we want Shoes" (53). Given Swift's position on these various ideas, Monk makes a strong case for considering Gulliver to be suffering from delusion, pride, and, finally, madness. Through the study of historical ideas, Monk arrives at an interpretation of a specific text.

## AGGELER: CONTEMPORARY PERSPECTIVES

Studies of ideas may also deal with contemporary authors and texts. In "Pelagius and Augustine in the Novels of Anthony Burgess," a discussion focusing particularly on Burgess's futuristic novel *The Wanting Seed*, Geoffrey Aggeler investigates Burgess's presentation of history as a cycle from liberal welfare states to conservative police states. Since *The Wanting Seed* describes liberal states as Pelagian and conservative ones as Augustinian, Aggeler turns to the original debate between the fourth-century British monk Pelagius, who emphasized humanity's natural goodness, and St. Augustine, who argued humankind's innate depravity and the need for grace. This debate, Aggeler believes, is political as well as religious and has been carried on through much of Western history. In *The Wanting Seed*, the Pelagian belief in natural goodness leads to a welfare state predicated on education and propaganda, a state that eventually fails and gives way to a repressive Augustinian regime based on force and coercion. The end of the novel, however, gives signs of a return to Pelagian ideas. Given the failures and weaknesses of both states, Aggeler sees Burgess's view as one in which "sanity and vision could lead men to a rejection of both 'Pelagianism' and 'Augustinianism' and a creation of a society based upon a realistic assessment of individual human potentiality" (55).

## Culture and Institutions

The preceding examples show some of the range of studies of ideas, from those primarily concerned with documenting and exploring the nature and history of certain ideas to those that apply this knowledge to the interpretation of specific literary texts. Although studies of culture and of institutions exist on a similar continuum, it is probably enough to note one example in each area.

A brief extract from Robert Gittings's biography *Young Thomas Hardy* indicates the worth of knowing about the culture—that is, the norms, values, and behavior—of a given time. Sue Bridehead, the main character of Hardy's *Jude the Obscure,* has frequently been interpreted as representing the "new woman" of the 1890s, when the novel was published. However, Gittings shows Sue to be very much a product of the 1860s in her values, attitudes, and behavior. Whereas the advanced woman of the 1890s was likely to have some university education, to be attracted to socialism, and to be working toward opening traditionally male professions to women, Sue demonstrates no interest in any of these. Instead, her intellectual interests are in John Stuart Mill and Auguste Comte, two thinkers popular in the 1860s but no longer in vogue among intellectual women in the 1890s. Gittings's close knowledge of nineteenth-century culture prevents an interpretation as misleading as that of representing attitudes of the 1950s as those of the 1980s.

A knowledge of significant institutions can also be important in understanding literary works. For example, Gervase Mathew's "Ideals of Knighthood in Late-Fourteenth-Century England" investigates the institution of knighthood and defines its principal tenets: prowess, loyalty, pity, generosity, franchise (or freedom and naturalness of spirit), and courtesy. To understand the implications of these ideals and how they were viewed at the time is nearly indispensable to an informed reading of a late-fourteenth-century poem such as *Sir Gawain and the Green Knight*, in which the main character is caught between conflicting duties. Loyalty, for instance, calls for Gawain's allegiance to his host, Bercilak; courtesy, on the other hand, limits the manner in which Gawain can fend off the romantic requests of Bercilak's lady. The reader's judgment of Gawain in this and other circumstances depends in part on a knowledge of the ideal behavior demanded by the institution Gawain represents.

## The New History and the New Historicism

Recently, there has been renewed interest in the theory of historical criticism and a rethinking of its assumptions, a reassessment signaled as early as 1969 by the founding of the journal *New Literary History*. As in many other areas of recent literary theory, historical criticism has begun to take greater account of the reader. For example, Ralph Cohen in *New Directions in Literary History* speaks of the literary work as "an 'event,' an 'action,' a relation established between reader and what he reads, audience and performance" (1). That is, the new literary history rejects any view of the literary work simply as an object of the past and instead emphasizes the interaction that takes place during the reading of the text. This position does not deny the significance of historical knowledge; indeed, critics argue that the pastness of the work is part of its present meaning and must inform any reading. As Robert Weimann says of Hamlet: ". . . On the one hand there is the Elizabethan context and meaning; on the other, the modern understanding and interpretation. There is no getting away from the inevitable tension between the historical and modern points of view" (106). A work is not simply a monument of the past, but it cannot be read meaningfully without recognizing its context.

During the 1980s, new ways of thinking about this relationship of present and past and of text and culture resulted in one of the more influential critical movements of the time: the new historicism. The term *new historicism* was used by Wesley Morris in his *Toward a New Historicism* in 1972 but seems to have been adopted widely after Stephen Greenblatt applied it to a series of historical Renaissance studies in a 1982 issue of the periodical *Genre*. Although the new historicism takes many forms, Anton Kaes isolates some of its main elements when he speaks of it as "a critical method that perceives the literary text as a communal product rather than the expression of an author's intention; that disputes the autonomy (and isolation) of the work of art and reconnects it to its cultural context; that scrutinizes artistic production as social intervention; that consistently crosses disciplinary boundaries; that draws on recent theoretical work, and nevertheless seeks historical and textual specificity" (210).

## GREENBLATT: AN EXAMPLE

What Kaes means by the new historicism's attempt to perceive the literary text as a communal product and to reconnect it to its cultural context may be clarified by briefly considering an illustration from Stephen Greenblatt's *Shakespearean Negotiations: The Circulation of Social Energy in Renaissance England*. Greenblatt begins one chapter, "Martial Law in the Land of Cockaigne," by recounting a sermon delivered by Hugh Latimer to Lady Catherine Bertie in 1552. In the sermon, Latimer tells of a woman convicted of murdering her child. Latimer, after rigorously questioning the woman, comes to believe in her innocence and acquires a royal pardon for her. However, he conceals the pardon up until near the moment of her execution because he believes her to hold a false doctrine concerning the need for a ritual of purification in order to attain salvation. Only when the woman comes to accept Latimer's doctrine does he produce the pardon.

Greenblatt notes particularly Latimer's manipulation of the woman through her anxiety and reminds the reader of Shakespeare's *Measure for Measure* in which Duke Vincentio causes Claudio to believe he is to be executed. Greenblatt recalls other uses of the manipulation of anxiety in *The Winter's Tale, The Comedy of Errors,* and *Othello*. Greenblatt's point is not that

Shakespeare knew Latimer's sermon but that the technique was available within the culture. As Greenblatt says, "The resemblance between the tales arises not because Latimer's sermon is one of Shakespeare's sources but because Latimer is practicing techniques of arousing and manipulating anxiety, and these techniques are crucial elements in the representational technology of the Elizabethan and Jacobean theater" (133).

This brief example may help to explain the new historicist's belief in the library text as a communal product. If Shakespearean drama uses certain strategies and techniques to raise anxiety, these techniques result not simply from the genius of a given author but from a community in which they were available and prevalent. As Greenblatt puts it: "Works of art, however intensely marked by the creative intelligence and private obsessions of individuals, are the products of collective negotiations and exchange" (vii). By calling attention to the collective and communal aspect of art, the new historicist also connects the text to its cultural context. For example, Greenblatt argues that Renaissance England was "institutionally committed to the arousal of anxiety" and points to public punishments and executions that "were designed to arouse fear and to set the stage for the royal pardons that would demonstrate that the prince's justice was tempered with mercy" (137). Thus, strategies used on the Renaissance stage are connected to a society's beliefs and behaviors.

Greenblatt's organization, in which he begins with an anecdote or story from which he teases out values, meanings, and interrelationships with other texts, is in itself significant and characteristic of the new historicism. For instance, the French historian and archaeologist Michel Foucault, whom many see as a seminal figure in the new historicism, begins his work *Discipline and Punish: The Birth of the Prison* with an account of the drawing and quartering of a would-be assassin of Louis XV. From this narrative, Foucault fashions a powerful study of the interconnections of discipline and power and of the way in which prisons express values within Western society, a study of what he calls the "coercive technologies of behavior" (293). The similarity of Greenblatt's structure to Foucault's seems to be no accident. Greenblatt is not beginning with a particular literary text or problem which he wants to solve, nor is he suggesting that one must understand historical background in order to read a literary work correctly. Rather, he is demonstrating how the literary work participates in a larger context and how it shares in the shaping of meaning within a culture.

As well, the use of such narratives as Latimer's sermon and the execution of the French regicide demonstrates the historical and textual specificity to which Kaes alludes when he speaks of "historical background" as "no longer confined to the world of ideas" but as "identified with the complex social and cultural processes of everyday life, with the 'slime of history'" (212). These narratives also show the practice of the new historicism to blur the usual boundaries between disciplines. As Ross Murfin argues, the new historicists have "discarded old distinctions between literature, history, and the social sciences" and "have erased the line dividing historical and literary materials, showing that the production of Shakespeare's plays was a political act and that the coronation of Elizabeth I was carried out with the same care for staging and symbol lavished on a work of dramatic art" (229).

## QUESTIONING THE CANON

Another aspect of the new ideas and methods in historical study is a severe questioning of the literary *canon,* that is, the list of works which by cultural consensus have come to be regarded as "masterpieces" or as being of special importance. Of course, the canon was under attack before the advent of the new historicism; charges have been made throughout the 1960s, 1970s, and 1980s that the canon as it is represented in critical discussions and college classrooms is ideologically elitist and a reflection of white, male values. However, in several ways, the assumptions of the new historicists encourage the reevaluation of canons. Certainly, both the view of literary texts as communal products rather than as results of individual inspiration and the blurring of distinctions between literary works and other texts and cultural artifacts militate against a canon of masterpieces of literary genius. As well, the new historicists' understanding of the interconnectedness of culture and values reinforces a recognition of canons as cultural productions reflecting time-bound values.

# Dissenting Views

Although the new historicism has rapidly become an important perspective in textual study, its assumptions and methods are not universally accepted. For example, M. H. Abrams in "On Political Readings of *Lyrical Ballads*" calls "misleading" Greenblatt's claim that "the traditional historical approach to literature . . . finds history to lie outside the texts, to function in effect as the object to which signs in the text point." Abrams finds this description simply not to "do justice to many [traditional] historical critics" who, he maintains, do "identify implicit social and political structures and values that are inscribed within the literary works themselves." Abrams's more crucial objection, though, is to what he does see as the distinguishing feature between traditional historical study and the new historicism: the view of new historicists "that history, not the author, shapes a literary work and forges its meaning" (365). Abrams argues that, in practice, this view frequently leads to self-confirming readings in which critics begin with their understanding of historical ideology and then "discover" evidence of that ideology in the literary work. It produces readings, Abrams suggests, in which there is no appeal to "what a poet undertook to say" (370).

Disagreement, debate, and controversy, however, may simply point to the current vitality of historical studies. Certainly, among many students of literature, there seems to be agreement with Brook Thomas's statement that "at this specific historical moment, the special quality of literature may well be its historicity" (520) because "our cultural amnesia has left us with no perspective on the present, thus making it more difficult than ever to shape the direction of the future" (510). It is the need for perspective and for even a provisional understanding of our position within our culture that may be the ultimate goal of both traditional and new historical studies.

Along with works already mentioned, some valuable discussions of traditional historical criticism are Ronald S. Crane's "Philosophy, Literature, and the History of Ideas," D. W. Robertson's "Historical Criticism," Lionel Trilling's "The Sense of the Past," and A. S. P. Woodhouse's "The Historical Criticism of Milton." Among important resources for recent theory and practice of historical study are the previously mentioned journal, *New Literary History*, and the journal *Representations*, founded in 1983. Anton Kaes's "New Historicism and the Study of German Literature" is a clear overview of the new historicism and as valuable for the student of English and American literature as for the Germanist.

## WORKS CITED AND RECOMMENDED

Abrams, M. H. "On Political Readings of *Lyrical Ballads." Doing Things with Texts*. Ed. Michael Fisher. New York: Norton, 1989.

Aggeler, Geoffrey. "Pelagius and Augustine in the Novels of Anthony Burgess." *English Studies* 55 (1974): 43–55.

Auerbach, Erich. *Mimesis: The Representation of Reality in Western Literature*. Princeton: Princeton UP, 1953.

Caspari, Fritz. *Humanism and the Social Order in Tudor England*. Chicago: Chicago UP, 1954.

Cohen, Ralph. *New Directions in Literary History*. Baltimore: Johns Hopkins UP, 1974.

Crane Ronald S. "Philosophy, Literature, and the History of Ideas." *The Idea of the Humanities*. Chicago: Chicago UP, 1967.

Foucault, Michel. *Discipline and Punish: The Birth of the Prison*. Trans. Alan Sheridan. New York: Pantheon, 1977.

Gay, Peter. *The Enlightenment: An Interpretation*. New York: Knopf, 1966–1969.

Gittings, Robert. *Young Thomas Hardy*. London: Heinemann, 1975.

Greenblatt, Stephen. *Shakespearean Negotiations: The Circulation of Social Energy in Renaissance England*. Berkeley: California UP, 1988.

Hamer, Mary. *Signs of Cleopatra: History, Politics, Representation*. London and New York: Routledge, 1993.

Kaes, Anton. "New Historicism and the Study of German Literature." *German Quarterly* 62 (1989): 210–219.

Lovejoy, Arthur. *The Great Chain of Being: A Study of the History of an Idea*. Cambridge: Harvard UP, 1936.

Mathew, Gervase. "Ideals of Knighthood in Late-Fourteenth-Century England." *Studies in Medieval History Presented to Fredrick Maurice Powicke*. Ed. R. W. Hunt, W. A. Pantin, and R. W. Southern. Oxford: Clarendon, 1948. 338–362.

Matthiessen, F. O. *American Renaissance*. New York: Oxford UP, 1941.

Monk, Samuel Holt. "The Pride of Lemuel Gulliver." *Sewanee Review* 68 (1955): 48–71.

Murfin, Ross C. "What Is the New Historicism?" *Heart of Darkness: A Case Study in Contemporary Criticism*. New York: St. Martin's, 1989.

Nicolson, Marjorie. *Newton Demands the Muse: Newton's Opticks and the Eighteenth-Century Poets*. Princeton: Princeton UP, 1946.

Robertson, D. W., Jr. "Historical Criticism." *English Institute Annual 1950*. New York: Columbia UP, 1951.

Spiller, Robert. "Literary History." *The Aims and Methods of Modern Scholarship in Languages and Literature*. Ed. James Thorpe. New York: MLA, 1963.

Taine, Hippolyte. *History of English Literature*. Trans. H. Van Laun. New York: Holt, 1871.

Thomas, Brook. "The Historical Necessity for—and Difficulties with—New Historical Analysis in Introductory Literature Courses." *College English* 49 (1987): 509–522.

———. *The New Historicism and Other Old-Fashioned Questions*. Princeton: Princeton UP, 1991.

Tillyard, E. M. W. *The Elizabethan World Picture*. New York: Macmillan, 1944.

Trilling, Lionel. "The Sense of the Past." *The Liberal Imagination*. New York: Viking, 1942.

Veeser, H. Aram, ed. *The New Historicism*. New York: Routledge, 1989.

Weimann, Robert. "Past Significance and Present Meaning." *New Literary History* 1 (1969): 91–109.

Willey, Basil. *The Seventeenth-Century Background: Studies in the Thought of the Age in Relation to Poetry and Religion*. London: Chatto, 1942.

Williams, Raymond. *Culture and Society 1780–1950*. New York: Columbia UP, 1958.

———. *Keywords: A Vocabulary of Culture and Society*. New York: Oxford UP, 1976.

Williamson, George. *Seventeenth Century Contexts*. Chicago: Chicago UP, 1969.

Woodhouse, A. S. P. "The Historical Criticism of Milton." *PMLA* 66 (1951): 1033–1044.

# BIOGRAPHICAL STUDIES

Biographical studies are familiar to most persons interested in literature; for many, the belief that discussions of literary works should take into account the author's life is an unshakable, if sometimes unexamined, conviction. In fact, however, the biographical interpretation of literature underwent severe questioning during the mid-twentieth century as part of the general attack on the "intentional fallacy," a term used by W. K. Wimsatt and Monroe Beardsley to signify the error of inquiring about an author's intended meaning (2–18). The main arguments came, first, from a need to describe and judge literary works in their own terms and on their own merits, not on the author's intention, and, second, from a disbelief in the possibility of determining such an intention. Many critics remain unconvinced by these arguments and continue to find biography an important aid to the appreciation and understanding of literary texts. As Frank Cioffi puts it in "Intention and Interpretation in Criticism," "A reader's response to a literary work will vary with what he *knows*; one of the things which he knows . . . is what the author had in mind, or what is intended" (224).

## Early Hagiography

Of course, the biography of a literary figure is only one kind of biography, and the elucidation of texts is only one purpose. Literary biography shares with other biographical writing essential features developed from a common history. Many early biographies, especially medieval Latin chronicles, are examples of hagiography; that is, they are idealized portraits of saints and rulers, the purpose of which is to glorify their subjects. However, as Robert Gittings points out in *The Nature of Biography,* the Renaissance brought a change in tone, with some biographies, such as Thomas More's on Richard III, serving as a warning by showing the vices of previous rulers and others by the greater use of "human detail and character" (22-23). By the seventeenth century, Gittings suggests, the biographer is becoming "for the first time . . . a conscious artist" as exemplified in the works of Izaak Walton. In these biographies, "there is a conscious attempt to give, from all sources, all the events of [the subjects'] lives, and to make them a rounded whole" (26).

## Boswell

In the eighteenth century are two supreme examples of literary biography: James Boswell's *Life of Samuel Johnson* and Johnson's own biographical works, particularly his *Lives of the English Poets*. In the *Lives*, Johnson combines biography and literary criticism, each life beginning with the events and details of the subject's life and concluding with a critical discussion of the poetry. In speaking of Johnson's conception of biography, Robert Folkenflik notes "the emphasis on private and domestic affairs, the use of minute particulars and anecdotes, and the concern for the uniform nature of man" (29). The use of intimate details and the attempt to show the humanity of the subject are nowhere better illustrated than in Boswell's *Life of Samuel Johnson*. Boswell, of course, spent much time with Johnson, but he combined his firsthand knowledge with through research and an artful presentation. Boswell's use of dialogue and his ability to construct dramatic scenes make the *Life* far more than a mere recounting of events.

## Strachey

The use of intimate detail and the presentation of the whole person is often not found in biographies of the nineteenth century, which frequently show only the public side of figures and disguise or ignore unsavory aspects. A reaction to this tendency is Lytton Strachey's biographies, which focus on the private and sometimes sordid details of their subjects' lives. Strachey's *Eminent Victorians* has come to represent an attitude toward biography best exemplified in Strachey's own words: "Ignorance is the first requisite of the historian, ignorance, which simplifies and clarifies, which selects and omits, with a placid perfection unattainable by the highest art" (vii). Strachey's point is the need for truth, not to every incidental fact, but to a design that enables the reader to see the essential nature of the subject. Biography is an art insofar as it clears away meaningless events and gives a unified conception of a person's real being. Strachey, though, as has often been noted, seems to have distorted his subjects through his own preconceptions about Victorian society and his own desire to debunk the legends that had grown up around his subjects.

## Recent Examples

The elements mentioned in this brief look at several earlier biographers are central to recent ideas about contemporary biography. Most agree that biography should not give an idealized or a public picture but make every attempt to describe the whole person by using intimate details and a thorough knowledge of the subject's life and times. There is also the need for the biography to be itself an artistic work, to be constructed not simply as a record of facts and events but also with a dramatic design. This design, however, is not to be imposed from without but should arise from the attempt to make sense of the subject's life and to see its essentials. Finally, there is the need for the biographer to recognize his or her own preconceptions and biases.

These aims are ones that literary biography shares with all biography, and some biographers of literary figures go no further. That is, they treat their subjects as they would treat any other figure, public or private, showing the mind and personality of the subjects but with no attempt to deal directly with their literary production. For example, Quentin Bell's two-volume *Virginia Woolf: A Biography* presents a detailed and compelling view of Woolf's life but gives no consideration to her literary works. Bell, in fact, clearly refuses to act as a literary critic: "Although I hope that I may assist those who attempt to explain and to assess the writing of Virginia Woolf, I can do so only by presenting facts which hitherto have not been generally known and by providing what will, I hope, be a clear and truthful account of the character and personal development of my subject" (xiii). Such a biography can be extremely useful to those interested in Woolf's novels, but as James Gindin points out, the most "creative fact" of a writer's life is likely to "involve her fiction deeply and centrally" (99).

Most literary biography does directly consider the subject's literary production, helping the reader understand the works more fully through knowledge about the author's life and thought. Very often, simply knowing certain facts can give new insights, and scholarly biography has traditionally worked toward a more nearly complete awareness of occurrences in an author's life. For example, Gittings in *Thomas Hardy's Later Years* considers a sequence of fifty poems written shortly after the death of Hardy's wife, Emma, and attempts to see the sequence in light of Hardy's life. Although these poems contain some of Hardy's best poetic work, Gittings believes their "full meaning" has never been clear because "the circumstances of [Hardy's] last years with Emma have never been fully understood or appreciated" (152). These poems, most filled with remorse, were, to use Hardy's word, an "expiation"; but until Gittings's work it was uncertain why Hardy should have felt so deeply the need for self-reproach. Gittings, however, documents Hardy's neglect of Emma, his nearly criminal refusal to recognize the seriousness of her illness. Hardy had, according to Gittings, "deliberately turned his eyes away and pretended not to notice" and was instead giving all his attention to a younger woman, Florence Dugdale. These facts, Gittings argues, explain "the profound remorse which gives these remarkable poems their secret, unspoken intensity and painful inward passion" (153). If readers accept Gittings's interpretation, they are likely to read the poems with new insight.

Gittings believes Hardy understood his motive for writing these poems but wished to keep it hidden from the world. Other biographers believe authors frequently are not fully aware of the meaning of their own works. Of course, those who accept the concept of the intentional fallacy see this as additional evidence of the impossibility of determining a writer's meaning: If motives are so complex and deeply hidden that even the author cannot know them, how can readers dare to speak of an intended meaning? The *psychobiography* is an attempt to answer this question by using formal psychological or psychoanalytic theory to uncover motives and meanings hidden from the writer as well as the reader.

## PSYCHOBIOGRAPHY

John Cody's *After Great Pain: The Inner Life of Emily Dickinson* attempts not only to determine the inner motives of Dickinson but also to reconstruct parts of her life through the application of psychoanalytic theory. Cody explains the process of reconstruction by analogy to a paleontologist reconstructing a skeleton from fossil remains or an engineer reassembling an exploded aircraft. In both the skeleton and the aircraft, there are underlying ordering principles that allow one to deduce the nature and placement of missing parts given the nature of existing fragments. Similarly, psychoanalytic theory makes it possible to assume certain kinds of occurrences in a life on the basis of existing evidence. Thus, Cody speculates that "early in Emily Dickinson's life, she experienced what she interpreted as a cruel rejection by her mother." Although Cody admits "no record of any concrete nature" exists, he contends that "many of her statements, her choices of certain recurring metaphors and symbols, and the entire course of her life, viewed psychoanalytically, argue for the truth of the assumption" (2). Among the symbols arising from this maternal deprivation are those that associate both food and home with affection and sometimes with erotic love. Although many critics disagree with Cody's findings and his method, both are far richer than any brief discussion can suggest, and they do lead to new perspectives on such poems as "I Had Been Hungry, All the Years" and "I Years Had Been from Home."

## PROCESSES OF THE MIND

Although most biography is concerned with exterior events and how they shape the mind of the subject, some biographies focus almost exclusively on the thoughts and processes of the mind itself. A fascinating example, though one too monumental to consider typical, is John Livingston Lowes's *The Road to Xanadu,* a study of Samuel Taylor Coleridge and two of his poems, *The Rime of the Ancient Mariner* and "Kubla Khan." Lowes's concern is with Coleridge's imagination and "how, in two great poems, out of chaos the imagination framed a thing of beauty" (xi). The process of which Lowes speaks may be as deep and complex as that which Cody investigates, but Lowes is intrigued not by emotional responses to external events but more simply by the reading Coleridge did. Lowes traces Coleridge's reading to determine the raw material that the imaginative faculty shaped into poetry. A brief example may show something of the method.

Several lines in *The Ancient Mariner* tell of water snakes moving in "tracks of shining white" :"Blue, glossy green, and velvet black. / They coiled, and swam; and every track / Was a flash of golden fire." Where, Lowes asks, do these ideas and images originate; especially, where does the idea of the shining track begin? Lowes finds in Joseph Priestley's *Opticks* a similar description, an account of a phosphorescent sea with fish leaving a luminous track. The question then becomes whether Coleridge had read the *Opticks.* Lowes discovers in Coleridge's notebook an entry showing that he had read at least part of the *Opticks,* but had he read the passage in question? Lowes then follows a footnote of Priestley, which refers to an account in the *Philosophical Transactions of the Royal Society* telling of fish leaving a "luminous track" and making "a kind of artificial Fire in the water." Could Coleridge have read the *Opticks* and then followed the footnote to the *Philosophical Transactions*? The answer is established almost conclusively when an initially puzzling statement in the notebook turns out to refer to another part of the *Transactions.* Lowes follows Coleridge's reading until he has accounted for every aspect of the lines on the water snakes and eventually nearly the whole of *The Ancient Mariner* and "Kubla Khan." Lowes's book is a fascinating record of research, but its importance lies in showing Coleridge's reading and especially in demonstrating the workings of his imagination. Lowes makes a solid case for the way in which ideas, fragments, and recollections in the unconscious are given shape by the imagination.

## New Views

These few examples of different types of biographical study represent a portion of the range of traditional biography. However, contemporary critical theory, particularly deconstructionist criticism, has held up to question nearly all of the traditional understandings of the relationship of writers to their texts. For example, Roland Barthes, in "The Death of the Author," argues that "it is language which speaks, not the author" (223). To give the writer preeminence, Barthes believes, is to close off the meanings of the text, to make the text, as Barthes puts it, "the 'message' of the Author-God" (224). Other critics speak less of the death of the author than of the author as a figure, in Brigitte Bailey's phrase, "constructed in the text" (87). That is, we can know the writer only as we see her or him in the language of the text. The assumptions that inform these views, particularly assumptions about language, are discussed more fully in the section titled "Structuralist and Deconstructionist Studies" in Chapter 1.

For the person interested in the latest work in biographical writing, the journal *Biography* includes articles, reviews, and up-to-date bibliographies. Good collections of essays on biography are Daniel Aaron, *Studies in Biography;* James Clifford, *Biography as an Art;* Anthony Friedson, *New Directions in Biography;* and Louis Martz and Aubrey Williams, *The Author in His Work.* An important discussion of authorial intention is found in E. D. Hirsch, Jr., *Validity in Interpretation;* and Gregory T. Polletta, *Issues in Contemporary Literary Criticism,* includes a sequence of articles on the question of intention.

## WORKS CITED AND RECOMMENDED

Aaron, Daniel. *Studies in Biography*. Cambridge: Harvard UP, 1978.

Altick, Richard. *Lives and Letters*. New York: Knopf, 1965.

Bailey, Brigitte. "Hawthorne and the Author Question." *College English* 57(1995): 89–97.

Barthes, Roland. "The Death of the Author." *Falling into Theory.* Ed. David H. Richter. Boston: Bedford, 1994. 222–226.

Bell, Quentin. *Virginia Woolf: A Biography*. New York: Harcourt, 1972.

Cioffi, Frank. "Intention and Interpretation in Criticism." *Issues in Contemporary Literary Criticism*. Ed. Gregory T. Polletta. Boston: Little, 1973.

Clifford, James. *Biography as an Art*. New York: Oxford UP, 1962.

Cody, John. *After Great Pain: The Inner Life of Emily Dickinson*. Cambridge: Harvard UP, 1971.

Edel, Leon. *Literary Biography*. Bloomington; Indiana UP, 1973.

———. "Literature and Biography." *Relations of Literary Study*. Ed. James Thorpe. New York: MLA, 1967.

Folkenflik, Robert. *Samuel Johnson, Biographer.* Ithaca: Cornell UP, 1978.

Friedson, Anthony. *New Directions in Biography*. Hawaii UP, 1981.

Gindin, James. "Method in the Biographical Study of Virginia Woolf." *Biography* 4 (1981): 95–107.

Gittings, Robert. *The Nature of Biography.* Seattle: Washington UP, 1978.

———. *Thomas Hardy's Later Years*. Boston; Little, 1978.

Hirsch, E. D., Jr. *Validity in Interpretation*. New Haven: Yale UP, 1967.

Lowes, John Livingston. *The Road to Xanadu*. Boston: Houghton, 1927.

Martz, Louis, and Aubrey Williams. *The Author in His Work*. New Haven: Yale UP, 1978.

Shelton, Alan. *Biography.* London: Methuen, 1977.

Strachey, Lytton. *Eminent Victorians.* New York: Harcourt, 1969.

Wimsatt, W. K. and Monroe Beardsley. *The Verbal Icon*. Lexington: Kentucky UP, 1954.

## STUDIES OF THE LITERARY TRADITION

In "Tradition and the Individual Talent," T. S. Eliot writes, "Someone said: 'The dead writers are remote from us because we *know* so much more than they did.' Precisely, and they are that which we know." Eliot's recognition of a line, or tradition, in which literary works build on those that went before is a central insight. However much we argue the uniqueness of each literary text, we also realize that *Hamlet* would not be precisely the same play had Shakespeare not known earlier tragedies of the Elizabethan and Jacobean stage. Similarly, tragedy today would surely be different if Shakespeare had never written. Studies of literary traditions do not always examine influences of one artist on another, but they do attempt to understand literary works more fully by viewing their relationships to preceding and succeeding ones.

Of course, such studies are one kind of literary history. But instead of considering the intellectual or social context of a work's origin or exploring the relation of the work to the artist's life, these studies investigate the literary background. Essentially, they attempt to explain a text by showing its use of traditional forms and materials and its departure from them. These studies will concern genre at times, especially the history and evolution of a genre, but with the purpose of understanding how a given work makes use of elements of the genre and, perhaps, how it adds to or changes these elements. At other times, tradition will be defined more broadly to include characteristic attitudes or uses of language or subject matter. The Romantic tradition, for example, is not limited to a certain genre but is recognized by a set of shared concerns and ways of looking at the world.

## The Pastoral: An Example

Whereas Eliot, when he writes of the literary tradition in the passage just quoted, seems to have in mind the whole of literature, most studies examine specific lines. The pastoral is one such line, running through hundreds of years of literary history. Taking its name from *pastor,* the Latin term for shepherd, the pastoral traditionally is a poem celebrating the joys of the bucolic life, usually at the expense of a more complicated urban society. A sketchy outline shows the pastoral running from the works of the Greek poet Theocritus in the third century BC to Virgil's *Eclogues* to the works to Spenser, Sidney, and Milton and then to Pope's pastorals in the eighteenth century and to some of Wordsworth's in the nineteenth; a few scholars trace the tradition into the twentieth century.

An early attempt to examine a poem in light of the pastoral tradition is James Hanford's "The Pastoral Elegy and Milton's *Lycidas.*" Although there could be no doubt Milton made use of pastoral conventions in this elegy on the death of his friend Edward King, Hanford's achievement is to trace specific sources of the poem and to show that it was "predetermined by the literary tradition of the pastoral elegy" (446). Hanford's concise account of this history cites earlier passages Milton is likely to have had in mind and, perhaps more important, shows that the pastoral developed conventions appropriate for Milton's purposes. For example, Hanford notes the similarity of Milton's lines "Bring the rathe Primrose that forsaken dies. / The tufted Crow-toe, and pale Gessamine, / The white Pink, and the Pansie freakt with jet" to those in Spenser's April eclogue:

Bring hether the pincke and purple cullambine,
    With gelliflowers;
Bring coronations, and sops in wine,
    Worme of paramoures.

Of more significance than individual lines, though, is the development of the pastoral to a point at which it could be used by a Christian for the dignified treatment of grief and consolation. Hanford discusses the change in the pastoral from Theocritus's relatively light and delicate lines to the loftier strains of Virgil, a change necessary for Milton to select the pastoral as appropriate to his theme. Similarly, Hanford notes that the pastoral had, long before Milton, developed the ability to incorporate Christian concepts, another necessity for Milton's choice. As a later writer, Richard P. Adams, puts it, "The conventions of pastoral elegy were appropriate because they had been hammered out over the centuries by poets concerned, as Milton was, with the problem and mystery of death" (183).

The tradition of the pastoral is seen not only in the poetic genre of the elegy but also in much other literature. For example, Leo Marx, in *The Machine in the Garden: Technology and the Pastoral Ideal in America,* examines the uses of pastoral in the "interpretation of American experience" (4). Marx views as a central metaphor in American literature the impingement of technology and the machine on the rural, natural landscape. Beginning with Nathaniel Hawthorne's account of a peaceful revery interrupted by the harsh shriek of a locomotive whistle, Marx follows the complex relationship between the ideal of America as a fresh, green land and the reality of its sophisticated, technological society.

For instance, Marx sees Jay Gatsby in F. Scott Fitzgerald's *The Great Gatsby* as a character unable to reconcile or even recognize the discrepancy between a sentimental vision of love among "the elegant green lawns of suburban Long Island" and the fact of the technological society that gives rise to those suburbs. Only after Gatsby's death does the narrator, Nick Carraway, begin to understand the title character's personality, a personality based on a pastoral dream that denies the reality of the sources of power and wealth in the United States. Nick, on the Long Island beach, looks over the water and has a momentary vision in which "the inessential houses began to melt away until gradually [he] became aware of the old island here that flowered once for Dutch sailors' eyes—a fresh, green breast of the new world." Such a vision, Marx believes, "locates the origin of that strange compound of sentiment and criminal aggressiveness in Gatsby" (360) and relates him to a line of pastoral figures who long for a retreat from the complexities and cruelty of urban society to the simplicity of a peaceful, natural world. Gatsby's tragedy, however, is his confusion of that vision with reality.

## Donne: The Profane and the Sacred

A somewhat different kind of study traces the line of influence of the works of a specific author. For example, George Williamson's *The Donne Tradition: A*

*Study in English Poetry from Donne to the Death of Cowley* argues the significance of John Donne's poetry for many lyric poets of the seventeenth century. In an appendix, Williamson lists twenty important seventeenth-century poets possibly influenced by Donne's work. Although this discussion cannot easily be reproduced in brief, it recognizes two lines to the Donne tradition—the "sacred line," including such poets as George Herbert, Richard Crashaw, and Henry Vaughn, and the "profane line," including Lord Herbert of Cherbury, Henry King, Andrew Marvell, and Aurelian Townsend. The lines reflect and carry on two major elements in Donne's poetry: love and religion. In Williamson's words, "Love poetry could never be quite the same after him and religious verse that is also poetry descends from him" (47).

If Donne was the source of a literary tradition, he was also the inheritor of one. Louis L. Martz, in *The Poetry of Meditation: A Study in English Religious Literature of the Seventeenth Century*, demonstrates the way in which the tradition of English religious meditation shaped the devotional poetry of Donne and other writers of that century. The religious meditation consisted of three parts, one for each of the "three powers of the soul"—memory, understanding, and will. The first element was calling to mind or remembering a specific religious problem or mystery; the second was an analysis of the problem; and the third was communication with God, expressing "affections, resolutions, thanksgiving, and petitions" (27). Martz clearly shows many of Donne's sonnets to be structured according to this pattern.

For example, Donne's "Holy Sonnet 12" begins by calling to mind a specific religious problem, the mystery of humanity's favored status among all creatures. Why, the sonnet asks, are we the beneficiary of animals who provide us food and clothing? The sonnet then moves on to a more detailed analysis of the mystery as it questions individual beasts—the horse and the bull—asking why these strong, pure animals submit to weak and sinful humans. The sonnet ends with the third element of meditation, in this case wonder and implicit thanksgiving for a creator who died for his creatures. The "greater wonder," the poem states, is not that animals are subject to human dominion but that "their Creator, whom sin, nor nature tyed, / For us, his Creatures, and his foes, hath dyed." Although a reader can understand this poem without knowing the tradition of the meditation, that knowledge clarifies the sonnet's structure by showing the relationship and purpose of the different parts and also enriches appreciation of the poem by locating it within the context of religious devotion.

## The Classical Tradition in Literature and Theory

The preceding examples have been relatively limited in scope, but some studies of literary tradition are extremely comprehensive. One such is Gilbert Highet's *The Classical Tradition: Greek and Roman Influences on Western Literature*, an attempt to trace classical influence from the Middle Ages to the mid-twentieth century. Of course, so pervasive is the classical tradition that

Highet's book becomes nearly a history of Western literature. A condensed example may indicate something of the tradition Highet investigates. Discussing Albert Camus's *The Myth of Sisyphus*, the tale of a man condemned to an eternity of pushing a boulder uphill only to have it roll down again, Highet refers to Camus's belief that true victory is the ability to realize the absurdity and pointlessness of human life and yet to take satisfaction from the struggle itself. Highet finds this idea not to be original with Camus and quotes from Byron's *Prometheus,* in which the speaker recognizes a human's ability to "foresee / His own funeral destiny," to defy that destiny, and thus to make even death a victory. The line can be traced, then, from Camus in the twentieth century back to Byron in the early nineteenth and on back to the earliest Greek tales of Prometheus.

A work somewhat more difficult to classify is M. H. Abrams's *The Mirror and the Lamp: Romantic Theory and the Critical Tradition.* As the title indicates, Abrams's interest is in tracing a tradition not of literature but of literary theory. Abrams sees the nineteenth century as a time when the conception of literature changed. Previously, literary works were viewed as mirroring exterior reality, as giving reflections of the "real" world. The main question to be asked of a literary text concerned its truth or fidelity to nature, its accuracy as a representation. In the nineteenth century, however, literature came to be seen as a lamp giving "insights into the mind and heart of the poet himself" (23). The appropriate question no longer concerned a work's truth but its genuineness or sincerity. Was the text a genuine expression of the writer's feelings? Obviously, so dramatic a change in literary theory, in the conception of what literature is and what it attempts to do, goes hand in hand with a shift in literature itself. In that sense, Abrams's book gives knowledge about the tradition of literature as well as that of literary theory.

This section has mentioned only a few representative examples of literary traditions. There are many more, as many as there are conventions, forms, and ideas that are handed down and built on. For instance, the utopian tradition, composed of works depicting ideal governments and societies, runs from Plato's *Republic* through the sixteenth and seventeenth centuries with Thomas More's *Utopia* and Francis Bacon's *New Atlantis* to the nineteenth century with Samuel Butler's *Erewhon* and on into the twentieth century. A relatively recent collection of critical essays by James Nagel and Richard Astro, *American Literature: The New England Heritage,* investigates a tradition of New England writing. The Romantic tradition is the subject of many books and articles. The list could go on, but the point is that no literary work stands solely on its own. Literary texts are unique and individual, but they are also the products of what has gone before.

Along with works already mentioned, the following list includes examples of studies of several of the traditions discussed in this section.

## WORKS CITED AND RECOMMENDED

Abrams, M. H. *The Mirror and the Lamp: Romantic Theory and the Critical Tradition.* New York: Norton, 1953.

Adams, Richard P. "The Archetypal Pattern of Death and Rebirth in *Lycidas.*" *PMLA* 64 (1949): 183-188.

Bush, Douglas. *Mythology and the Romantic Tradition.* New York: Norton, 1963.

Eliot, T. S. "Tradition and the Individual Talent." *Selected Essays 1917-1932.* New York: Harcourt, 1932.

Empson, William. *Some Versions of Pastoral.* London: Chatto, 1950.

Gregg, W. W. *Pastoral Poetry and Pastoral Drama.* London: Bullen, 1906.

Hanford, James. "The Pastoral Elegy and Milton's *Lycidas.*" *PMLA* 25 (1910): 403-447.

Hertzler, J. A. *The History of Utopian Thought.* New York: Macmillan, 1923.

Highet, Gilbert. *The Classical Tradition: Greek and Roman Influences of Western Literature.* New York: Oxford UP, 1949.

Lincoln, Eleanor. *Pastoral and Romance: Modern Essays in Criticism.* Englewood Cliffs: Prentice, 1969.

Marinelli, Peter. *Pastoral.* London: Methuen, 1971.

Marts, Luis L. *The Poetry of Meditation: A Study in English Religious Literature of the Seventeenth Century.* New Haven: Yale UP, 1954.

Marx, Leo. *The Machine in the Garden: Technology and the Pastoral Ideal in America.* Oxford: Oxford UP, 1964.

Mumford, Lewis. *The Story of Utopias.* New York: Boni, 1922.

Murray, Gilbert. *The Classical Tradition in Poetry.* New York: Vintage, 1957.

Nagel, James, and Richard Astro, eds. *American Literature: The New England Heritage.* New York: Garland, 1981.

Walsh, Chad. *From Utopia to Nightmare.* New York: Harper, 1962.

Williamson, George. *The Donne Tradition: A Study in English Poetry from Donne to the Death of Cowley.* New York: Noonday, 1930.

# Chapter 3

# THE INSIGHT OF OTHER FIELDS

The mirror is one of the most ancient and persistent metaphors for literature: Writers from Plato's time to the present day have often described literature as a mirror reflecting life. In a sense, the six approaches presented in this chapter—moral and religious, sociological and political, feminist, ethnic and minority, archetypal, and psychological—may be said to be predicated on the assumption that literature is at least to some extent a mirror offering the reader images of human beings and societies. As much as these approaches differ in their emphases and techniques, they all take the connection between life and literature very seriously indeed. Critics using these approaches tend to see the literary work not as an independent artifact existing in an aesthetic universe, but as very much a reflection of and a part of the human universe. And just as the study of literature provides insights into human life, other disciplines that study human life can provide insights into literature.

All these approaches, then, are more or less interdisciplinary: Critics may be guided by their knowledge of another discipline as well as by their knowledge of literature, and they may see their work as contributing to that discipline as well as to literary study. A critic undertaking a psychological study of *Hamlet*, for example, may draw on a knowledge of Freudian theory as well as a knowledge of Elizabethan drama and may hope to improve the reader's understanding both of the play itself and of the Oedipus complex. Some would say that such a critic subordinates literature to something else, violating the artistic integrity of the literary work by intruding upon it foreign concepts and, perhaps, inappropriate standards of judgment. One reply to such a charge is that it is no denigration of literature to see it as capable of illuminating and being illuminated by a number of other disciplines. Psychological critics do not see *Hamlet* as no more than a footnote to Freud; on the contrary, they are drawn to the play because they regard Shakespeare's portrait of the Oedipus complex as genuine and unique. Literature shares with many other disciplines the common goal of examining human emotions, ideas, relationships, and societies. The interdisciplinary critic may be said to pay literature a profound compliment by recognizing its true importance—its relevance to every area of human thought and action, its ability to provide what Matthew Arnold would call an interpretation of life.

Still, some would deny the validity—and, indeed, the separate identities—of several of the approaches represented in this chapter. Is there, for example, really such a thing as a feminist approach to literary criticism? Or is it simply that some critics, employing a variety of approaches, find a feminist significance in the literary works they study? Is a critic who discusses the religious ideas in literary works using a definable critical approach or simply examining the influence of religious ideas on the literature of a certain period? Some would argue that the approaches here described as moral and religious, sociological and political, feminist, and ethnic and minority are in fact usually varieties of historical studies; some would charge that those who do identify themselves as Marxist or feminist critics, for example, are in fact engaged not in true literary criticism but in dubious sorts of special pleading.

Admittedly, some of these approaches cannot be defined in the same ways that approaches such as the structuralist and the rhetorical can. Feminist critics, for example, do not all share the same methodology: Some feminist critics are primarily formalists, some rely heavily on the insights afforded by biography, and some focus on matters of literary history. Thus, some of the critics discussed in the section on feminist criticism could also be mentioned in other chapters as examples of formalists, biographical critics, and literary historians. It also seems appropriate, however, and is perhaps more truly informative, to group them together as feminist critics. These critics, despite their different methodologies, are united by their feminist perspectives, and their criticism is informed by their feminist ideas and commitments. Their primary interest is in offering feminist interpretations of literature, and they adopt the critical tools that they consider most likely to enable them to achieve that goal. It would be misleading to describe Elaine Showalter, for example, as a literary historian who has happened to discover matters of feminist significance; it seems far more accurate to describe her as a feminist critic, which is indeed how she describes herself. Nor does it seem either respectful or sensible to say that those who define themselves as feminist critics are somehow not engaging in literary criticism in the true sense: If they contribute to the understanding of literature, they deserve the title of literary critics. If a feminist critic's work degenerates into special pleading and fails to say anything valuable about literature, that is a failing of the individual critic and not of the approach itself. No critical approach can guarantee all its adherents freedom from bias. Even a purely formalist reading may be colored by the critic's personal religious or political beliefs—and, indeed, many feminists charge that the critic's traditional claim to objectivity is often no more than a mask for sexism and prejudice.

Similar arguments might be made about the critics who take the other approaches described in this chapter. These critics share a compelling interest in uncovering a particular kind of significance found in literary works; most would readily admit that literature has other kinds of significance as well, but they see one as preeminent. It has seemed to us most helpful to group these critics according to the kinds of questions they ask about literature and the kinds of significance they hope to find. Moreover, the critics using each of these approaches have a common debt to a discipline or field of knowledge other than literature: The value of Carl Woodring's criticism, for example, derives in part from his understanding of literature and in part from his understanding of politics. Limited space has made it impossible to include discussions of approaches that explore the relationships between literature and such fields as philosophy, economics, music, and the visual arts. The approaches described here can provide no more than a sampling of current interdisciplinary studies of literature, a partial indication of their variety and vigor.

## MORAL AND RELIGIOUS STUDIES

"The best poetry," Matthew Arnold declares in his 1880 essay "The Study of Poetry," has "a power of forming, sustaining, and delighting us, as nothing else can." Literature that possesses "high seriousness" and offers a worthy "criticism of life" has a vital mission in modern times: "More and more mankind will discover that we have to turn to poetry to interpret life for us, to console us, to sustain us. Without poetry, our science will appear incomplete; and most of what now passes with us for religion and philosophy will be replaced by poetry." For Arnold, then, literature is a supremely important source of moral guidance and spiritual inspiration, and indeed the probable successor to both philosophy and religion. In seeing literature as a worthy substitute for religion, Arnold takes an extreme position. His insistence on the moral and religious significance of literature, however, is very much in harmony with critical tradition. Plato acknowledges literature's power as a teacher by believing it capable of corrupting morals and undermining religion; other classical thinkers, notably Aristotle and Horace, consider literature capable of fostering virtue. Although some modern critical theories may make us resist the idea that literature has a didactic purpose, we cannot deny that many, perhaps most, of the greatest writers have considered themselves teachers as well as artists. Some have seen themselves as providing sound ethical advice and models of virtuous action; some have seen themselves as encouraging morality by enlarging their readers' sympathies or refining their sensibilities; some have seen themselves as guardians of religion and moral traditions; and some have seen themselves as critics and liberators challenging established beliefs. Criticism that focuses on the moral and religious ideas in and significance of literature, then, invites the reader to take a perspective shared by many great writers and to examine what they saw as one of their most important purposes.

### Babbitt, More, and Fuller: Three Examples

Critics who concentrate on the moral dimensions of literature often judge literary works by their ethical teachings and by their effects on readers: Literature that is ethically sound and encourages virtue is praised, and literature that misguides and corrupts is condemned. Irving Babbitt, probably the most influential and controversial moral critic of this century, held that literature must help us recognize the reality of evil and the necessity of controlling our impulses. In

"Genius and Taste," originally written in 1918, Babbitt attacks critics who value "primitivism" and "enthusiasm" above decorum and restraint; they are "corrupters of the literary conscience" who have turned the imagination into "the irresponsible accomplice of the unchained emotions" (175). Truly great literature, Babbitt argues, conforms to standards, to "the ethical norm that sets bounds to the eagerness of the creator to express himself." Literature that does not abide by such standards leads to self-indulgence and, ultimately, moral degeneration (164–165). Given this view, it is not surprising that Babbitt is critical of romanticism. In one of his major works, *Rousseau and Romanticism,* Babbitt condemns romantic morality: "The ideal of romantic morality . . . is altruism. The real . . . is egoism" (192). Babbitt sees Blake as "the extreme example" of the dangerous romantic rejection of limits and restraints: "He proclaims himself of the devil's party, he glorifies a free expansion of energy, he looks upon everything that restricts this expansion as synonymous with evil" (196). Poets such as Blake, Babbitt believes, have contributed to a moral decline in society.

Paul Elmer More, a friend of Babbitt, takes a similar approach to criticism. It is the critic's duty, More declares in an essay entitled "Criticism," to determine the moral tendency of literary works and to judge them on that basis; the greatest critics, he says, are "discriminators between the false and the true, the deformed and the normal; preachers of harmony and proportion and order, prophets of the religion of taste" (80). In "The Praise of Dickens," More attempts to practice this sort of criticism by pointing out what is "false" and what is "true" in Dickens's work. More values Dickens's "divine tenderness" and "human delicacy" revealed, for example, in his treatment of Emily in *David Copperfield.* But "a strain of vulgarity runs through Dickens," More says, because he lacks the "restraining faculty": Because he does not understand self-discipline, his attempts to portray gentlemen are always unsuccessful (166).

A third example of criticism focusing on moral considerations is found in Edmund Fuller's *Man in Modern Fiction: Some Minority Opinions on Contemporary American Writing.* Fuller's definition of criticism is similar to More's. "At least one part of the critic's task," Fuller says, "is to appraise the validity and the implications of the image of man projected by the artist's use of his materials" (xvii). Like Babbitt and More, Fuller sees standards and restraint as essential for moral action. He condemns much of modern fiction for rejecting these guides in the name of compassion. True compassion, Fuller says, must be based on "a large and generous view of life and a distinct set of values"; the compassion found in many modern novels, by contrast, is a "teary slobbering over the criminal and degraded, the refusal to assign any share of responsibility to them, and a vindictive lashing out against the rest of the world" (34–37). Many would view both Fuller's language and his judgments as unduly harsh and would consider his standards too narrow—much narrower than Matthew Arnold's, for example. Certainly, the approach that Babbitt, More, and Fuller epitomize has become less popular and influential during the last few decades. Whether this decline is attributable to the excesses of the critics or to the deficiencies of the approach itself—or, perhaps, to the moral laxness of other critics—is a matter for debate.

## Contemporary Critics: Reevaluating Moral Considerations

It would be a mistake, however, to think that literary critics no longer give any weight to moral considerations. Moral fervor can be detected in the writings of many contemporary critics who cannot be considered disciples of Babbitt or More. For example, feminist critics who call attention to sexual stereotypes in literary works clearly seem to be applying moral as well as aesthetic criteria when they judge such works inferior to ones that offer other sorts of portrayals of male and female characters. In "Aristotle's Sister: A Poetics of Abandonment," Lawrence Lipking notes that, in addition to winning critical attention for many neglected works by women writers, feminist criticism has sparked a reevaluation of many works traditionally granted high, secure places in the canon. "Something peculiar has been happening lately to the classics," he writes. "Some of them now seem less heroic, and some of them less funny. Those 'irrelevant' scenes of cruelty to women, those obsessions with chastity and purity, those all-male debates about the nature and future of the human race, those sacrifices of feeling to duty have changed their character" (79). It would be hard to argue that the critics who have helped to bring about such changes have been blind to moral concerns.

Furthermore, some critics have recently called for a renewed, explicit acknowledgment of the relationship between literary and moral judgments. In *The Ethics of Criticism*, Tobin Siebers declares that "literary criticism is inextricably linked to ethics" (1). At its best, he says, literary criticism "accepts the task of examining to what extent literature and life contribute to the nature and knowledge of each other" (42). Attempts to extract literature from an ethical context are misguided and ultimately unsuccessful. Siebers faults the New Criticism, for example, for trying to treat literary works as completely autonomous creations, for arguing that any interest either in an author's intentions or in a work's effect on its audience is irrelevant to the true business of criticism. By insisting on this false division between "literature" and "the human," the New Critics become mired in contradictions. "If critics forget their relation to the human world," Siebers writes, "they risk misunderstanding the nature of their own judgments" (66–68).

Similarly, in *The Moral Imagination: Essays on Literature and Ethics*, Christopher Clausen attacks "the superstition that aesthetic categories are more intrinsic to the nature of literature than ethical or cognitive ones" (2). In fact, Clausen says, "literary works usually embody moral problems and reflect moral attitudes, sometimes even moral theories. There is no good reason for criticism to tiptoe around one of the major reasons that literary works endure" (xi). Clausen cites Donne's "A Valediction: Forbidding Mourning" as an example of a poem that is often analyzed only in terms of its technical excellence but actually matters to readers largely because of what it says about love: "The famous metaphors, the twists and turns of technique, are after all used in the service of expressing a moral ideal." Critics who praise Donne's metaphors but neglect his teaching are doing the poem a disservice and failing to understand it fully (9-11). Clausen acknowledges the difficulty of attempting moral criticism in an age when no standards of right and wrong are universally accepted, but he argues that such criticism need not be narrow or doctrinaire, and that it can promote an understanding of literature's true meaning and significance. "When carried out responsibly," Clausen writes, moral criticism can "dignify literature by taking account of more of its facets than a purely aesthetic criticism"; even more important, moral criticism "reaffirms the status of poetry as an art that illuminates our other acts of living" (20-22).

## Religious Criticism

Religious studies of literature often share this focus on moral issues, but some studies have taken other directions as well. As Giles Gunn says in "Literature and Religion," the scope of these studies "extends far beyond the boundaries of apologetic theology to the theory of aesthetics on the one hand, and to literary history and the history of ideas, on the other" (48). Some students of religion and literature are essentially formalists, some are structuralists, and others employ any number of other critical methods. The kinds of literature these critics study also vary greatly. Some critics have made what may seem to be the obvious choice by discussing devotional poetry or other literature explicitly religious in theme and purpose. Kenneth B. Murdock's *Literature and Theology in Colonial New England,* for example, analyzes Puritan works ranging from sermons to poems. Murdock notes the Puritans' preference for a plain writing style and their disapproval of "any art which seemed only to please the senses"; he also calls attention to the "homeliness" and "realism" of the imagery found in Puritan theological writing—"the sea, the forest, the field, and the village household appear vividly on every page, even those devoted to the most lofty points of doctrine" (59). His study of sermons and other theological writings gives Murdock a special insight into the works of Puritan poets such as Edward Taylor. Although Taylor is in many ways a metaphysical poet, Murdock says, his poems "differ essentially" from those of Donne and Herbert, for Taylor's poetry "is made out of characteristically Puritan elements." Taylor's Puritanism is reflected not only in his ideas but also in his language: Like Puritan sermon writers, Taylor is distinguished by "his startling realism in diction and imagery, his love for the homeliest of colloquial words and for figures out of the most commonplace aspects of life" (154-158). Murdock's interpretation of Taylor's poetry is thus informed by his study of its religious context.

Other critics have examined the religious elements in seemingly secular works. In *Religion and Literature*, Helen Gardner argues that although Elizabethan drama "cannot in any sense be called a sacred drama," it is "not necessarily irreligious" (62). Indeed, Shakespeare's tragedy is fundamentally Christian, not in the sense of expounding Christian doctrine but because "the mysteries it exposes are mysteries that arise out of Christian formulations, and . . . some of its most characteristic features are related to Christian religious feeling and Christian apprehensions" (72). She notes that some of the plays contain "most beautiful and impressive expressions of distinctively Christian conceptions"—for example, Claudius's soliloquy on penitence (71). She devotes a good deal of attention to *Hamlet*, asserting that it is "a Christian tragedy in the sense that it is a tragedy of the imperatives and torments of the conscience." Another important Christian element in the play is Hamlet's gradual discovery of all the evil and corruption in the world, including the corruption of the flesh: "there grows throughout the play a sense of horror at man's entanglement in the flesh, at the indecencies of physical existence." Some have seen Hamlet's "horror at carnality" as morbid, but Gardner maintains that we must recognize his attitude as a fundamentally Christian one that can be traced to St. Paul: "Among religions Christianity is remarkable for the severity with which it regards 'the flesh' and the sins of the flesh, finding that there is a law in a man's members that wars against the law of his mind" (80-84). It would be a mistake, then, to see Hamlet's attitude as a mere idiosyncrasy or psychological aberration. Gardner believes that one can understand Hamlet's revulsion at "the flesh" more accurately by recognizing its theological antecedents and implications.

Stanley Romaine Hopper similarly argues that much modern literature is fundamentally religious. In *Spiritual Problems in Contemporary Literature*, he says that "the problems of the literary artist today bring him more and more firmly upon the crucial centers of all human reflection" (ix). In our time, Hopper asserts, the most important "confessional" and "prophetic" writing "will be found, chiefly, in the best modern poetry." In the works of poets such as Auden and Eliot, a central theme is "the quest of the Prodigal . . . a narrative of alienation and return" (161-163). If Hopper is right, an analysis of such poetry would be incomplete if it did not take religious themes into account; moreover, studying such poetry can help the reader understand vital religious issues.

Those interested in learning more about the moral and religious perspectives in criticism might begin with some of the works mentioned earlier in this section—for example, Babbitt's *Rousseau and Romanticism* or Fuller's *Man in Modern Fiction: Some Minority Opinions on Contemporary American Writing*. Some of More's most important essays are collected in *The Essential Paul Elmer More: A Selection of His Writings*. Keith F. McKean's *The Moral Measure of Literature* includes chapters on Babbitt, More, and Yvor Winters.

Giles Gunn's "Literature and Religion" in Jean-Pierre Barricelli and Joseph Gibaldi's *Interrelations of Literature* provides a survey of important work in this field and a short annotated bibliography. Several collections of essays might also provide a helpful introduction to studies of literature and religion—for example, *Spiritual Problems in Contemporary Literature*, edited by Nathan A. Scott, Jr. Hoxie Neale Fairchild's six-volume *Religious Trends in English Poetry* is a historical study surveying literature from 1700 to 1965; readers might observe some similarities between Fairchild's perspective and those of Babbitt and More. A list of these and other important works follows.

## WORKS CITED AND RECOMMENDED

Alter, Robert. *The Art of Biblical Narrative.* New York: Basic, 1981.

Babbitt, Irving. *Rousseau and Romanticism.* Boston: Houghton, 1919.

———. "Genius and Taste." *Criticism in America: Its Function and Status.* New York: Haskell, 1924. 152–175.

Buell, Lawrence. "*Moby-Dick* as a Sacred Text." *New Essays on Moby-Dick.* Ed. Richard H. Brodhead. Cambridge: Cambridge UP, 1986. 53–72.

Clausen, Christopher. *The Moral Imagination: Essays on Literature and Ethics.* Iowa City: Iowa UP, 1986.

Fairchild, Hoxie Neale. *Religious Trends in English Poetry.* 6 vols. New York: Columbia UP, 1939–1968.

Fraser, Hilary. *Beauty and Belief: Aesthetics and Religion in Victorian Literature.* Cambridge: Cambridge UP, 1986.

Frye, Northrup. *The Double Vision: Language and Meaning in Religion.* Toronto: Toronto UP, 1991.

Fuller, Edmund. *Man in Modern Fiction: Some Minority Opinions on Contemporary American Writing.* New York: Random, 1958.

Gardner, Helen. *Religion and Literature.* London: Faber, 1971.

Gunn, Giles. "Literature and Religion." *Interrelations of Literature.* Ed. Jean-Pierre Barricelli and Joseph Gibaldi. New York: MLA, 1982. 47–66.

Hopper, Stanley Romaine, ed. *Spiritual Problems in Contemporary Literature.* New York: Harper, 1952.

Johnson, Peter. *Politics, Innocence, and the Limits of Goodness.* New York: Routledge, 1988.

Larson, Janet L. *Dickens and the Broken Scripture.* Athens: Georgia UP, 1985.

Liking, Lawrence. "Aristotle's Sister: A Poetics of Abandonment." *Critical Inquiry* 10 (1983): 61–81.

McKean, Keith F. *The Moral Measure of Literature.* Denver: Alan Swallow, 1961.

More, Paul Elmer. *The Essential Paul Elmer More: A Selection of His Writings.* New Rochelle: Arlington, 1972.

Murdock, Kenneth B. *Literature and Theology in Colonial New England.* Harvard UP, 1949.

Ong, Walter J. *The Barbarian Within.* New York: Macmillan, 1962.

Scott, Nathan A., Jr., ed. *The New Orpheus: Essays toward a Christian Poetic.* New York: Sheed, 1964.

Siebers, Tobin. *The Ethics of Criticism.* Ithaca: Cornell UP, 1988.

Tennyson, G. B., and Edward Ericson, Jr., eds. *Religion and Modern Literature: Essays in Theory and Criticism.* Grand Rapids: Eerdmans, 1975.

Williams, Bernard Arthur. *Shame and Necessity.* Berkeley: California UP, 1993.

## SOCIOLOGICAL AND POLITICAL STUDIES

Many people regard sociological and political approaches to the study of literature with skepticism and hostility. The world of polls, press conferences, and party conventions seems far distant from that of the poet or novelist, who is often envisioned as a solitary, introspective figure. In particular, those who think of literature primarily in terms of form, as an intricate construction of words and images, may suspect that the only literature concerned with social conditions or politics is propagandistic and inferior; how, then, could sociological or political approaches afford any insights into truly valuable literature? It is important to remember, however, that poets and novelists themselves have often insisted that literature is in fact very much bound up with politics and society. "Poets," Percy Bysshe Shelley declares in "A Defense of Poetry," "are the unacknowledged legislators of the world." And George Orwell, in "Why I Write," says that his primary purpose in all his serious works is political, a "desire to push the world in a certain direction, to alter other people's idea of the kind of society that they should strive after. . . . [N]o book is genuinely free from political bias. The attitude that art should have nothing to do with politics is itself a political attitude." Although many may think that Shelley overestimates literature's impact on society or that not all writers are as politically committed as Orwell, it nevertheless seems clear that some important writers, at least, see political ideas as central to their works and hope to influence society. And many modern critics believe that sociological and political considerations are often important to the analysis of literary works. Irving Howe, for example, attacks "the notion that abstract ideas invariably contaminate a work of art and should be kept at a safe distance from it"; rather, as he says in *Politics and the Novel*, "ideas, be they in free isolation or looped into formal systems, are indispensable to the serious novel" (22). C. M. Bowra, similarly, argues in *Poetry and Politics, 1900–1960* that "public themes have for centuries been common in many parts of the world and the conscious avoidance of them is more often the exception than the rule"; he cites Aeschylus, Virgil, and Dante as examples of writers whose works are deeply concerned with political matters (1). If political and sociological themes are in fact central to many works of literature, critical approaches that focus on these themes are at least worth exploring.

## The Marxist Critics

Among the most influential and controversial critics to use such approaches are the Marxist critics. Two articles in the November 1972 issue of *College English* can help explain some of the essential characteristics of this approach. Richard Wasson writes that the Marxist critics, while appreciating the New Critics' discoveries about such matters as verbal irony and paradox, reject formalistic approaches because their "methods could not deal with the relation between literature and the lived lives of men and women"; both formalism and historicism, Wasson thinks, "make us forget that writers are concerned with class, race, and sexism, and the recovery of that awareness is vital to a reinvigorated criticism" (170–171). Ira Shor, in "Notes on Marxism and Method," identifies ways in which Marxist critics differ from other critics. His explanation of materialism touches on several important Marxist doctrines.

> Being materialist indicates that a Marxist critic confronts the actual configuration of society in the contemporary age or in the age of the work in question.

> Moral, emotional and psychological problems are not thought of as eternally unchanging forms of human life, but are cast against the dominant mode of living every age manifests. A dominant mode includes the forces which make society function—labor which earns a living, laws and customs which regulate work, sexuality, property, political groups contending for power, and so on. Marxists tend to evaluate human action against its immediate social atmosphere. Materialism here suggests that there are tangible and material forces, people and objects in every person's life, in every book's narrative, and in the societies out of which every book has come, to explain why things happened as they did. (174-176)

Thus, *Marxist criticism* often focuses on the ways in which the sorts of forces Shor mentions can be seen to operate within a literary work, or on the ways in which such forces influenced the author of the work. Shor describes Marxist criticism as "moral" because "all the material circumstances are judged for their impact on human beings." Since literary works may be considered "material circumstances" to the extent that they influence what Marxists see as the "transcendent drama of history . . . the progress of humanity toward socialism," literature should be judged primarily on the basis of whether it promotes or impedes that progress. Marxist criticism is partisan, Shor says, because it deals harshly with "authors whose works fail to take sides or fail to evoke the necessity of revolution." Marxist critics are primarily concerned with theme because "literature's content is more accessible to attack than is literary form" (174-176).

A look at several examples of Marxist literary criticism supports Shor's description of it as materialist, moral, and partisan. Christopher Caudwell (the pseudonym of Christopher St. John Spriggs) argues in *Illusion and Reality: A Study of the Sources of Poetry* that the study of literature and the study of society are inextricably intertwined: "Art is the product of society, as the pearl is of the oyster, and to stand outside art is to stand inside society. The criticism of art differs from pure enjoyment or creation in that it contains a sociological component" (11). Thus, in reviewing the course of English poetry, Caudwell analyzes its connections with economic and political developments. He sees Milton as "England's first openly revolutionary poet," representing "a stage of the illusion where [the bourgeois] sees himself as defiant and lonely, challenging the powers that be" (81); Tennyson's image of nature as brutal and indifferent "in fact only reflects the ruthlessness of a society in which capitalist is continually hurling down fellow capitalist into the proletarian abyss" (100). Caudwell's analysis thus reflects the Marxist belief that people's lives and ideas are shaped by the material conditions of their times.

Two other prominent Marxist critics illustrate the belief that literature should be judged according to its ability to contribute to the class struggle. In *The Great Tradition,* Granville Hicks identifies a tradition in American literature that begins with James Russell Lowell and Walt Whitman and extends to such writers as John Dos Passos. Ralph Waldo Emerson and Henry David Thoreau, for example, are included in this tradition because they were "rebels against the shams and oppressions of their day" (305). Writers such as Henry James, Willa Cather, Emily Dickinson, and Robert Frost, however, must be excluded from the great tradition of American literature: Their works prove that "it has been increasingly difficult to those who ignore industrialism to create a vital culture" (301–302). For example, although Hicks praises Dickinson's craft and her insight into love and renunciation, he finds her poetry "undeniably fragile and remote" (126); her isolation from the world "permitted her to avoid all the contamination of an era of uncertainty and false values, but at the same time it meant that she could have none of the vigor that is found in an artist for whom self-expression is also the expression of the society of which he is a part" (130). Georg Lukacs, often regarded as the greatest Marxist literary critic, offers in *Studies in European Realism: A Sociological Survey of the Writings of Balzac, Stendhal, Zola, Tolstoy, Gorki, and Others* some criteria for interpreting and evaluating literature, especially modern fiction. More important than a writer's conscious beliefs is "the essence of realism: the great writer's thirst for truth, his fanatic striving for reality." By realistically describing social conditions, the greatest writers have inevitably "aided the development of mankind and the triumph of humanist principles." Thus, Lukacs praises Balzac, who, despite his royalist beliefs, "nevertheless inexorably exposed the vices and weaknesses of royalist feudal France and described its death agony with magnificent poetic vigor" (10–13). Hicks and Lukacs do not completely disregard aesthetic considerations, but their assessments of literary works rest primarily on the sorts of moral concerns Shor describes.

## BEYOND MARXIST CRITICISM

Although Marxist critics have been very influential, they have not completely dominated sociological and political studies of literature. "In some sense," Priscilla B. Clark says in "Literature and Sociology," "every sociology of literature today can be traced to Marx"; however, most literary critics ultimately reject Marxism's deterministic view of literature (112). Jeffrey Sammons, in *Literary Sociology and Practical Criticism: An Inquiry,* says that Marxism has contributed to literary criticism because it "militates against any isolation of literature from the total realm of experience." Still, Sammons sees Marxist criticism as limited and reductive: Because Marxism claims to have discovered the whole truth of human history and society, Marxist critics can decide only whether or not a literary work reflects this truth—"there is little that a Marxist literary inquiry can learn, apart from illustrative detail, for the truth is one and is known." Sammons contrasts the Marxist position with that of the "liberal scholar" of sociology and literature, who "will look upon literary sociology as the pursuit of a large number of open questions about the relationship of literature and society. He will hope for some illumination of literature and its relation to social environment on the one hand, and some understanding of society and history on the other" (7–8). Marxist criticism, then, is not the only approach open to those interested in studies of literature and sociology.

# Sociological Analyses

Clark sees sociological analyses of literature as a valuable supplement to other approaches, not as a substitute for them. Without denying the uniqueness of an author or a literary work, the "sociological perspective . . . links the individual person, act, or work to collective phenomena, to social groups, institutions, and forces" (108). "Where others tie literature to myth, to linguistic structures, or to psychological constructs," Clark says, "sociological readings view literature as either a document of social phenomena or a product of those same phenomena. One may read from society into a text or one may reverse the procedure" (114). Thus, by studying a literary work in the context of sociological phenomena, the critic hopes to gain a fuller understanding of the work, of the phenomena, or of both.

## THE AUTHOR'S AUDIENCE

For example, some critics have focused on the relationship between authors and their audiences. An early example of this sort of study is Alfred Harbage's *Shakespeare's Audience,* published in 1941. Using such evidence as letters, diaries, and financial and dramatic records, Harbage challenges the standard image of Shakespeare's audience as "rabble." The people who came to see Shakespeare's plays at the Globe, Harbage maintains, were a varied and, on the whole, a respectable lot: There were more women and university students than most people usually imagine, and most of the playgoers were working people who were at least refined enough to choose the theater over the other two amusements they could afford—drinking and animal baiting. It is a mistake, then, to think that Shakespeare achieved greatness despite having to write for a crude, boisterous mob; on the contrary, Harbage believes, the audience "must be given much of the credit for the greatness of Shakespeare's plays" (159). Shakespeare's much admired "universality" must be attributed in part to his "socially, economically, educationally heterogeneous audience" (162). Harbage's study thus offers insight both into the plays themselves and into the social conditions that foster the creation of great literature.

Ian Watt's *The Rise of the Novel* also pays a good deal of attention to audience, this time to the eighteenth' century reading public in England. Examining evidence about such matters as the prices of books, wages, and school attendance, Watt concludes that the novel was accessible to "an ever-widening audience"—for example, merchants, manufacturers, women, apprentices, and household servants. For the first time, the middle class had a "dominating position" in the reading public. "The new literary balance of power," Watt concludes, "probably tended to favor ease of entertainment at the expense of obedience to traditional critical standards, and it is certain that this change of emphasis was an essential permissive factor for the achievements of Defoe and Richardson" (37–49).

**THE BOOK AND MAGAZINE TRADE**

William Charvat, another well-known proponent of the sociological approach, argues that it is important to recognize the role of "the whole complex organism of the book and magazine trade—a trade which, for the last two centuries at least, has had a positive and dynamic function in the world of literature." He describes in *The Profession of Authorship in America, 1800-1870* a "triangle" consisting of author, reader, and publisher, each influencing and being influenced by the others. For example, he points out that the discount policies of the early nineteenth century may have helped make English authors popular in America, for their works could be obtained more cheaply than those by native authors; he argues that publishers' changing requests for three-volume, then two-volume, and then one-volume novels profoundly influenced novelists; and he suggests that Longfellow shifted from writing sonnets to writing "poems in space-consuming quatrains" because the editor of *Graham's Magazine* was reluctant to pay large fees for short poems (284–289). To some, it may seem that the conclusions Charvat and other sociological critics reach are too speculative or that the matters they investigate are relatively unimportant; to others, however, sociological approaches offer an opportunity to see literature in a richer and more realistic way.

# Political Analyses

Other critics have focused not on sociological considerations but on the political ideas explicit or implicit in literary works. An examination of these ideas, such critics argue, is often essential to fully understand a work, an author, a period, or a genre. For example, William Chace, in *The Political Identities of Ezra Pound and T. S. Eliot,* maintains that these two poets "were more than interested in politics; they were entangled in, even obsessed by politics" (xvii). Still, many critics ignore the political elements in both poets' works, and particularly in Pound's: Since they found Pound's political beliefs so repellent, critics "have for the most part preferred either to analyze Pound's work without reference to his ideas or to analyze his ideas without reference to his work." Chace finds such analysis unbalanced and unsatisfactory: A purely formalist study of Pound's poetry, he says, reduces ideas "to the level of an arbitrarily chosen raw material on which the poet, for unspecified reasons, chose to exercise his consummate constructive skills" (3–4). Chace's comments remind us that writers are seldom, if ever, purely ethereal creatures who care only about form; like the rest of us, poets and novelists often have definite and deeply held political beliefs, and these beliefs often permeate their works.

Carl Woodring's *Politics in English Romantic Poetry* demonstrates how examining writers' political ideas can lead to new insights into both the content and the form of their works. Woodring sees politics as a central concern for all the major Romantic poets: "Romantic poems involve political theory, political convictions, and practical politics, as well as many traditions and conventions of political writing" (vii). Sometimes, poets express their political ideas directly—for example, Shelley in "Song to the Men of England." And sometimes, Woodring says, we can see the influence of the poet's political beliefs even in poems that ostensibly have little or nothing to do with politics. For example, in the opening lines of "Tintern Abbey," William Wordsworth's description of the cottages and farms along the Wye shows his lasting respect for "democratic individualism" (98). Even Wordsworth's innovations in the language and form of poetry, Woodring asserts, were based on more than aesthetic concerns; many of these innovations are linked to Wordsworth's democratic ideals. For example, he "attacks poetic diction, which is aristocratic and privileged," and he "attacks urbane generalizations about the rustic poor, who are actually individual farmers, shepherds, cottagers . . . speaking and acting at particular times from unique combinations of human feelings" (11-12).

Some critics who take a political perspective hope to gain a better understanding not only of the works they study but also of politics itself. Such critics question the assumption that poets, novelists, and dramatists can have nothing important or original to say about politics. "Literature," Joseph Blotner argues in *The Modern American Political Novel, 1900-1960,* "can provide insights into man as political animal as well as marital or amorous animal. As it can treat the individual, so it can treat the group . . ." (7). Nor can one assume that only members of English departments are able to analyze the political ideas in or the political significance of literary works. What Allan Bloom, a professor of political philosophy, says of Shakespeare could be said of other writers as well: "Shakespeare is not the preserve of any single department in the modern university . . . He presents us man generally, and it is not to be assumed that a department of literature possesses any privileged position for grasping his representations comprehensively" (Bloom and Jaffa 4). Most conventional Shakespearean criticism, Bloom thinks, fails to take Shakespeare's political ideas seriously, thereby robbing his works of much of the interest they should hold and most of the influence they should exert. "To the extent that Shakespeare's plays are understood to be merely literary productions," Bloom writes, "they have no relevance to the important problems that agitate the lives of actual men"; if we can put aside fashionable critical theories and read Shakespeare more "naively," Bloom says, his plays will become more exciting to us as readers and more useful to us as citizens (2-3). For example, Bloom argues that *Julius Caesar* teaches a great deal about republican government. Brutus and Cassius reflect two different "elements in the republican character; the one represents the principles, the other the passions which must be combined for a republican regime to endure" (93). Although Shakespeare portrays both men as noble and shows great sympathy for their cause, he also shows us their weaknesses, making it clear that neither Brutus's idealism nor Cassius's realism provides an adequate basis for understanding and controlling politics (104-105). Bloom's analyses, and other like them, assert that Shakespeare's hold on our imaginations and emotions cannot be attributed only to the charm of his words or the pleasing intricacies of his plots; rather, Shakespeare and other great writers intrigue us largely because they can enrich our understanding of all areas of human life, including politics.

Those interested in learning more about sociological and political approaches to the study of literature might begin with two articles in *Interrelations of Literature,* edited by Jean-Pierre Barricelli and Joseph Gibaldi: Clark's "Literature and Sociology" and Matei Calinescu's "Literature and Politics." Each article provides a concise summary of its field and a short but helpful annotated bibliography. Those interested in Marxist criticism can find a useful introduction in the November 1972 issue of *College English* mentioned earlier. Along with articles explaining and applying theories of Marxist literary criticism, the journal contains a short annotated bibliography on Marxism and literature, compiled by M. L. Raina. The following list suggests a number of other studies useful to those exploring various sociological and political approaches to the study of literature.

## WORKS CITED AND RECOMMENDED

Albrecht, Milton C., James H. Burnett, and Mason Griff, eds. *The Sociology of Art and Literature: A Reader*. New York: Praeger, 1970.

Alvis, John, and Thomas G. West, eds. *Shakespeare as Political Thinker*. Durham: Carolina Academic, 1981.

Bakhtin, M. M. *Art and Answerability: Early Philosophical Essays*. Austin: Texas UP, 1990.

Bardes, Barbara, and Suzanne Gossett. *Declarations of Independence: Women and Political Power in Nineteenth-Century American Fiction*. New Brunswick: Rutgers UP, 1990.

Baxandall, Lee. *Marxism and Aesthetics–An Annotated Bibliography*. New York: Humanities, 1968.

Bergonzi, Bernard. *The Myth of Modernism and Twentieth-Century Literature*. New York: St. Martin's, 1986.

Bloch, E. *The Utopian Function of Art and Literature*. Cambridge: MIT P, 1987.

Bloom, Allan, and Harry Jaffa. *Shakespeare's Politics*. New York: Basic, 1964.

Blotner, Joseph. *The Modern American Political Novel, 1900–1960*. Austin: Texas UP, 1966.

Bowra, C. M. *Poetry and Politics, 1900–1960*. Cambridge: Cambridge UP, 1966.

Burke, Kenneth. *On Symbols and Society*. Ed. Joseph R. Gusfield. Chicago: Chicago UP, 1989.

Calinescu, Matei. "Literature and Politics." *Interrelations of Literature*. Ed. Jean-Pierre Barricelli and Joseph Gibaldi. New York: MLA, 1982. 123–149.

Caudwell, Christopher. *Illusion and Reality: A Study of the Sources of Poetry*. 1937. New York: International, 1963.

Chace, William M. *The Political Identities of Ezra Pound and T. S. Eliot*. Stanford: Stanford UP, 1973.

Charvat, William. *The Profession of Authorship in America, 1800–1870*. Columbus: Ohio State UP, 1968.

Clark, Priscilla B. "Literature and Sociology." *Interrelations of Literature*. Ed. Jean-Pierre Barricelli and Joseph Gibaldi. New York: MLA, 1982. 102–122.

Des Pres, Terrence. *Praises and Dispraises: Poetry and Politics in the 20th Century.* New York: Viking, 1988.

Eagleton, Terry. *Marxism and Literary Criticism*. Berkeley: California UP, 1976.

Euben, J. Peter. *Greek Tragedy and Political Theory.* Berkeley: California UP, 1987.

Gibson, Colin, ed. *Art and Society in the Victorian Novel: Essays on Dickens and His Contemporaries*. New York: St. Martin's, 1988.

Goodin, George. *The Poetics of Protest: Literary Form and Political Implication in the Victim-of-Society Novel.* Carbondale: Southern Illinois UP, 1985.

Harbage, Alfred. *Shakespeare's Audience*. New York: Columbia UP, 1941.

Hicks, Granville. *The Great Tradition*. New York: Macmillan, 1933; Quadrangle, 1939.

Howe, Irving. *Politics and the Novel*. 1957. New York: Avon, 1970.

Jameson, Frederic. *The Political Unconscious: Narrative as a Socially Symbolic Act.* Ithaca: Cornell UP, 1981.

Johnson, Claudia L. *Jane Austen: Women, Politics, and the Novel.* Chicago: Chicago UP, 1988.

Knapp, J. F. *Modernism and the Transformation of Work*. Evanston: Northwestern UP, 1988.

LaCapra, Dominick. *History, Politics, and the Novel.* Ithaca: Cornell UP, 1987.

Lukacs, Georg. *Studies in European Realism: A Sociological Survey of the Writings of Balzac, Stendhal, Zola, Tolstoy, Gorki, and Others*. Trans. Edith Bone. 1950. New York: Grosset, 1964.

Raina, M. L. "Marxism and Literature—A Select Bibliography." *College English* 32 (1972): 308–314.

Reynolds, Larry J. *European Revolutions and the American Literary Renaissance.* New Haven: Yale UP, 1988.

Sammons, Jeffrey L. *Literary Sociology and Practical Criticism: An Inquiry*. Bloomington: Indiana UP, 1977.

Shor, Ira. "Notes on Marxism and Method." *College English* 32 (1972): 173–177.

Tucker, Robert C. *The Marx-Engels Reader*. New York: Norton, 1978.

Wasson, Richard. "New Marxist Criticism: Introduction." *College English* 32 (1972): 169–172.

Watt, Ian. *The Rise of the Novel*. 1957. Berkeley: California UP, 1962.

West, James L. W. *American Authors and the Literary Marketplace Since 1900.* Philadelphia: Pennsylvania UP, 1988.

Woodring, Carl. *Politics in English Romantic Poetry*. Cambridge: Harvard UP, 1970.

# FEMINIST STUDIES

Matthew Arnold, in an 1864 essay entitled "The Function of Criticism at the Present Time," declares that literary criticism must abide by a "rule" that "may be summed up in one world—*disinterestedness*." Dismayed because the English literary reviews of his time are controlled by various parties and factions, Arnold argues that literary criticism loses its validity and its value when it is used to further political or religious goals, or to serve any "practical" purpose; whatever the political interests of the time, criticism should be "not the minister of these interests, not their enemy, but absolutely and entirely independent of them." The critic's only motive, Arnold argues, must be "to see the object as in itself it really is," for all true criticism is "a disinterested endeavor to learn and propagate the best that is known and thought in the world." Although most critics have conceded—and felt—the difficulty of meeting these ideals, until recently few have openly challenged Arnold's opinion that criticism should at least strive to be objective and independent. Writers advocating *feminist criticism*, however, reject the idea of a totally disinterested criticism as both impossible and undesirable. Such critics freely admit that their interpretations of literature are deeply influenced by their feminist perspectives; further, many argue that exposing sexism, elucidating feminist ideals, and thereby contributing to the liberation of society can be a proper function of literary criticism.

## Barnes: Basic Feminist Beliefs

Annette Barnes, for example, argues that a critic "cannot come to the task as an ideal spectator devoid of culture, history, political perspective"; no critic, she says, is "able to escape some classificatory system, some way of perceiving the world." The ways in which critics approach literary works, the questions they ask, and the answers they reach will all to some extent be determined by their beliefs—whether these beliefs are Christian or atheist, democratic or communist, sexist or feminist (1–3). Is there a core of beliefs to which all feminists subscribe? Barnes identifies beliefs that she considers "the minimal criteria for feminism":

> [A]ll feminists, I argue, would agree that women are not automatically or necessarily inferior to men, that role models for females and males in the current Western societies are inadequate, that equal rights for women are necessary, that it is unclear what by nature either men or women are, that it is a matter for empirical investigation to ascertain what differences follow from the obvious physiological ones, that in these empirical investigations the hypotheses one employs are themselves open to question, revision, or replacement. (9)

Feminist critics will be influenced by these beliefs, Barnes maintains, just as Freudian critics will be influenced by their beliefs in the unconscious or in infantile sexuality (9).

## Approaches to Feminist Criticism

Even if we accept Barnes's list of basic feminist beliefs, the question of defining feminist literary criticism itself remains. Arlyn Diamond and Lee R. Edwards, in the foreword to *The Authority of Experience: Essays in Feminist Criticism*, point out that "feminist critics, obviously, are distinguished by virtue of their particular concern with society's beliefs about the nature and function of women in the world, with the transformation of these beliefs into literary plots, with the ways in which artistic and critical strategies adjust and control attitudes toward women" (x). Although they share some common beliefs and concerns, however, feminist critics use a variety of methodologies: Feminist criticism is not "a school of criticism with a rigidly defined methodology," Diamond and Edwards say, but rather involves "a general orientation, an attitude toward literature which can turn a wide variety of existing techniques to its own ends" (xiv). As Elaine Showalter points out, feminist criticism "differs from other contemporary schools of critical theory in not deriving its literary principles from a single authority figure or from a body of sacred texts." Feminist critics, she says,

> do not look to a Mother of Us All or a single system of thought to provide their central ideas. Rather, these have evolved from several sources—from extensive readings in women's literature; from exchanges with feminist theorists in other disciplines, especially history, psychology, and anthropology; and from the revision and reconsideration of literary theory itself. Linguistics, psychoanalysis, Marxism, and deconstruction have all provided feminist critical theory with important analytical tools. (*The New Feminist Criticism* 4)

Similarly, Annette Kolodny argues that feminist criticism gains much of its vitality from its willingness to draw on a variety of critical approaches. Feminist criticism, she says, is characterized by "a playful pluralism, responsive to the possibilities of multiple critical schools and methods, but captive of none" (19).

Despite this diversity of approaches, it seems safe to say that most, if not all, feminist critics consider the formalist approach inadequate by itself, believing that at least some attention must be paid to such matters as social and economic history. For example, Annis Pratt calls for "a new feminist critic" who "should be a 'new critic' . . . in judging the formal aspects of individual texts; she should be a 'feminist' in going beyond formalism to consider literature as it reveals men and women in relationship to each other within a socio-economic context." Feminist criticism, Pratt believes, should involve both "textual" and "contextual" analysis; a feminist critic must, for example, be able to "consider certain fictional conventions as politico-economic strategies without for a moment suspending her critical judgment" ("The New Feminist Criticism" 873–874). Diamond and Edwards agree that it is not enough to consider works or authors in isolation; Feminist critics "point constantly to the need to measure literary reality on the one side against historical and personally felt reality on the other" (x).

## Varieties of Feminist Criticism

In the last three decades, feminist critics have reached out in so many directions that any attempt to classify the varieties of feminist criticism must be tentative, temporary, and probably incomplete. We can, however, at least identify a few of the major varieties.

## STEREOTYPICAL FEMINIST CRITICISM

Pratt uses the term "stereotypical criticism" to describe works "in which the image of woman in both male and female literature is examined for bias" ("The New Feminist Criticisms" 176). Kate Millett's *Sexual Politics* in an early, controversial example of such criticism. In this 1970 book, Millett examines the works of D. H. Lawrence, Henry Miller, Norman Mailer, and Jean Genet, arguing that some major modern writers, including ones usually considered liberal, perpetuate sexual stereotypes by portraying male power and domination as natural and desirable. In her analysis of Lawrence's *Sons and Lovers,* for example, Millett describes Paul Morel as "the perfection of the male ego": The female characters in the novel "exist in Paul's orbit and to cater to his needs." Lawrence endorses his hero's brutal treatment of Miriam, his exploitation and rejection of Clara, and even his murder of his mother when she has "ceased to be of service" to him. Throughout the novel, Paul is sustained by his "faith in male supremacy," a faith that Lawrence, according to Millett, shares without reservation (245-257). Judith Fryer's *The Faces of Eve: Women in the Nineteenth-Century American Novel* can also be considered a work of stereotypical criticism. Building on the idea of America as a "New World Garden of Eden," Fryer describes the images of women found in a number of novels, all but one of them by male authors. She identifies four distinct types of female characters, or faces of Eve: the Temptress, the American Princess, the Great Mother, and the New Woman.

Not all stereotypical criticism is devoted to attacking works by male authors; often, feminist critics find much to praise even in works that might at first be considered sexist. Although we cannot ignore "resonant and craftsman-like" literature even if it is chauvinist, Pratt says, "it would seem better to turn one's attention from attack to defense, from examples of distorted images of women to examples of healthier representation" ("The New Feminist Criticism" 877). Miriam Lerenbaum, for example, defends *Moll Flanders* for offering a healthier representation of women than most readers think it does. In "Moll Flanders: 'A Woman on Her Own Account,'" Lerenbaum takes issue with critics who see Moll as masculine or monstrous: Moll's nature and behavior are "essentially feminine," Lerenbaum says, and Defoe's portrayal of her is both realistic and sympathetic. For example, to answer the charge that Moll's willingness to leave her children in the care of others is abnormal and cruel, Lerenbaum examines historical and psychological evidence and concludes that "Moll is neither unnatural, culpable, nor unfeminine in her indifference to her children, certainly not by the standards of her own time and probably not even by the standards of ours" (102, 106-107). Lerenbaum's article illustrates what Diamond and Edwards describe as feminist criticism's ability to salvage some of the literature of the past, to show that some of our classic male authors are "finally more and not less humane than we have perhaps been willing to think them" (xiii).

Even while defending such authors, feminist critics often find fault with critics they consider sexist. Pratt uses the term "phallic criticism" to describe criticism that is sexist because it ignores or undervalues literature by women or because it offers distorted, chauvinist interpretations of works by either women or men ("The New Feminist Criticisms" 176). Carol Ohmann's "Emily Brontë in the Hands of Male Critics" analyzes reviews that appeared when *Wuthering Heights* was first published as well as two recent interpretations of the novel. Ohmann points to critical biases that have, she says, persisted for more than a century: Both Brontë's contemporaries and our own assume, for example, that Brontë had little conscious control over her material and that her lack of experience and understanding limits her achievement. Such statements, Ohmann says, are often used to dismiss or denigrate the works of women writers.

Nina Baym makes a related point in "Melodramas of Beset Manhood: How Theories of American Fiction Exclude Women Authors." American literary criticism, she says, has always had a "nationalist orientation"—American literary works are judged "great" not if they meet some standard of formal excellence but if they seem to capture the essence of the American experience. Typically, this experience has been defined as a protagonist's struggle for complete freedom and selfhood. The problem is that the protagonist has almost universally been assumed to be male and that women are automatically identified with the "encroaching, constricting, destroying society" that seeks to frustrate his desires (71-72). Through "strenuous critical revisions of the text," Baym says, even *The Scarlet Letter* has often been read as a work with a male protagonist— Arthur Dimmesdale—resisting the temptations of seductress Hester Prynn (73-74). Moreover, in addition to distorting our interpretations of important works by male authors, popular critical theories have excluded all works by female authors. Since "the matter of American experience is [seen as] inherently male," Baym writes, it seems "highly unlikely that American women could write fiction encompassing such experience" (70). Thus, "if one accepts current theories of American literature, one accepts as a consequence—perhaps not deliberately but nevertheless inevitably—a literature that is essentially male" (65).

## GYNOCRITICS

Some have argued that feminist criticism should move away from analyzing works by either male authors or male critics, for such criticism may become derivative and defensive, a matter of women responding to what men have written. What is needed, according to Elaine Showalter, is "a feminist criticism that is genuinely women centered, independent, and intellectually coherent." In an essay titled "Feminist Criticism in the Wilderness," Showalter calls for what she terms *gynocritics,* the study of women *as writers*; "its subjects," she says, "are the history, styles, themes, genres, and structures of writing by women; the psychodynamics of female creativity; the trajectory of the individual or collective female career; and the evolution and laws of a female literary tradition." In recent years, Showalter believes, feminist criticism has quite properly "gradually shifted its focus from revisionary readings to a sustained investigation of literature by women" (14-15).

Showalter's *A Literature of Their Own: British Women Novelists from Brontë to Lessing* is an important contribution to gynocritics. Most criticism of novels by women, Showalter says, focuses only on the few novelists long recognized as major figures—Jane Austen, the Brontës, George Eliot, Virginia Woolf. Because we have neglected important minor novelists, "we have not had a very clear understanding of the continuities in women's writing, nor any reliable information about the relationships between the writers' lives and the changes in the legal, economic, and social status of women" (7). Showalter sets out to correct this problem by writing about minor novelists as well as major ones. For example, she examines the works of Olive Schreiner, a feminist novelist who wrote around the turn of the century. Showalter does not consider her an excellent literary artist: Schreiner was "sadly underambitious," and her novels are "depressing and claustrophobic." Still, Showalter says, it is important to realize that Schreiner contributed to the female literary tradition through "her use of female symbolism, her commitment to feminist theory, and her harshly physical allegories"; moreover, she influenced later women writers such as Doris Lessing (194-204). To fully understand the development of women's literature, we must, according to Showalter, recognize the Schreiners as well as the Austens.

In drawing attention to the works of writers such as Schreiner, feminist critics have contributed to the reshaping of the literary canon, the body of works regarded as deserving of serious study. Novelist and critic Alice Walker, for example, has brought renewed attention to the works of Zora Neale Hurston, an African American novelist whose writings were well regarded earlier in the century but had drifted into virtual obscurity. Other feminist critics have made similar efforts on behalf of such authors as Charlotte Perkins Gilman, Kate Chopin, Susan Glaspell, and many others. Minority and lesbian feminist critics—for example, Barbara Smith in "Toward a Black Feminist Criticism" and Becky Birtha in "Is Feminist Criticism Really Feminist?"—have often faulted both traditional critics and early feminist critics for failing to take due notice of works by minority and lesbian authors.

Some feminist critics have argued that, in order to appreciate the merits of women's writings, we must reexamine our ideas about what makes a literary work excellent or important. Should judgments of a work's merits be based on purely aesthetic criteria, or should other considerations also influence our evaluations? In *Feminist Scholarship: Kindling in the Groves of Academe*, Ellen Carol DuBois and her coauthors describe the reconsidering of not only individual works but also "entire genres of writing long dismissed as inherently minor, popular, transient, and (of course) feminine." Nineteenth-century sentimental fiction, for example, is usually dismissed as "unworthy of serious critical attention," perhaps largely because it was the work of "female authors who wrote for an audience of other women." However, feminist critics who regard the sentimental novel "as a social as well as a literary document" see it as far from trivial. Through questioning traditional standards of judgment, DuBois and her coauthors say, feminist literary critics have "expanded their field and the definition of literature itself to include women's diaries, journals, private poetry, and letters" (60-61). Many feminist critics see such questioning and such redefinitions as central to the development of gynocritics.

## CHALLENGING MYTHS CREATED BY MEN

In *Madwoman in the Attic: The Woman Writer and the Nineteenth-Century Literary Imagination,* Sandra M. Gilbert and Susan Gubar present the two major kinds of feminist criticism discussed so far—stereotypical criticism and gynocritics—as interdependent. The ultimate goal of the woman writer may be "literary autonomy," and the ultimate goal of the feminist critic may be to construct a "feminist poetics" and to "understand literature by women"; still, before they can achieve these ultimate goals, both the woman writer and the feminist critic "must come to terms with . . . those mythic masks male artists have fastened over [woman's] human face." Male artists, Gilbert and Gubar argue, have created two principal masks, or images, for women—the passive, submissive "angel" and the destructive, sinister "monster"—and women cannot create freely unless they first understand and destroy these masks (16-17). Gilbert and Gubar contend, for example, that Milton's "inferior and Satanically inspired Eve" has "intimidated women and blocked their view of possibilities both real and literary"; accordingly, many women writers have "devised their own revisionary myths and metaphors" in order to come to terms with and, sometimes, free themselves of the inhibiting image Milton created (187-189). Gilbert and Gubar analyze at length two works they see as creative "misreadings" or "rewritings" of *Paradise Lost*—Mary Shelley's *Frankenstein*, in which both Victor Frankenstein and his monster may be identified with Eve, and Emily Brontë's *Wuthering Heights,* in which the fall from heaven is transformed and parodied. Thus, although Gilbert and Gubar concentrate on analyzing literature by women, they often look at that literature in the context of literature and myths created by men.

## FOCUS ON WOMEN'S CREATIVE PROCESSES

Feminist critics have also focused on questions relating to the creative process, imaginations, and writing styles of women. A few brief examples will have to suffice here to attest to the variety and vitality of this branch of feminist criticism. The interest in women's creative processes may be traced back at least as far as Virginia Woolf's 1929 *A Room of One's Own*. Here, Woolf analyzes some of the forces that have hampered women writers in the past and explores the many implications of her thesis that "a woman must have money and a room of her own if she is to write fiction" (4). Woolf also suggests some standards for evaluating literature: Truly great literature, whether written by a woman or by a man, must be androgynous, must transcend self-consciousness about gender, must be calm and at peace.

A continuing interest in the issues Woolf raises is evident in more recent works, such as "Writing as a Woman," in which poet Anne Stevenson discusses both her own experience and that of other women writers in order to explore the relationship between the desire for fulfillment as a woman and the quest for creative achievement. Patricia Meyer Spacks, in *The Female Imagination,* asks whether we can identify a "female point of view" that is distinct from the male and that seems largely independent of time and place, whether we can point to recurring themes in the works of women writers and in the lives of women everywhere.

## PROMOTING SOCIAL CHANGE

Some feminist critics have attempted to establish standards for evaluating literature or to use literature and criticism to promote social change. Carolyn G. Heilbrun, in *Reinventing Womanhood,* makes literary criticism a part of her effort to promote "the struggle for female selfhood" (202). Arguing that we must reinterpret the mythology and literature of the past in order to help women, Heilbrun offers, for example, a feminist reinterpretation of the *Oresteia,* in which the murder of Clytemnestra becomes a symbolic overthrowing of traditional ideas about motherhood (152–159). Toril Moi, in *Sexual/Textual Politics: Feminist Literary Theory*, agrees that feminist criticism can and should contribute to social change. "The principal objective of feminist criticism," she says, "has always been political: it seeks to expose, not to perpetuate, patriarchal practices" (xiv). Similarly, DuBois and the other authors of *Feminist Scholarship: Kindling in the Groves of Academe* point out that much feminist criticism, especially in the early years of the movement, "is actually criticism that relies on literary—or at least textual—phenomena as the basis for discussion of social experience." They cite *Sexual Politics* as an example of such criticism: "[E]ven though Kate Millett anchored her opening argument in a discussion of Henry Miller, Norman Mailer, and D. H. Lawrence as sexist writers, her chief target was the society that generated their oppressive displays, rather than the novelists themselves" (35).

## CONCERN WITH LANGUAGE

Another important element in feminist literary criticism is a continuing concern with language. In the first volume of *No Man's Land: The Place of the Woman Writer in the Twentieth Century,* significantly entitled *The War of the Words,* Sandra M. Gilbert and Susan Gubar declare that "a major campaign in the battle of the sexes is the conflict over language and, specifically, over competing male and female claims to linguistic primacy" (228). It is not enough, some feminist critics argue, to challenge the way women have been portrayed in literature, or the extent to which male authors have dominated the canon;

rather, we must recognize that language itself has been shaped by men, in ways that denigrate and alienate women. The work of several French feminist critics deserves special mention here. Hélène Cixous, Luce Irigaray, and Julia Kristeva, among others, see Western cultures and languages as profoundly male-dominated or *phallogocentric*. Just as the phallus is implicitly—and sometimes explicitly—assumed to be the only significant sexual organ, the masculine is accepted as the central point of reference, the only source of validity and authority. Women are defined only in terms of their relations to men, only in terms of what they lack. As Cixous argues in "Castration or Decapitation?" the categories that traditionally order culture inevitably relegate women to a secondary status:

> It's the classic opposition, dualist and hierarchical. Man/Woman automatically means great/small, superior/inferior . . . means high or low, means Nature/History, means transformation/inertia. In fact, every theory of culture, every theory of society, the whole conglomeration of symbolic systems—everything, that is, that's spoken, everything that's organized as discourse, art, religion, the family, language, everything that seizes us, everything that acts on us—it is all ordered around hierarchical oppositions that come back to the man/woman opposition, an opposition that can only be sustained by means of a difference posed by cultural discourse as "natural." (44)

It is a mistake, Cixous warns, to fail to recognize these dualities and hierarchies, to think that language is objective or gender-neutral. Until recently, most women writers saw themselves as "writing not as women but as writers," believing "that sexual difference means nothing, that there's no attributable difference between masculine and feminine writing." As a result, such women "do someone else's—man's—writing, and in their innocence sustain it and give it voice, and end up producing writing that is in effect masculine" (51–52).

Such dangers can be overcome, however, through uses of language that celebrate the feminine rather than repressing it. In an influential 1976 essay called "The Laugh of the Medusa," Cixous describes an emerging women's writing (*écriture féminine*) that rejects phallogocentrism in favor of a joyful acknowledgment of women's sexuality: "A woman's body, with its thousand and one thresholds of ardor—once, by smashing yokes and censors, she lets it articulate the profusion of meanings that run through it in every direction—will make the old single-grooved mother tongue reverberate with more than one language" (256). Similarly, Luce Irigaray, in "This Sex Which Is Not One," stresses the need to break free from traditional notions of logic and coherence. Women's speech, she says, will be "inaudible for him who listens with ready-made grids, a code prepared in advance": "One must listen to her differently in order to hear an 'other meaning' which is constantly in the process of weaving itself, at the same time ceaselessly embracing words and yet casting them off to avoid becoming fixed, immobilized" (103). In another attempt to provide a model for *écriture féminine*, Julia Kristeva calls attention to the earliest communication between mother and infant. Before the infant's sexuality has been rigidly defined, before communication has been limited by words that symbolize fixed concepts, mother and infant communicate through rhythm, sound, and movement. By defying conventional notions of language, Joyce and some avant-garde poets have been able to rediscover the richness and spontaneity of this early communication. Such writing, Kristeva declares in *Desire in Language: A Semiotic Approach to Literature and Art,* "is slated to become the laboratory of a new discourse," one that "rejects all discourse that is either stagnant or eclectically academic, preempts all its knowledge where it does not impel it, and devises another original, mobile, and transformative knowledge" (92). Kristeva thus holds out the hope that both women and men can contribute to the liberation of language.

Those interested in learning more about feminist criticism might well begin with Woolf's seminal *A Room of One's Own.* The next step might be to examine some of the collections of essays that provide introductions to the concerns and scope of feminist criticism. *The Authority of Experience: Essays in Feminist Criticism,* edited by Arlyn Diamond and Lee R. Edwards, includes several essays discussing feminist theory, several focusing on male authors, and several analyzing works by women authors. Elizabeth Abel's *Writing and Sexual Difference* and Elaine Showalter's *The New Feminist Criticism: Essays on Women, Literature, and Theory* offer a similar range of essays. For an introduction to French feminist criticism, *New French Feminism: An Anthology,* edited by Elaine Marks and Isabelle de Courtivron, is especially helpful. Both Carol Fairbanks Myers and Cheri Register have prepared helpful bibliographies of feminist criticism. A number of other important works of feminist criticism are included in the following list.

## WORKS CITED AND RECOMMENDED

Abel, Elizabeth, ed. *Writing and Sexual Difference*. Chicago: Chicago UP, 1982.

Barnes, Annette. "Female Criticism: A Prologue." *The Authority of Experience: Essays in Feminist Criticism*. Ed. Arlyn Diamond and Lee R. Edwards. Amherst: Massachusetts UP, 1977. 1-15.

Bauer, Dale M. and S. Jaret McKinstry. *Feminism, Bakhtin, and the Dialogic*. Albany: State of New York P, 1991.

Baym, Nina. "Melodramas of Beset Manhood: How Theories of American Fiction Exclude Women Authors." *The New Feminist Criticism*. Ed. Elaine Showalter. New York: Pantheon, 1985. 63-80.

——. *Woman's Fiction: A Guide to Novels by and about Women in America, 1820-1870*. Ithaca: Cornell UP, 1980.

Birtha, Becky. "Is Feminist Criticism Really Feminist? *Lesbian Studies*. Ed. Margaret Cruikshank. Old Westbury: Feminist, 1982.

Cixous, Hélène. "Castration or Decapitation?" Trans. Annette Kuhn. *Signs* 6 (1981): 36-55.

——. "The Laugh of the Medusa." Trans. Keith Cohen and Paula Cohen. *New French Feminisms: An Anthology*. Ed. Elaine Marks and Isabelle de Courtivron. New York: Schocken, 1981. 245-264.

Diamond, Arlyn, and Lee R. Edwards, eds. *The Authority of Experience: Essays in Feminist Criticism*. Amherst: Massachusetts UP, 1977.

DuBois, Ellen Carol, Gail Paradise Kelly, Elizabeth Lapovsky Kennedy, Carolyn W. Korsmeyer, and Lillian S. Robinson. *Feminist Scholarship: Kindling in the Groves of Academe*. Urbana: U of Illinois P, 1987.

Fetterley, Judith. *The Resisting Reader: A Feminist Approach to American Fiction*. Bloomington: Indiana UP, 1978.

Frye, Joanne. *Living Stories, Telling Lies: Women and the Novel in Contemporary Experience*. Ann Arbor: Michigan UP, 1986.

Fryer, Judith. *The Faces of Eve: Women in the Nineteenth-Century American Novel*. New York: Oxford, 1976.

Gilbert, Sandra M., and Susan Gubar. *Madwoman in the Attic: The Woman Writer and the Nineteenth-Century Literary Imagination*. New Haven: Yale UP, 1979.

———. *The War of the Words*. Vol. 1 of *No Man's Land: The Place of the Woman Writer in the Twentieth Century*. New Haven: Yale UP, 1988. 3 vols.

Grosz, Elizabeth. *Sexual Subversions: Three French Feminists*. Sydney, Australia: Allen, 1989.

Heilbrun, Carolyn G. *Reinventing Womanhood*. New York: Norton, 1979.

Irigary, Luce. "This Sex Which Is Not One." Trans. Claudia Reeder. *New French Feminisms: An Anthology*. Ed. Elaine Marks and Isabelle de Courtivron. New York: Schocken, 1981. 98-106.

Jacobus, Mary. *Reading Woman: Essays in Feminist Criticism*. New York: Columbia UP, 1986.

———. *Women Writing and Writing about Women*. New York: Harper, 1979.

Kolodny, Annette. "Dancing through the Minefield: Some Observations on the Theory, Practice, and Politics of a Feminist Literary Criticism." *Feminist Studies* 6 (1980): 1-25.

Kristeva, Julia. *Desire in Language: A Semiotic Approach to Literature and Art*. Ed. Leon S. Roudiez. Trans. Thomas Gora, Alice Jardine, and Leon S. Roudiez. New York: Columbia UP, 1980.

Lerenbaum, Miriam. "Moll Flanders: 'A Woman on Her Own Account.'" *The Authority of Experience: Essays in Feminist Criticism*. Ed. Arlyn Diamond and Lee R. Edwards. Amherst: Massachusetts UP, 1977. 101-117.

Marks, Elaine, and Isabelle de Courtivron. *New French Feminisms: An Anthology*. New York: Schocken, 1981.

Millett, Kate. *Sexual Politics*. Garden City: Doubleday, 1970.

Moi, Toril. *Sexual/Textual Politics: Feminist Literary Theory*. New York: Methuen, 1985.

Myers, Carol Fairbanks. *Women in Literature: Criticism of the Seventies*. Metuchen: Scarecrow, 1976.

Ohmann, Carol. "Emily Brontë in the Hands of Male Critics." *College English* 32 (1971): 906-913.

Pratt, Annis V. "The New Feminist Criticism." *College English* 32 (1971): 872-878.

———. "The New Feminist Criticisms." *Beyond Intellectual Sexism: A New Woman, A New Reality*. Ed. Joan I. Roberts. New York: McKay, 1976. 175-195.

Register, Cheri. "American Feminist Literary Criticism: A Bibliographical Introduction." *Feminist Literary Criticism: Explorations in Theory*. Ed. Josephine Donovan. Lexington: Kentucky UP, 1975. 1-28.

Showalter, Elaine. "Feminist Criticism in the Wilderness." *Writing and Sexual Difference*. Ed. Elizabeth Abel. Chicago: Chicago UP, 1982. 9-35.

———. *A Literature of Their Own: British Women Novelists from Brontë to Lessing.* Princeton: Princeton UP, 1977.

———. *The New Feminist Criticism: Essays on Women, Literature, and Theory.* New York: Pantheon, 1985.

Smith, Barbara. "Toward a Black Feminist Criticism." *Women's Studies International Quarterly* 2 (1978): 183–194.

Spacks, Patricia Meyer. *The Female Imagination.* New York: Knopf, 1975.

Stevenson, Anne. "Writing as a Woman." *Women Writing and Writing about Women.* Ed. Mary Jacobus. New York: Harper, 1979. 159–176.

Woolf, Virginia. *A Room of One's Own.* New York: Harcourt, 1929.

## ETHNIC AND MINORITY STUDIES

Studies of ethnic and minority literature bear important and readily apparent similarities to feminist studies. Like feminist studies, studies of ethnic and minority literature often challenge traditional ideas about the canon, about which works deserve to be most widely read and to receive the most serious critical attention. Furthermore, both sorts of studies often take an interdisciplinary approach, and both often call attention to issues involving stereotyping, oppression, resistance, and social justice. And, like feminist studies, studies of ethnic and minority literature might be said not to represent a critical approach at all.

The authors of these studies, it might be argued, do not always share a common methodology; they share only a common area of interest. Thus, it might be more appropriate to compare them to students of a particular period or genre rather than to adherents of a more clearly definable approach such as the psychological or the structuralist. These objections have some merit. Nevertheless, as with feminist studies, it seems, in the end, most useful to define critics in the way that they define themselves; to recognize that many people doing important work see themselves primarily as critics of ethnic and minority literature rather than as members of any other school; and to attempt to analyze a growing current in literary criticism in its own right and on its own terms.

### Expanding the Canon of American Literature

Fundamental to many studies of ethic and minority literature is a desire to win recognition for works whose merits and significance have often been overlooked or denied. In "Canonical and Noncanonical Texts: A Chicano Case Study," Juan Bruce-Nuova criticizes anthologists and others who have, he says, "been in charge of trimming the canon to . . . isolationist proportions." Traditionally, anthologies and curricula in American literature have stressed the works of white, English-speaking writers to the exclusion of all others: In most courses in early American literature, for example, the sermons of Puritan theologian Cotton Mather are studied, but writings such as the journals of French and Spanish explorers are not. "The literary and historical canon," Bruce-Nuova charges, "has been forged at the expense of a pluralistic perspective more genuinely reflective of the country's development" (198).

In *Minority Language and Literature: Retrospective and Perspective*, Dexter Fisher agrees that the works of Asian Americans, African Americans, Chicanos, Native Americans, and Puerto Ricans have not received the attention they deserve; as a result, our understanding of American literature is partial and distorted. Students of American literature, Fisher says, will benefit greatly from examining a broader range of works:

> It is the juxtaposition of ideas, world views, and linguistic variations through literature that revitalizes our notions of man and culture, making such terms as "dominant" and "minority" ultimately irrelevant. By revising the canon of American literature, we challenge some values and affirm others with the result that our understanding of tradition is deepened, our appreciation of neglected literatures refined, and our concept of genre expanded. (14)

Both Bruce-Nuova and Fisher, thus, see challenging the traditional canon of American literature as a crucial critical task.

## CONTRIBUTIONS OF AFRICAN AMERICAN LITERATURE

Marion Wilson Starling's pioneering *The Slave Narrative: Its Place in American History* is an example of an attempt to draw attention to writings that had long been neglected. Starling argues that some of these narratives, such as Frederick Douglass's autobiography, are "readily acceptable as literary achievements," meeting the standards of excellence by which literary works are traditionally judged. Some of the other narratives, Starling says, are "admittedly low in artistic value": "The untutored condition of the slave authors and the rush market for their stories as abolitionist propaganda mitigated against the development of literary excellence" (264). Nevertheless, literary historians cannot afford to discount the narratives' influence on antislavery novels such as *Uncle Tom's Cabin*. More important, the narratives demand our attention because they can contribute to "the universal brotherhood of man" by providing "a long and fascinating autobiographical record of a race under the yoke of a grotesque institution" (312).

Nick Aaron Ford agrees that the canon should not be closed to all works that do not meet a rigid standard of literary excellence. In "Black Literature and the Problem of Evaluation," he chastises educators who have "with few exceptions, completely ignored . . . the whole corpus of Black literature," partly because they rely too exclusively on narrowly defined "aesthetic" criteria. Ford proposes a new set of criteria for judging works of literature and admitting them to the canon. For example, "the test of *human values*" is "worthy of a high place on the scale of literary evaluation": A work can legitimately be judged excellent on the basis of "the extent and degree to which it responds to human needs," including "the desire for simple entertainment" and for "vicarious experiences in alien cultures and religions." If we adopt more comprehensive criteria for judging literature, Ford says, we can more fully appreciate works that deserve our attention not only because of their aesthetic merits but also because they "may be extremely rich in other human values" (65).

## AMENDING THE NEW CRITICS' STANDARDS

As critics who focus on ethnic and minority literature have sought to broaden the literary canon and the critical standards that influence it, the New Critics have often come under particular attack. In "Black Literature and the Critic," Charles T. Davis faults the New Critics for engaging in a "narrow formal analysis" that leads them to overrate some writers and underrate others. Misled by an exaggerated "affection for the tight structure and the well-integrated rhetoric" of poets such as Donne, the New Critics fail to appreciate works that incorporate "matter defying easy ordering, matter that often has a source in popular culture." Such critics will find it very difficult to understand Black literature, which often draws on such "folk materials" as sermons, works songs, and jazz (53-54). Furthermore, the political and social unrest of recent years has freed many black artists from conventional ways of thinking, sparking "bold and rewarding experimentation" in literature. Traditional critical approaches, Davis says, "do not fully describe the creative revolution that is taking place in the black world around us." Accordingly, he advocates fundamental changes in critical assumptions, standards, and practices. Although he does not wish to "abandon Aristotle," Davis says, he seeks "to amend the tradition that has flowed from him—to force an adjustment to the realities of a history, form, and language in the black world, seek an appreciation for a music, indeed, for a literary performance, that is off as well as on the beat" (60-62).

Paul Lauter, in "The Literatures of America: A Comparative Discipline," issues a similar challenge to the critical standards advocated by the New Critics and others. While he admits the merits of "complex poetic structures" and "the dense, allusive modernist line," he declares that these "are not the only virtues in poetry, nor are they the only means for representing the modern world":

> "Complexity" in language can be, in fact, a mask for privilege, a screen behind which power sustains itself—in criticism as in poetry. Gwendolyn Brooks had no need for obscurity of language when she set her poetic sensibility to observe the ordinariness of hate in Little Rock. . . . To what extent is the manner in which one uses language dependent upon where one is placed in "our" civilization, or upon one's audience, or upon one's conception of the function of art? (26)

If traditional critical standards are indeed masks for "privilege" and "power," a way of excluding the literary works of oppressed peoples, it is all the more urgent for critics of ethnic and minority literature to evolve new standards by which this literature can be more fairly judged and appreciated.

## POSTMODERN CRITICISM AND NATIVE AMERICAN LITERATURE

Some critics of ethnic and minority literature have turned to more recent critical approaches. Gerald Vizenor, for example, in *Narrative Chance: Postmodern Discourse on Native American Indian Literatures,* finds that some features of postmodern criticism are well suited to the discussion of Native American literature:

Native American Indian literatures are unstudied landscapes, wild and comic rather than tragic and representational, storied with narrative wisps and tribal discourse. Social science theories constrain tribal landscapes to institutional values, representationalism and the politics of academic determinalism. . . . Postmodernism liberates imagination and widens the audience for tribal literatures; this new criticism rouses a comic world view, narrative discourse and language games on the past. (5-6)

## SKEPTICISM ABOUT EXISTING THEORIES

Other critics of ethnic and minority literature view all existing critical theories with skepticism. In "Canon Formation, Literary History, and the Afro-American Tradition: From the Seen to the Told," Henry Louis Gates, Jr., declares that "no critical theory—be it Marxist, feminist, post-structuralist, Kwame Nkrumah's 'consciencism,' or whatever—escapes the specificity of value and ideology. . . . To attempt to appropriate our own discourses by using Western critical theory uncritically is to substitute one mode of colonialism for another." Instead of borrowing established critical methods, Gates says, "theorists have turned to the black vernacular tradition . . . to isolate the signifying black difference through which to theorize" (27). Gates's own *The Signifying Monkey: A Theory of Afro-American Literary Criticism* turns to African and African American traditions to find the figures of Elu-Elegbara and the Signifying Monkey, tricksters who provide, Gates says, metaphors for understanding several distinctive features of African American literature—for example, "the tension between the oral and written modes of narration" (21). Houston Baker's *Blues, Ideology, and Afro-American Literature: A Vernacular Theory* provides another example of an attempt to root critical theory in elements of popular culture.

# Taking an Interdisciplinary Approach

In searching for an appropriate approach, other critics of ethnic and minority literature stress the importance of taking an interdisciplinary perspective. Kenneth Lincoln, for example, describes his *Native American Renaissance* as "neither anthropology nor literary criticism, strictly speaking, but a hybrid" (9). The nature of the literature he is analyzing, Lincoln says, demands such an approach: "Art is not on the decorative edges of Indian cultures, but alive at the functional heart: in blankets that warm bodies, potteries that store food, songs that gather power, stories that bond people, ceremonies that heal, disciplines that strengthen spirits" (12). Understanding Native American literature thus requires careful attention to all of Native American culture. The critic must collate "literature, folklore, history, religion, handcraft, and the expressive arts" (9). Lincoln begins his own study of Native American literature with a chapter discussing such concepts as "tribe" and briefly tracing Native American history since the arrival of the first European settlers; throughout his book, he frequently points out connections between the literature he analyzes and various aspects of Native American life. In his discussion of Simon Ortiz, for example,

Lincoln draws many parallels with Pueblo architecture and pottery to explain concepts central to the poet's work (189–196).

Other critics of ethnic and minority literature also emphasize the need to study works in a broad cultural context. King-Kok Cheung, for example, in "Self-Fulfilling Visions in *The Woman Warrior* and *Thousand Pieces of Gold*," writes that understanding these works requires some insight into Chinese culture, which traditionally places a higher value on sons than it does on daughters. It is the authors' "innovative and subversive uses of their Chinese legacies," Cheung says, that enable their protagonists to develop personalities that "depart radically both from the original Chinese models and from the stereotypes of Asian women in American" (143–144).

Bernard W. Bell, in *The Afro-American Novel and Its Tradition,* warns that the critic must not try to isolate literature from society. The Afro-American novel, he argues, "is not the culmination of an evolutionary process in the narrative tradition, but the product of social and cultural forces that shape the author's attitude toward life"; it is "not a solipsistic, self-referential signifying system, but a systematic sociocultural act" (339). It would be a mistake, according to Bell, to see Euro-American and Afro-American novels as part of the same literary tradition. The Euro-American novel is characterized by "the search for innocence and the Adamic vision"; the Afro-American novel is characterized by "the Manichean drama of white versus black, a messianic belief in freedom, an apocalyptic destiny, and the quest to reconcile the double-consciousness of Afro-American identity" (341). Thus, understanding differences in racial concerns and aspirations plays a crucial part in analyzing literary works.

## LITERATURE VERSUS SOCIOLOGY: PORTRAYING CHICANO CULTURE

Rudolph O. de la Garza and Rowena Rivera, in "The Socio-Political World of the Chicano: A Comparative Analysis of Social Scientific and Literary Perspectives," make a different sort of argument about the relationship of literature and society. After comparing several studies by Chicano social scientists and three novels by Chicano authors, de la Garza and Rivera conclude that the novelists often depict Chicano life more fully and realistically than the social scientists do. The realities of racism and discrimination are clearly reflected both in the sociological studies and in the novels. However, although the sociologists have accurately described Chicano voting patterns, community structures, and political attitudes, they have been so intent on dispelling negative stereotypes of the Chicano that they have tended to gloss over some painful facts—for example, that "many Chicanos are fatalistic and superstitious, and men do exploit 'their' women." Chicano novelists have generally been more successful at portraying the community's strengths while also acknowledging its problems. "The tools of social science," de la Garza and Rivera conclude, "seem too clumsy to focus on both the individual and the structure" (60–62). Thus, Chicano novels are important not only because of their literary excellence but also because they complement and to some extent correct the findings of social science.

Other writers have focused on what is sometimes called stereotypical criticism, on the portrayals of members of minority groups. Barbara Christian, in "Images of Black Women in Afro-American Literature: From Stereotype to Character," examines the images of black women in works by both black and white authors. She identifies several common stereotypes—the "mammy figure," the "tragic mulatta," the "sex kitten"—that appear not only in white Southern literature but also in the works of such distinguished black novelists as Richard Wright, James Baldwin, Chester Himes, and Ralph Ellison. It is only in the works of such black women writers as Paule Marshall, Nikki Giovanni, and Toni Morrison that real freedom from these stereotypes is achieved (15–16). Indeed, Christian concludes, the most "prevalent trend" in the works of black women writers is "the movement away from the stereotype," the attempt to accurately portray "the diversity of the black woman's experience in America" (28). By helping readers more fully appreciate the value of such works, Christian joins her efforts to those of other critics of ethnic and minority literature.

*Redefining American Literary History*, edited by A. LaVonne Brown Ruoff and Jerry W. Ward, Jr., contains short but helpful bibliographies on African American literature, Native American literature, Asian American literature, Chicano literature, and Puerto Rican literature in the United States, as well as a more general bibliography on "Minority and Multicultural Literature, Including Hispanic Literature."

A number of journals are of special interest to students of ethnic and minority literature—for example, *Afro-Hispanic Review, Amerasia Journal, Black American Literature Forum,* and *Melus: Critical Approaches to Ethnic Literature.* Some especially helpful books and articles are also listed below.

## WORKS CITED AND RECOMMENDED

Baker, Houston A., Jr., and Patricia Redmond, eds. *Afro-American Literary Study in the 1990's.* Chicago: Chicago UP, 1989.

———. *Blues, Ideology, and Afro-American Literature: A Vernacular Theory.* Chicago: Chicago UP, 1984.

———. *Working of the Spirit: The Poetics of Afro-American Women's Writing.* Chicago: Chicago UP, 1991.

Bell, Bernard W. *The Afro-American Novel and Its Tradition.* Amherst: Massachusetts UP, 1987.

Bruce-Nuova, Juan D. "Canonical and Noncanonical Texts: A Chicano Case Study," *Redefining American Literary History.* Ed. A. LaVonne Brown Ruoff and Jerry W. Ward, Jr. New York: MLA, 1990. 196–209.

———. *Chicano Poetry: A Response to Chaos.* Austin: Texas UP, 1982.

Chapman, Abraham, ed. *Literature of the American Indians.* New York: MLA, 1975.

Cheung, King-Kok. "Self-Fulfilling Visions in *The Woman Warrior* and *Thousand Pieces of Gold.*" *Biography* 13 (1990): 143–153.

Christian, Barbara. "Image of Black Women in Afro-American Literature: From Stereotype to Character." *Black Feminist Criticism: Perspectives on Black Women Writers.* New York: Pergamon, 1985. 1–30.

Davis, Charles T. "Black Literature and the Critic." *Black Is the Color of the Cosmos: Essays on Afro-American Literature and Culture, 1942–1981.* Ed. Henry Louis Gates, Jr. New York: Garland, 1982. 49–62.

de la Garza, Rudolph O., and Rowena Rivera. "The Socio-Political World of the Chicano: A Comparative Analysis of Social Scientific and Literary Perspectives." *Minority Language and Literature: Retrospective and Perspective.* Ed. Dexter Fisher. New York: MLA, 1977. 42–64.

DiPietro, Robert J., and Edward Ifkovic. *Ethnic Perspectives in American Literature: Selected Essays on the European Contribution.* New York: MLA, 1977.

Fisher, Dexter. *Minority Language and Literature: Retrospective and Perspective.* New York: MLA, 1977.

Fleck, Richard F., ed. *Critical Perspectives on Native American Fiction.* Washington, D. C.: Three Continents, 1993.

Ford, Nick Aaron. "Black Literature and the Problem of Evaluation." *The Black Writer in Africa and the Americas.* Ed. Lloyd W. Brown. Los Angeles: Hennessey, 1973. 45–68.

Gates, Henry Louis, Jr. "Canon Formation, Literary History, and the Afro-American Tradition: From the Seen to the Told." *Afro-American Literary Study in the 1990s.* Ed. Houston A. Baker, Jr., and Patricia Redmond. Chicago: Chicago UP, 1989. 14–39.

———. *The Signifying Monkey: A Theory of Afro-American Literary Criticism.* New York: Oxford UP, 1988.

Hymes, Dell. *"In Vain I Tried to Tell You": Essays in Native American Ethnopoetics.* Philadelphia: Pennsylvania UP, 1981.

Jimenez, Francisco. *The Identification and Analysis of Chicano Literature.* New York: Bilingual, 1979.

Lauter, Paul. "The Literatures of America: A Comparative Discipline." *Redefining American Literary History.* Ed. A. LaVonne Brown Ruoff and Jerry W. Ward, Jr. New York: MLA, 1990. 9–34.

Lincoln, Kenneth. *Native American Renaissance.* Berkeley: California UP, 1983.

Margolies, Edward, and David Bakish, eds. *Afro-American Fiction, 1853–1976.* Detroit: Gale, 1979.

Marken, Jack. *The American Indian: Language and Literature.* Arlington Heights: AHM, 1978.

Mohr, Eugene. *The Nuyorican Experience: Literature of the Puerto Rican Minority.* Westport: Greenwood, 1982.

Morrison, Toni. *Playing in the Dark: Whiteness and the Literary Imagination.* Cambridge: Harvard UP, 1992.

Owens, Louis. *Other Destinies: Understanding the American Indian Novel.* Norman: U of Oklahoma P, 1992.

Paredes, Raymond A. "The Evolution of Chicano Literature." *Melus* 5 (1978): 71–110.

Pettit, Arthur G. *Images of the Mexican American in Fiction and Film.* College Station: Texas A & M UP, 1980.

Ruoff, A. LaVonne Brown, and Jerry W. Ward, Jr. *Redefining American Literary History.* New York: MLA, 1990.

Starling, Marion Wilson. *The Slave Narrative: Its Place in American History.* Boston: Hall, 1981.

Vizenor, Gerald. *Narrative Chance: Postmodern Discourse on Native American Indian Literatures.* Albuquerque: U of New Mexico P, 1989.

# ARCHETYPAL STUDIES

Literary works at their best touch something deep in readers and provide a sense of participation in universal experience. Whether in Hamlet's quest for vengeance or the ancient mariner's confrontation at sea or Huck and Jim's trip down the Mississippi, readers encounter events that seem to transcend time and geography. Archetypal critics account for this universality in literature by pointing to recurring patterns and images that appear so deeply embedded in the human mind and culture that they strike a responsive chord in everyone. Archetypal studies explore the relationship of such patterns in a literary work to those found in myth, ritual, and other pieces of literature.

## Frazer and Myth

Archetypal criticism, sometimes called *myth criticism,* has its roots in anthropological and psychological studies of the late nineteenth and early twentieth centuries, particularly in the works of Sir James George Frazer and Carl Gustav Jung. Frazer, the foremost of a group of Cambridge anthropologists, examined primitive rituals that indicated similar patterns of behavior and belief among diverse and widely separated cultures. In *The Golden Bough: A Study in Magic and Religion,* a monumental compendium of ancient myths and rituals eventually running to twelve volumes, Frazer's avowed purpose was the explanation of the motives behind a single custom—the strange rule of kingly succession among an Italian people who had inhabited the shores of Lake Nemi, a rule in which the potential successor plucked a bough from a sacred tree and then killed the old king in individual combat. Frazer's investigation led to the documentation of a vast array of similar or connected customs, causing him to suspect an "essential similarity in the working of the less developed human mind among all races, which corresponds to the essential similarity in their bodily form revealed by comparative anatomy" (123).

### MURRAY'S CONCLUSIONS

Although many of Frazer's facts are now disputed, his conclusion soon became significant to literary study. Gilbert Murray's "Hamlet and Orestes" in *The Classical Tradition in Poetry* is an early but still important example. Murray finds in the characters of Shakespeare's Hamlet and the Greek Orestes similarities so striking that they can hardly be explained as chance or accident. Both Hamlet and Orestes are sons of kings slain by younger kinsmen who then marry the dead king's wife. Both are driven by supernatural forces to avenge their father's death and end not only by slaying the new king but also by being responsible for their mother's death. Since there seems no possibility of influence or imitation, Murray explores connections in the mythic patterns underlying the Greek Orestes saga and the Scandinavian Hamlet saga. Behind both, he concludes, is the "world-wide ritual story of what we may call the

Golden-Bough Kings" (228)—that is, the pattern identified by Frazer in which life is renewed through the slaying of an old monarch and succession by a new one. Aegisthus and Claudius slay the old king but are themselves doomed to be slain in a repeating cycle. Thus, Murray believes that certain stories and situations are "deeply implanted in the memory of the race, stamped, as it were, upon our physical organism" (238–239).

## Jung and Archetypes

Murray's metaphor of a racial memory has psychological implications that are more fully developed by Carl Jung, the psychologist who first gave prominence to the term *archetype*. On the bases of clinical studies and wide reading, Jung became convinced that all humans share a "collective unconscious," an unconscious "which does not derive from personal experience and is not a personal acquisition but is inborn" (*The Basic Writing of C. G. Jung* 287). Jung called the contents of the collective unconscious *archetypes,* which he defined as primordial or "universal images that have existed since the remotest times" (288). These archetypes, according to Jung, were formed during the earliest stages of human development. Although the theory may seem almost mystic, Jung found no other way to account for the appearance of nearly identical images and patterns in the minds of individuals from wholly different cultures and backgrounds. For example, Jung notes instances, ranging from the dreams of a Protestant clergyman to the legends of African tribes, which suggest that water is a symbol of the unconscious and the action of descending to the water is a symbol of the frightening experience of confronting the depths of one's unconscious. A particularly striking example of the unconscious nature of universal symbols is Jung's account of a patient who in 1906 related visions containing odd symbolic configurations. Only later did Jung encounter similar symbols—in a Greek papyrus first deciphered in 1910. The theory of archetypes would explain not only such instances as these but also the similarity of myths and rituals found by Frazer, for archetypes are universal patterns from which myths derive.

### BODKIN'S STUDY

Among the first literary studies in the Jungian tradition is Maud Bodkin's *Archetypal Patterns in Poetry,* which is still an outstanding example of the application of psychological knowledge to works of literature. In a long chapter on *The Rime of the Ancient Mariner,* Bodkin finds the powerful effect of the poem to reside in its articulation of the "rebirth archetype," a pattern sometimes called the "night journey under the sea" and given expression in the biblical story of Jonah. Just as Jonah is thrown into the sea, devoured by a whale, and cast "reborn" on the land, the mariner journeys on the sea, confronts death, and is returned to land "a sadder and wiser man." The wisdom, of course, comes from the meeting with and acceptance of the individual's own unconscious;

going down to the water, to the depths of one's own being, is the death that precedes a rebirth in greater wisdom and self-knowledge. The general pattern, according to Bodkin, is an image sequence composed of "a movement downward, or inward toward the earth's centre, or a cessation of movement . . . balanced by a movement upward and outward—an expansion or outburst of activity, a transition toward reintegration and life-renewal" (52–53).

## Frye and the Anatomy of Criticism

Although Murray has an extensive knowledge of myth and Bodkin brings to bear nearly all the major psychological theories of her day, critics need not be psychologists or anthropologists to use the archetypal approach. In fact, the value of Frazer and Jung comes less from the details of their specific theories than from their having focused attention on underlying recurrent patterns. Many recent archetypal studies consciously reject reliance on other fields and draw their patterns or archetypes solely from literature itself. Northrop Frye, for instance, writes of the theory of the collective unconscious as "an unnecessary hypothesis in literary criticism" (112). Accordingly, he shifts the definition of archetype from the psychological to the literary. For Frye, an archetype is "a symbol, usually an image, which recurs often enough in literature to be recognizable as an element of one's literary experience as a whole" (365).

This shift is essential to Frye's attempt to discover the "conceptual framework" of literature—that is, to determine the organization of the field of literature. To accomplish this task, Frye argues, one cannot go outside literature; one cannot organize literature around the concepts of another field, whether that field be history, anthropology, psychology, or sociology. Instead, one must make an inductive survey of literature itself. The results of Frye's survey show the organization of literature to be mythic. Types of literature constitute aspects of "a central unifying myth," and within individual examples of each type are found similar archetypes and patterns. These patterns, however, do not necessarily derive from ritual or myth; they are simply analogous to those found there. As Frye states, "To the literary critic, ritual is the *content* of dramatic action, not the source of it" (109).

For Frye, there are four types of literature or four narrative patterns, each of which he terms a *mythos* and each of which is one part of a larger pattern. The large pattern, or unifying myth, is analogous to the season of the year or to the story of the birth, death, and rebirth of the mythic hero. In this scheme, the mythos of summer is the romance, the kind of fiction we know from medieval tales such as *Sir Gawain and the Green Knight* as well as from popular romances and even from old-fashioned cowboy movies. The romance is analogous to the birth and youthful adventures of the mythic hero insofar as it suggests innocence and triumph. It is a narrative of wish-fulfillment, with unambiguously good characters triumphing over the bad. The mythos of autumn is tragedy, its major movement toward the death or defeat of the hero. Oedipus, once the triumphant savior of the city, is reduced to blindness and exile;

Lear, no longer the all-powerful king, dies on the rack of the cruel world. The mythos of winter is irony or satire. The hero now absent, society is left without effective leadership or a sense of norms or values. In a work like Swift's "A Modest Proposal," social norms are turned upside down for artistic purposes, and in many of the works of Kafka or even of Camus or Conrad there is a sense of hopelessness and bondage, a kind of death in life. However, comedy, the mythos of spring, brings the rebirth of the hero, a renewal of life in which those elements of society who would block the hero are overcome. Hero and heroine take their rightful place, and order is restored. For Frye, every work of literature has its place within this scheme or myth, and every piece of literature adds to the myth.

## Fiedler and Cultural Patterns

Another critic who begins with the examination of literary works themselves rather than with universal patterns is Leslie Fiedler. Fiedler is especially concerned with defining unique cultural patterns within literature; and in *An End to Innocence: Essays on Culture and Politics, Love and Death in the American Novel,* and to some extent in his more recent work on Shakespeare, he uses the insights of archetypal criticism to isolate telling patterns within literature of a given culture or author. For example, as Fiedler views nineteenth-century American novels in *An End to Innocence,* he sees a single, though controversial, archetype": "the mutual love of a white man and a colored . . . the boy's homoerotic crush, the love of the black . . ."(146). Although he has been accused of myopia, Fiedler argues that where in European novels we would expect to find heterosexual passion we discover in James Fenimore Cooper the affection of Natty Bumpo and Chingachgook, in Herman Melville the love of Ishmael for Queequeg, and in Mark Twain the feeling of Huck for Jim. This is an American pattern and one that may be limited historically; however, insofar as it is a pattern that repeats itself and seems widely shared at a level beneath consciousness, it is for Fiedler "a symbol, persistent, obsessive, in short, an archetype" (146).

## Archetypes and the Writer

Although archetypal studies have most frequently been used to identify the significance and meaning of patterns within a text, they may also be used to illuminate aspects of the writer. In *The Elusive Self: Archetypal Approaches to the Novels of Miguel de Unamuno*, Gayana Jurkevich attempts to show that "the archetypes that surface in [Unamuno's] novels, and the repetition of psychological configurations found among his fictional characters, [are] analogous of the same or similar archetypes within the author's own unconscious" (4). Jurkevich argues that the so-called mother archetype is dominant in Unamuno's novels because of certain traumatic events occurring before the beginning of his career, the childhood loss of his father and a later spiritual crisis. Although

Jurkevich explicitly rejects any claim to the production of psychobiography, her work clearly demonstrates the use of archetypal criticism to connect the writer and the text.

## The Archetypal Rationale

As the discussion so far may have suggested, some critics are skeptical about the value of the archetypal approach, believing such criticism to be reductionistic. Archetypal studies, so the argument goes, ignore the particularity of individual literary works and reduce all pieces of literature to a few simple patterns, frequently the pattern of death and rebirth. Archetypal critics have several answers to such an argument. First, archetypal studies do not reduce but universalize works of art. To recognize the universal patterns that exist in literature is to see the relationship of literature to larger areas of human experience and activity. Second, archetypal studies are indeed concerned with the particularity of literary works, that each work makes its own unique articulation of the underlying myth. The sensitive archetypal critic attempts to define the special context and statement of the archetypal pattern in each piece of literature. Archetypal criticism at its best seeks the achievement Stanley Edgar Hyman finds in Maud Bodkin's analysis of *The Rime of the Ancient Mariner* when he writes, "She not only has used the poem to illustrate her archetypal pattern, but has made the pattern illustrate the poem and its effects, fix it in the corpus of major poetry, and greatly heighten and inform enjoyment" (137).

Although the archetypal approach seems to be used less frequently in the 1970s and 1980s than in earlier years, it is responsible for some of the more significant critical works of the twentieth century and remains a kind of study with which persons interested in literature should be familiar. Along with books already mentioned, early works such as F. M. Cornford's *The Origin of Attic Comedy,* James Harrison's *Themis: A Study of the Social Origins of Greek Religion,* and Jessie Weston's *From Ritual to Romance* explore the relationship of myth and ritual to literature. Each of these brings to bear ideas formulated by Frazer and later developed by Murray on a specific literary subject: Cornford on Aristophanic comedy, Harrison on Homeric poetry, and Weston on the medieval Grail legend. Somewhat later, Francis Ferguson in *The Idea of a Theater: A Study of Ten Plays; The Art of Drama in Changing Perspective* assumes as background the work of Frazer, Cornford, Harrison, and Murray for his study of "landmarks" of drama. Joseph Campbell makes particular use of Jung's ideas in *The Hero with a Thousand Faces,* an attempt to decipher the language and symbols of myth through the insights of psychoanalysis.

Somewhat more recently, James Baird has studied the symbolism of *Moby-Dick* by discussing the archetypes of primitivism in *Ishmael: A Study of the Symbolic Mode in Primitivism,* and John J. White in *Mythology in the Modern Novel: A Study of Prefigurative Techniques* analyzes various patterns of correspondence between contemporary novels and classical prefigurations. Robert Richardson's *Myth and Literature in the American Renaissance* turns from twentieth-century myth theory to show how nineteenth-century writers made conscious use of myth in their work. Other significant studies are also included in the following list.

## WORKS CITED AND RECOMMENDED

Baird, James. *Ishmael: A Study of the Symbolic Mode in Primitivism.* Baltimore: Johns Hopkins UP, 1956.

Bodkin, Maud. *Archetypal Patterns in Poetry.* London: Oxford UP, 1934.

Campbell, Joseph. *The Hero with a Thousand Faces.* New York: Pantheon, 1949.

Cornford, F. M. *The Origin of Attic Comedy.* London: Arnold, 1914.

Fergusson, Francis. *The Idea of a Theater: A Study of Ten Plays; The Art of Drama in Changing Perspective.* Princeton: Princeton UP, 1949.

Fiedler, Leslie. *An End to Innocence: Essays on Culture and Politics.* Boston: Beacon, 1955.

——. *Love and Death in the American Novel.* Cleveland: World, 1962.

Frazer, Sir James George. *The Golden Bough: A Study in Magic and Religion.* 1922. New York: Macmillan, 1940.

——. *The New Golden Bough.* Ed. Theodor H. Gaster. Garden City: Doubleday, 1961.

Frye, Northrop. *Anatomy of Criticism: Four Essays.* Princeton: Princeton UP, 1957.

Harrison, Jane. *Themis: A Study of the Social Origins of Greek Religion.* Cambridge: Cambridge UP, 1912.

Hays, Peter. *The Limping Hero: Grotesques in Literature.* New York: New York UP, 1971.

Hyman, Stanley Edgar. *The Armed Vision: A Study in the Methods of Modern Literary Criticism.* New York: Random, 1955.

Jung, Carl Gustav. *The Basic Writings of C. G. Jung.* Ed. Violet Staub De Laszlo. New York: Modern, 1959.

——. *Modern Man in Search of a Soul.* New York: Harcourt, 1956.

——. *Psyche and Symbol.* Garden City: Doubleday, 1958.

Jurkevich, Gayana. *The Elusive Self: Archetypal Approaches to the Novels of Miguel de Unamuno.* Columbia and London: U of Missouri P, 1991.

Knapp, Bettina. *Music, Archetype, and the Writer.* University Park: Pennsylvania State UP, 1988.

Murray, Gilbert. *The Classical Tradition in Poetry.* Cambridge: Harvard UP, 1927.

Richardson, Robert, Jr. *Myth and Literature in the American Renaissance.* Bloomington: Indiana UP, 1978.

Sugg, Richard P., ed. *Jungian Literary Criticism.* Evanston: Northwestern UP, 1992.

Vogler, Christopher. *The Writer's Journey: Mythic Structure for Storytellers and Screenwriters.* Studio City: Wiese, 1992.

Weston, Jessie. *From Ritual to Romance.* Cambridge: Harvard UP, 1920.

Wheelwright, Philip. *The Burning Fountain: A Study in the Language of Symbolism.* Bloomington: Indiana UP, 1954.

White, John J. *Mythology in the Modern Novel: A Study of Prefigurative Techniques.* Princeton: Princeton UP, 1971.

# PSYCHOLOGICAL STUDIES

Given the almost inescapable concern of literature with human relationships and human behavior, it is not surprising that the insights of psychology have become important tools in literary criticism. In order to understand characters and actions, readers continually turn to psychology, sometimes to their own intuitive and experiential understanding of why people act as they do, but frequently to more formal psychological theory. However, a fuller understanding of characters and actions is not the only result of psychological studies. They may also help to explain the motivations of authors and enrich one's understanding of the creative process, and they can further knowledge of the way in which literature touches readers and of the reasons readers respond.

Psychological studies of literature are probably as old as literary criticism. Certainly, both Plato and Aristotle were concerned with the psychological relationship between the literary work and its audience. Plato, for instance, argued that poetry inflamed the emotions of the audience, that it fed passions that should be starved. On the other hand, Aristotle, although recognizing the emotional appeal of literature, contended that literature, especially tragedy, purged the emotions it raised. It left the audience not inflamed but satisfied. Somewhat later, Longinus examined how certain elements of a literary work elevate and transport the reader.

## Freud and the Unconscious

It is, however, with the emergence of depth psychology and particularly with the theories of Sigmund Freud that contemporary psychological criticism is usually associated. Obviously, no full explanation of Freudian psychoanalytic theory is possible in a brief discussion. For the student of literature, however, the single most important concept may be Freud's theory of the unconscious, his belief that within each person is a vast reservoir of mental processes and phenomena of which the person is unaware. Even though the concept of the unconscious has become commonplace in twentieth-century thought, its significance is sometimes minimized. Yet the recognition that authors, readers, and, in a sense, characters may be unaware of the reasons for their own behavior transforms the way we think about the literary process. We cannot assume an author's intention is known even to him- or herself; we cannot necessarily account for our responses as readers on grounds of which we are conscious; and we cannot suppose actions within a work will necessarily be explicable solely through reliance on the text. If we accept these implications of the theory of the unconscious, we are likely to turn to psychology for a fuller understanding of literary works and our reaction to them.

## The Unconscious and Fictional Characters

When we take a psychological approach to literary criticism, we find hypotheses that supply clues to the meaning of otherwise inexplicable behavior and events. One such hypothesis is the Oedipal complex, the name given to the developmental situation in which children attach themselves to the parent of the other sex and feel hostility and jealousy toward the parent of the same sex. Although elements of his theory have come under attack in recent years, it has been widely used to explore literary texts. Of course, the origin of the term *Oedipal* is literary. Freud borrowed it from Sophocles's *Oedipus Rex*, in which the protagonist unknowingly kills his father and marries his mother. Freud also alluded to the Oedipal situation in Shakespeare's *Hamlet*. Ernest Jones picked up on Freud's brief remarks about *Hamlet* and, in 1910, published the first modern psychological study of literature, "The Oedipus Complex as an Explanation of Hamlet's Mystery." The mystery is Hamlet's procrastination in avenging the death of his father. Though Hamlet clearly understands the need for vengeance, he postpones action time and again. Bringing to bear wide reading in *Hamlet* criticism as well as a thorough, professional knowledge of depth psychology, Jones found the solution to the mystery in Hamlet's repressed desires for his mother, Gertrude. Claudius, by murdering Hamlet's father and marrying Gertrude, has acted out Hamlet's own unconscious desires and has become, in effect, both Hamlet's father (his mother's husband) and a symbol of Hamlet himself. For Hamlet, to kill Claudius is to be guilty symbolically of patricide and incest; thus, Jones indicated, Hamlet suffers from a paralysis of will brought on by Oedipal conflicts.

Psychological insights concerning the relationship of parent and child have continued to inform literary criticism since the time of Jones's seminal work. Simon Lesser in *Fiction and the Unconscious* finds no less a mystery in Hawthorne's short story "My Kinsman, Major Molineux" than Jones found in *Hamlet*, and again the mystery concerns delay and procrastination. The story is of a boy, Robin, who comes to the city in search of his uncle, Major Molineux, an official who has promised to help Robin make his way in the world. After a desultory search, Robin is suddenly confronted by his kinsman, tarred and feathered, the subject of ridicule in a noisy, chaotic procession. Robin joins in the humiliation of Molineux and then prepares to leave the city but is invited to stay by a new acquaintance. Why, asks Lesser, is Robin's attempt to locate his uncle so half-hearted and easily postponed, and why does he participate in the humiliation when he does discover his uncle? Lesser's answer is that the major represents the authority of a father, an authority toward which young Robin unconsciously feels hostile and from which he must try to escape.

Several points should be clear from this brief discussion of the studies of Jones and Lesser. The first, already mentioned, is the significance of the theory of the unconscious. Although many good critics disagree with these particular interpretations, unexplained motives do seem to exist within the play and the short story. Hamlet vacillates inexplicably. Robin insists he is searching for his uncle yet does not take advantage of the most obvious ways of finding him. A second point is that to speak of characters as if they have unconscious motivation is to treat them as "real" people. Jones, in effect, diagnoses Hamlet, dealing with the literary character as a patient having a certain kind of childhood. The dilemma is probably obvious. On the one hand, we speak of characters as having a life of their own, as being real. On the other hand, we recognize literary characters as fictional constructs that exist only in the words on the page and, in a sense, as concepts in the minds of author and reader. Hamlet has no childhood although Shakespeare could have written one for him. The question becomes whether or not fictional characters can be said to have an unconscious.

## The Unconscious and the Writer

One way to deal with the question is to recognize the unconscious as the author's. Freud viewed literature as the fantasy projection of the artist, and psychological critics since have been concerned with the unconscious mind of the author. In this view, the work of art is the symbolic statement of unconscious fantasies that the artist could not otherwise admit. In a relatively early study, Geoffrey Gorer confronts this relationship between artist and work. Reading Jane Austen's novels, Gorer finds a pattern in which the female protagonist rejects a charming young lover and eventually marries a man whom she admires rather than loves passionately. In most of the novels, the heroine's misfortunes are due to the mother, and the man whom she marries stands in an almost paternal relation to her. Only in *Persuasion,* Austen's last novel, is the pattern broken. Here, the heroine eventually marries the dashing lover she originally rejected, and the father is viewed with contempt.

Gorer suggests the novels are Austen's unconscious attempt to work out her own "central fantasy." In her life, Gorer speculates, Austen gave up love and passion to remain committed, almost married, to her family. In *Persuasion,* she comes to question this decision and cries "out against her starved life, and the selfishness of the father and sisters on whose account it had been starved" (203). The basic Oedipal situation is evident—the rejection of the parent of the same sex and marriage to a surrogate parent of the other sex—but the fantasy and unconscious motivations are not those of characters but those of the author. The critic need not treat the fictional Emma Woodhouse or Elizabeth Bennet as if they were real; instead, the critic investigates the historical Jane Austen.

## The Unconscious and the Reader

If fantasies exist in the unconscious of artists, they also reside in the unconscious of an audience. Psychological criticism has always given attention to the mind of the reader or viewer, and I. A. Richards as early as the 1920s and 1930s was especially concerned with the relationship of text and reader. Recently, however, the examination of reader response has become even more significant in psychological criticism, as it has in many other approaches. Particularly influential has been Norman Holland's *The Dynamics of Literary Response,* which makes a full-scale effort "to develop a model for the interaction of literary works with the human mind" (x). In Holland's model, literary works remain fantasies but fantasies that have "defense mechanisms" built in. That is, the literary text embodies a fantasy that is deeply disturbing to many people (the Oedipal situation, for example) but it then finds a way for the reader to master or defend against the disturbing elements.

Holland believes literature uses essentially the same defenses as those defined by psychologists—such mechanisms as repression, denial, reversal, projection, symbolization, sublimation, and rationalization. Projection, for example, displaces one's own wish to an agent in the outside world. Oedipus displaces responsibility for killing his father and marrying his mother by projecting it onto the gods and oracles. He does not wish to perform the acts but is destined to perform them. In all the defense mechanisms, fantasies too dangerous to contemplate directly are denied or changed into a socially acceptable form. Austen's Emma does not marry her father but weds a character with fatherly attributes. For Holland, then, the dynamics of literature occur in the interplay between the powerfully disturbing fantasy and the displacement of it into terms the reader can manage. A work that offers no defenses against the fantasy may be pornographic or disgusting: The son clearly desires to possess the mother and does so. A work too heavily defended is simply bland and uninteresting; it has no power to move the reader.

Whereas *The Dynamics of Literary Response* focuses mainly on unconscious fantasies common to all readers, Holland in two later books, *Poems in Persons: An Introduction to the Psychoanalysis of Literature* and *5 Readers Reading*, joins other critics who have become more concerned with the mind of the individual reader. Using the term *identity theme* to refer to an individual's unique set of unconscious needs, fantasies, and defenses, Holland suggests that the meaning of a literary work resides in the transaction between the reader and the text, the reader receiving from the work only what his or her own identity theme allows. Thus, a piece of literature will have different meanings for different readers, depending on their expectations and defenses. In this and similar theories, the unconscious fantasy is that not of the character but of the reader.

## Bloom and the Anxiety of Influence

Three elements have so far been discussed separately: characters and actions within works, the relationship of the author to the work, and the relationship of the reader to the work. Although some critics may emphasize one of these elements, most critics recognize their interplay and attempt to account for all three: artist, work, and audience. Harold Bloom deals with the three in a slightly different way. He suggests, first in *The Anxiety of Influence: A Theory of Poetry* and later in *Poetry and Repression: Revisionism from Blake to Stevens* and *A Map of Misreading,* that an artist is moved to create by the work of a previous artist, a "precursor" who comes to stand in relation of a father to a son. In the literary situation as in the family situation, the son has ambiguous feelings toward the father—part admiration and love; part hate, envy, and jealousy. The literary process becomes an attempt to eclipse the work of the precursor, both to outdo the father and repress debt and influence. The literary text becomes "a psychic battlefield upon which authentic forces struggle for the only victory worth winning, the divinating triumph over oblivion" (*Poetry and Repression* 2). Tennyson, for example, must struggle against Keats, writing poems that go beyond those of Keats, and which repress his domination. Thus, for Bloom, "every poem is a misinterpretation of a parent poem" (*Anxiety of Influence* 17).

Similarly, every reading is a misreading. As the poet makes the literary work a struggle against a previous text, the reader makes his or her reading a struggle against the text. Readers, that is, read in terms of their own anxieties and defenses rather than attempting to determine something "meant" by the author. Bloom's view of the literary work as a misreading, which is then to be misread by the audience, is certainly not accepted by all, or even most, recent psychological critics; and Bloom, in fact, does not consider himself a psychological critic as such. However, the attempt to understand the psychology of the relationship of writer, text, and reader is the focus of many contemporary studies.

Those interested in pursuing the psychological study of literature should, of course, do substantial reading in the works of Freud, including *The Psychopathology of Everyday Life, The Interpretation of Dreams,* and *Jokes and Their Relation to the Unconscious.* John Rickman's *A General Selection from the Works of Sigmund Freud* is a helpful collection for the person beginning a study of psychoanalytic theory. One also needs to be aware of newer developments in psychology and of the relationship of Freud's theories to recent ideas and attitudes. Bernard Paris's *A Psychological Approach to Fiction* is especially valuable in its summary of the theories of Karen Horney and Abraham Maslow and their application to literary texts. *Holland's Guide to Psychoanalytic Psychology and Literature and Psychology* by Norman Holland is up-to-date and enormously helpful to anyone interested in the field.

Of growing importance are studies making use of the insights of cognitive psychology. Norman Holland's *The Brain of Robert Frost* blends ideas from Freudian and cognitive psychology and clearly explains theories of cognition. Henry Herring's reading of the "tomorrow" speech from *Macbeth* in Joseph Natoli's *Psychological Perspectives on Literature* is particularly helpful in its comparison of Freudian and cognitive approaches. John Hill, in *Chaucerian Belief,* applies cognitive psychology to the *Canterbury Tales.*

Particularly significant to much poststructuralist thought are the ideas of the French psychologist Jacques Lacan. Lacan's own writing is exceedingly complex, but Robert Con Davis's *The Fictional Father: Lacanian Readings of the Text* offers a helpful discussion of Lacanian criticism as well as essays from the Lacanian perspective. Juliet Mitchell's *Psychoanalysis and Feminism* analyzes the relationship of feminist thought to Lacanian and other psychoanalytic approaches.

## WORKS CITED AND RECOMMENDED

Bloom, Harold. *The Anxiety of Influence: A Theory of Poetry*. New York: Oxford UP, 1974.

———. *A Map of Misreading*. New York: Oxford UP, 1975.

———. *Poetry and Repression: Revisionism from Blake to Stevens*. New Haven: Yale UP, 1976.

Crews, Frederick. *Psychoanalysis and Literary Process*. Cambridge: Winthrop, 1970.

———. *The Sins of the Fathers: Hawthorne's Psychological Themes*. London: Oxford UP, 1966.

Davis, Robert Con. *The Fictional Father: Lacanian Readings of the Text*. Amherst: Massachusetts UP, 1981.

Erikson, Erik. *Childhood and Society*. New York: Norton, 1963.

Freud, Sigmund. *A General Selection from the Works of Sigmund Freud*. Ed. John Rickman. Garden City: Doubleday, 1957.

———. *The Interpretation of Dreams*. New York: Avon, 1965.

———. *Jokes and Their Relation to the Unconscious*. New York: Norton, 1960.

———. *The Psychopathology of Everyday Life*. New York: Norton, 1965.

George, Diana. *Blake and Freud*. Ithaca: Cornell UP, 1980.

Gorer, Geoffrey. "Myth in Jane Austen." *American Imago* 2 (1941): 197–204.

Hill, John M. *Chaucerian Belief: The Poetics of Reverence and* Delight. New Haven and London: Yale UP, 1991.

Hoffman, Frederick. *Freudianism and the Literary Mind*. Baton Rouge: Louisiana State UP, 1957.

Holland, Norman. *The Brain of Robert Frost: A Cognitive Approach to Literature*. New York: Routledge, 1988.

———. *The Dynamics of Literary Response*. New York: Oxford UP, 1968.

———. *5 Readers Reading*. New Haven: Yale UP, 1975.

———. *Holland's Guide to Psychoanalytic Psychology and Literature and Psychology*. New York: Oxford UP, 1990.

———. *Poems in Persons: An Introduction to the Psychoanalysis of Literature*. New York: Norton, 1973.

Jones, Ernest. *Hamlet and Oedipus*. New York: Norton, 1949.

———. "The Oedipus Complex as an Explanation of Hamlet's Mystery." *American Journal of Psychiatry* 21 (1910): 72–113.

Klein, George. *Psychoanalytic Theory: An Exploration of Essentials*. New York: International Universities, 1976.

Kris, Ernst. *Psychoanalytic Explorations in Art*. New York: International Universities, 1952.

Lesser, Simon. *Fiction and the Unconscious*. Boston: Beacon, 1957.

Mitchell, Juliet. *Psychoanalysis and Feminism*. New York: Pantheon, 1974.

Natoli, Joseph, ed. *Psychological Perspectives on Literature: Freudian Dissidents and Non-Freudians*. Hamden: Archon, 1984.

Paris, Bernard. *Character and Conflict in Jane Austen's Novels: A Psychological Approach*. Detroit: Wayne State UP, 1978.

———. *A Psychological Approach to Fiction: Studies in Thackeray, Stendhal, George Eliot, Dostoevsky, and Conrad*. Bloomington: Indiana UP, 1974.

Richards, I. A. *Practical Criticism*. New York: Harcourt, 1929.

———. *Science and Poetry*. New York: Norton, 1926.

Schacer, Roy. *A New Language for Psychoanalysis.* New Haven: Yale UP, 1976.

Skura, Meredith. *The Literary Use of the Psychoanalytic Process.* New Haven: Yale UP, 1981.

Strouse, Jean. *Women and Analysis: Dialogues on Psychoanalytic Views of Femininity.* New York: Viking, 1974.

# PART 2

---

# The Critical Essay

# *Chapter 4*

# ELEMENTS OF CRITICAL ESSAYS

The reasons for writing a critical essay about literature are many: People may write to fulfill a class assignment or to publish in order to gain promotion or tenure or, more ideally, because they are convinced of the significance of their own ideas. Probably, in fact, most writers are motivated by a combination of reasons. Whatever the immediate cause for writing, however, the best essays seem to come ultimately from a sincere desire to find the answer to some question about a literary work. That a study may be the requirement of a class or a job does not make it any less an opportunity to inquire about matters of importance and to satisfy one's own curiosity. In attempting to discover answers and to communicate their findings to an audience, most writers face several common problems. They need to determine the most useful procedures or approach; they need to organize clearly and structure their ideas effectively; and they need to develop an appropriate language and style. Obviously, there exists no formula for accomplishing any of these tasks, but a knowledge of contemporary critical practice can suggest strategies and procedures other writers have found useful.

## THE APPROACH

As stated earlier, the kinds of questions a person asks and the method of answering them combine to form a writer's approach, but that approach depends on assumptions about literary study and on other values and knowledge. It seems, then, that there is not a specific point at which a person adopts a given approach. It is seldom a matter of deciding to be a formalist or psychological or historical critic. Rather, a person's attitudes and assumptions are likely to develop over time, and new experiences and wider reading usually force a continuing, if sometimes subtle, modification of the person's stance. The reading of critical essays may lead some people to lines of inquiry which they find especially fruitful and with which they feel comfortable. The kinds of questions raised by a certain critic may be particularly intriguing or may match the reader's interests, and he or she may then begin to look more closely at the precise nature of this critic's approach. A given literary work may seem nearly to demand a certain kind of question or a certain mode of analysis. On the other hand, some persons are quite sure of the area they want to investigate. They know, for instance, that they want to deal with feminist issues in a text, but they are uncertain how to shape their questions and how to work with them in a literary discussion. At that point, a teacher, a colleague, or a book such as this one may suggest an approach or perhaps a single article that can demonstrate possible ways of proceeding.

The point is that an individual's approach to literature is not so much chosen as developed—and it cannot easily be developed without knowledge of literary study, experience with criticism, and some experimentation. At times, simply trying out approaches can help. Wilbur Scott in *Five Approaches of Literary Criticism* indicates the benefit of this strategy: "In my teaching experience, I have concluded that the student who knows he has things to say about a work of literature, but has no direction by which to shape his perceptions, finds his problems solved by taking on the discipline and organization of" a given approach (13). Experimenting with an approach, for the space at least of a single paper, can teach much about its assumptions and values and can provide a means of giving form to one's own responses to a work.

## Example: Drawing on the Pastoral Tradition

For example, a reader may be intrigued by William Gass's short story "In the Heart of the Heart of the Country" and find especially compelling the contrasts between a small town's peaceful beauty and its ugliness and decay. If the reader is aware of literary tradition, it soon becomes apparent Gass is using pastoral ideas and images. The narrator, "in retirement from love," has retreated to the heart of the country, "a small town fastened to a field in Indiana." The town is described in pastoral terms: It is "outstandingly neat and shady"; its "lawns are green, the forsythia is singing." That the narrator is aware of the pastoral traditions is clear from his quoting Wordsworth: "That man, immur'd in cities still retains / His inborn inextinguishable thirst / Of rural scenes." By this point, the reader might decide to try approaching the story through its relationship to the pastoral tradition.

Works such as Leo Marx's *The Machine in the Garden: Technology and the Pastoral Ideal* would alert the reader to the way in which technology is likely to impinge on the pastoral ideal, especially of how "the railroad . . . guts the town" and maples have been "maimed" to accommodate electric wires, which "deface the sky." Even the tillers of the soil are not simple rural folk but men in "refrigerated hats" driving great tractors with "transistors blaring." Eventually, the narrator decides the pastoral ideal of living "in harmony with the alternating seasons" is "a lie of old poetry." Of course, the reference to "old poetry" seems a direct allusion to the pastoral. Whether or not the reader decides to pursue studies of literary traditions beyond this application, the use of the approach here would probably clarify some implications of the story and lead to an appreciation of the possibilities of that approach.

# Taking Intellectual Risk

That Gass seems conscious of his use of the pastoral makes an investigation of that tradition clearly appropriate. Frequently, though, employing an approach calls for more intellectual risk. For example, many critics are highly suspicious of archetypal studies, and artists are unlikely to be conscious of archetypes in their own work. Still, a reader familiar with the writings of Carl Jung or James Frazer may find confirmation of their ideas in literary texts and decide to explore the implications of their theories. The person who has read Jung's discussion of water as a symbol of the unconscious and of fish as the ideas or archetypes arising from the unconscious may feel a shock of recognition when encountering Henry Thoreau's description of fishing in *Walden:* A lake "is earth's eye, looking into which the beholder measures the depth of his own nature" or "They plainly fished more in the Walden Pond of their own natures." The reader of Saul Bellow's *Henderson the Rain King* may recognize the character Dahfu to be in the line of Frazer's Golden Bough kings. Dahfu explains to Henderson that at the first sign of failing sexual prowess, he, Dahfu, will be strangled and his soul will pass first into a lion and then into the new king.

Such similarities may prove to be minor, interesting congruences without larger significance for the works. On the other hand, they may lead the reader to think afresh about the literature and to ask about larger and more revealing patterns. For example, Thoreau has come to Walden Pond to explore the depths of his own nature, to rid himself of the encumbrances of society and to be reborn. He leaves Walden with that rebirth: "I had several more lives to live." Henderson has likewise gone to African in an attempt to leave behind the "junk of civilization" and to discover himself. Tremendously self-conscious and egocentric, Henderson begins to find himself only in the death of his friend Dahfu. In recognizing that he must continue Dahfu's existence, he submits himself to the age-old pattern of death and rebirth. Obviously, *Henderson the Rain King* and *Walden* are dissimilar in many ways, but even these brief comments begin to point to a shared, universal pattern: the individual, whether fictional character or historical personage, who leaves civilization behind in order to confront his or her own elemental nature and who returns from the confrontation renewed and reborn.

# Using the Approach to Gain Insight

Although employing the insights and methods of a given approach may provoke new and valuable ways of thinking about a text, it also demands sensitivity and tact. Every critic faces the temptation to apply an approach as if it were a set of formulae that could be used in all literary contexts. This may be especially apparent in approaches derived from scientific and social scientific disciplines, but it is not restricted to them. The kind of formalist critic who finds every poem to be ironic or the biographical critic for whom all characters in a novel are thinly disguised portraits of the author's friends and relatives is close kin to the psychological critic who turns every literary cave into a womb and every banquet scene into a symbol of oral gratification. The indiscriminate use of general principles is not the fault of a particular kind of criticism but a weakness of the individual critic.

## HOLLAND'S CRITERIA

Although there is no recipe for wisdom or sensitivity, Norman Holland in *Poems in Persons: An Introduction to the Psychoanalysis of Literature* suggests several criteria for distinguishing good psychological criticism from bad—in Holland's words, "for telling lilies from weeds." Holland's questions may be adapted to fit many kinds of studies and are as useful to the writer as to the reader. First, Holland asks, does the study "recognize that we perceive both conscious, intellectual content as well as unconscious fantasies," or does it settle for the "'secret, unconscious meaning' rigmarole"? Second, does the study treat the formal aspects of the literature? Third, does the study show a sense of the "style" or "essence" or "character" of the text? Fourth, does the study deal with what the text says or translate it immediately and reductively by means of symbolic decoding"? Finally, does the study consider the language of the text (175)? Except for the first question, none of these is limited to psychological criticism, and even that question may be rephrased and applied more generally: Does the study recognize that we perceive conscious intellectual content as well as underlying, "hidden" meanings?

## EXAMPLE: APPROACHES TO AUSTEN'S *EMMA*

The point is that an understanding of literature is informed and given direction by the insights of an approach; the approach does not substitute for understanding or guarantee it. The best literary studies, regardless of approach, begin with a clear recognition of the essentials of a text. The critic or reader considering Jane Austen's *Emma*, for example, surely must examine the language and point of view of the narrative voice, an ironic, somewhat detached voice, which hints at the implications of the novel's actions. The reader would need to take account of the form and structure of the novel, the gradual "education" of Emma as she discovers her errors and enlarges her understanding; and the reader would need to see how the audience itself is led to many of the same errors as Emma. The reader will also probably conclude that the text, at least on the surface, is developed to show the values of Knightley and, ultimately, of Emma as the right and proper values. These considerations are not the property of any single approach; rather, they are likely observations drawn from carefully attending to such essential areas as Holland has defined: the work's intellectual content, its form, its style, and its language.

Of course, these observations are debatable, but they do give a place from which to begin a more specific investigation. Even those who would read "against the grain" need to determine the original direction of the grain. With these essentials in mind, the critic might start to approach the work from the perspective of her or his own stance. The sociological critic might examine the values of Knightley, Emma, and the narrator to determine their effect on those of various socioeconomic classes. Is the novel a defense of the status quo or a shrewd critique of it? The biographical critic might look closely at Austen's life and ideas to find evidence for a more complete reading. Would the historic Jane Austen approve the eventual conclusions of her heroine? The rhetorical critic might trace the strategies used to guide the reader to certain responses. Does the narrative in any way undercut the reader's acceptance of the novel's public attitudes, or is it designed to cause the reader to agree with Emma and Knightley's view of the world? Different critics using these and other approaches might focus on widely varying aspects of the novel, but they would ignore essential elements of content, language, form, and style only at the risk of seriously distorting the work.

## STRUCTURE AND ORGANIZATION

Whatever an individual's specific approach, literary papers usually share certain elements of structure and organization, not because there exists a single correct way to write but simply because of what any literary study tries to do—to investigate and answer a question about literature. This means that any essay about literature is likely to pose the question and perhaps indicate its significance, state the procedure by which the question is to be investigated, perform the investigation, and answer the question. Since literary papers mean to break some new ground or to have fresh insights or knowledge to offer, they are also likely to spell out the usual assumptions about the question and the way in which their findings alter these assumptions. These elements may be stated more or less explicitly, and they may be variously ordered, but they are found in one form or another in nearly all critical discussions.

Of course, these elements are often found in other sorts of essays as well. Those writing literary essays for the first time may find it helpful to recognize the similarities in substance and structure between these essays and other, perhaps more familiar kinds of essays. One might, for example, think of a literary essay as an argument about what a work means or how it should be read; such an argument might well contain some of the same elements as other sorts of argumentative essays, perhaps arranged in a similar order. Edward P. J. Corbett's *Classical Rhetoric for the Modern Student* lists the elements that often make up an argumentative essay; introduction, statement of fact, confirmation, refutation, and conclusion (299). This section will from time to time point out the parallels between these elements and those in many critical essays about literature.

# Introduction: Posing the Question

The opening paragraphs of two critical essays may indicate how some of these elements can be expressed. The first is from Geoffrey Gorer's "Myth in Jane Austen," already mentioned in the section on psychological criticism in Chapter 3. Gorer opens as follows:

> Everybody, or at any rate nearly everybody, who is fond of English literature is devoted to the works of Jane Austen; that is pretty generally agreed. It is so generally agreed that it never seems to have occurred to anybody to inquire why these "pictures of domestic life in country villages," to use her own phrase, are able to excite such passionate adoration, or, if the inquiry is made, it is answered in terms of technique and observation. But I do not consider this answer adequate—after all, the almost unread Miss Emily Eden was not lacking in either of these qualities—and I wish to suggest there are profounder reasons for the excessive love which she excites in so many of her admirers from Scott and Macaulay to Rudyard Kipling and Sir John Squire. The adoration of Miss Austen has at times nearly approached a cult—the sect of "Janeites"—and I propose to try to uncover the mystery behind the worship. The mystery is no unfamiliar one. (197).

The second example is from a formalist study, James Smith's discussion of Shakespeare's *As You Like It:*

> It is a commonplace that Jacques and Hamlet are akin. But it is also a commonplace that Jacques is an intruder into *As You Like It*, so that in spite of the kinship the plays are not usually held to have much connection. I have begun to doubt whether not only *As You Like It* and *Hamlet*, but almost all the comedies and tragedies as a whole are not closely connected, and in a way which may be quite important. (9)

Each of these paragraphs poses a question that the essay will attempt to answer. Gorer does so explicitly, asking what in Austen's work so excites readers. Smith's question is slightly more implicit, but he clearly intends to answer a question concerning the relationship of Shakespeare's comedies and tragedies.

## THE QUESTION'S SIGNIFICANCE

Each essay also links the question to common assumptions about the works being investigated. For Gorer, in fact, the question concerns those common assumptions, this widespread agreement about the value of Austen's novels and the nearly universal love for them. Smith states the usual assumptions in the context of his question and also hints that he will challenge at least one of the assumptions—the belief that *As You Like It* and *Hamlet*, and more generally Shakespeare's comedies and tragedies, are not closely connected. By the end of each paragraph, the general purpose of each essay is clear. Gorer directly states his purpose—"I propose to try to uncover the mystery behind the worship"— but Smith's purpose, to determine the connection between the comedies and the tragedies, is no less evident (198). Finally, each essay indicates its own significance or importance by contrasting its purpose with the common assumptions. If everybody likes Austen's novels but no one has shown why, it seems important to do so. If there are unrecognized connections between Shakespeare's comedies and tragedies, it is surely significant to demonstrate them.

These paragraphs thus serve the two functions traditionally assigned to introductory paragraphs in essays of all sorts, literary and nonliterary: They announce the writer's topic, and they attempt to make the reader receptive by showing that topic to be interesting and important. The similarities between Gorer's and Smith's paragraphs come not from some rule about raising a question at the beginning of an essay but from the nature of literary study and the nature of argumentation. If essays about literature are attempts to show readers something they have not fully understood before, the literary questions are those that have not frequently been confronted or, if confronted, have, in the writer's view, not been properly answered; if essays about literature are arguments, the author must show that the question being posed concerns a point worth arguing, one that is not only significant but also controversial, or at any rate not easily resolved.

## Background Information

The introductory paragraphs or pages of an essay about literature may also include a section analogous to the statements of fact found in most argumentative essays. As Corbett explains, the statement of fact is basically expository: Here the writer provides background information that will help the reader understand and appreciate the significance of the argument that is to follow (314–316). A trial lawyer, for example, might summarize the essential facts of a case before beginning to argue the defendant's guilt or innocence; a student writing an article for a college newspaper might describe a problem before proposing measures designed to alleviate it. In a literary essay, the statement of fact may take various forms. It might present information about a historical period or an author's life to help the reader see a work or an idea in context. Only rarely is a summary of a work's plot included in a statement of fact; generally, the writer assumes that readers are familiar with a work and would find a plot summary tedious and perhaps even insulting. Information not essential to the reader's understanding is superfluous.

Frequently, the statement of fact invites readers to consider the writer's argument in the context of earlier critical opinion. Of course, not every essay should begin with statements about "agreements," "common assumptions," or "usual views"; and in fact, Richard Altick in *The Art of Literary Research* warns against one strategy for stating common ideas—what he calls the "plodding initial Review of Previous Knowledge (or Opinion) on the Subject" (210). It is true that restating the findings or assumptions of previous criticism can become a mechanical and tedious formula, a way to begin that calls for little thought. Still, the attempt to indicate to readers the background of critical work on a question is a laudable goal and should not be forsaken simply because attempts to achieve it have sometimes been unskillful. When a literary essay results from a direct disagreement with other critics and means to debate the findings of others, the statement of fact is likely to be an account of the disagreement. William Bysshe Stein, for example, begins "The Lotus Posture and *Heart of Darkness*" with a clear statement of his disagreement with an earlier article: "Although Robert O. Evans' 'Conrad's Underground' offers some interesting 'epic' parallels to the 'Heart of Darkness,' it fails, I think, to cope with the moral experience in terms of the structure of the story" (235).

The statement of the context in which a literary question is being raised is not limited to the opening paragraph or to a few sentences, as the illustrations up to this point might suggest. In theses and books, whole introductory chapters are often devoted to establishing a context and stating the question; in term papers, opening sections may be given to these tasks. Irving Howe's *Politics and the Novel,* for example, starts with a chapter entitled "The Idea of the Political Novel," in which Howe discusses the kinds of questions the book will consider and suggests what he means by the term *political novel.* Holland begins *The Dynamics of Literary Response* by suggesting that his questions are not so different from those asked by Aristotle: "What is our emotional response to a literary work? What arouses it? What dampens it? Why do men enjoy seeing mimeses of the real world . . .?" (3).

## Procedures and Approach

To answer these or any questions posed by a literary essay calls for a procedure, an approach; and critical discussions differ widely on how explicitly procedures and assumptions are stated. Some critics, especially those using traditional approaches, may say relatively little about their assumptions, instead taking for granted the reader's knowledge of the approach. Usually, however, essays give at least subtle indications of their stance. For example, Gorer's brief reference to those who have attempted to account for Austen's popularity "in terms of technique and observation" almost certainly alludes to formalist critics and, perhaps, to certain biographical procedures as well (198). That is, Gorer is stating that he will not rely on an examination of technique, as some formalist critics might do, or on a discussion of Austen's powers of observation, as some biographical critics might. On the other hand, Stein's suggestion that Evans does not "cope with the moral experience in terms of the structure of the story" reveals Stein's intent to emphasize structure (235).

The critical approach to be used is indicated even more clearly in the following introductory paragraph, taken from a college student's essay on a Wordsworth poem:

Wordsworth's "Ode: Intimations of Immortality from Recollections of Early Childhood" is one of his most powerful poems but also one of his most puzzling. Its very title is puzzling: In what sense in this a poem about immortality? The words "immortality" and "mortality" appear several times, but the poem's focus seems restricted to this life, with some metaphorical references to a pre-existent state; the afterlife does not seem to be discussed at all. The poem presents other difficulties as well. The "Ode" falls naturally into three parts: In the first four stanzas, the speaker mourns the loss of the visionary gleam; in the next four he attempts to explain this loss; and in the last three he declares he will grieve no more. Presumably he has been comforted by the ideas in the central section, but how? How could his rather dismal reflections on the loss of the visionary gleam spark the joy and reconciliation he expresses at the end? If answers to these questions exist, they must lie in those difficult central stanzas. To understand these more fully, it seems necessary to turn to an outside source for help, a source to which Wordsworth himself refers us: the dialogues of Plato, and particularly the Phaedrus. The Phaedrus can help us to understand the nature of the consolation provided in the central stanzas, and also help us to see that the "Immortality Ode" is indeed about immortality. Useful as this dialogue is, however, the most important source of an understanding of the poem continues to be a close examination of the poem itself.

Like the paragraphs by Gorer and Smith, this introductory paragraph begins by posing questions: How do we explain the title's reference to immortality and the poem's progression from grief to joy? There is no explicit statement of the author's thesis—the paragraph does not actually answer the questions posed—but there is a promise of definite answers to come. The essay's specific focus is also indicated: Although the structure of the entire poem will be discussed, the central stanzas will be emphasized. Further, the paragraph indicates the importance of the topic to be discussed by stating that this poem is one of Wordsworth's "most powerful" poems but also one of his "most puzzling": Presumably, readers would want to understand why they can be moved by a poem that seems confusing in some ways. The paragraph ends by revealing that the analysis to follow will be essentially formalist: The author asserts that "a close examination of the poem itself" is the most important step toward understanding it. Turning to the *Phaedrus* for additional insight is secondary, and is justified only because "Wordsworth himself" alludes to that dialogue during the poem. The paragraph, thus, clearly reveals the essay's purpose, focus, importance, and approach.

Some critical works, of course, spell out their procedures and assumptions in great detail. Dorothy Van Ghent devotes the introduction of *The English Novel: Form and Function* to explaining her assumptions about literature and literary study and, in particular, the function and purpose of novels. Tzvetan Todorov uses about twenty pages in *The Fantastic: A Structural Approach to a Literary Genre* to indicate how he will proceed. Holland uses the preface to *The Dynamics of Literary Response* to "set out some of the objective assumptions that inform this book" and to state explicitly his approach, in this case a procedure that begins by considering "literary works as purely formal entities" and then moves to the use of psychoanalytic psychology (xiii, xv).

## The Investigation: Two Methods

It is in the body of the essay, however, in the investigation itself, that procedures are put into practice and the effectiveness of an approach is shown. In general, literary studies, like other essays, follow one of two methods. The first uses a thesis followed by the marshaling of evidence to prove it. That is, the essay poses the question, gives the critic's answer or thesis, and then supports that answer. The second method poses the question, works through an investigation, and then answers the question as a result of the investigation. Either organization can be effective in skilled hands. The first has some advantage in clarity. The essay's point is made explicitly and early, and the reader is never in doubt about the direction of the essay or the relationship of evidence to question. The second method may seem more natural and, for some, more persuasive since it retraces the investigation and moves the reader through a process of discovery.

The opening paragraph of Smith's essay on *As You Like It* illustrates a statement of thesis, although in this instance it is phrased in almost negative terms: "I have begun to doubt whether not only *As You Like* It and *Hamlet,* but almost all the comedies and tragedies as a whole are not closely connected. . . ." Clearly, the essay will argue the connection of the plays. On the other hand, Gorer does not state a thesis, as distinguished from his statement of purpose, but guides the reader through a process of investigation leading to an answer in the essay's last paragraph: "In the midst of her satirical observation Jane Austen had hidden a myth which corresponded to a facet of universal apprehension, a hidden myth which probably holds good for her myriad admirers. . . ." Austen's works are widely admired because they reflect certain deep truths to which readers respond at some level.

## Readings

No two essays are alike in the details of their presentation of evidence or their recounting of an investigation but are individually shaped, partly by the assumptions of the author's approach, partly by the decision to state a thesis or discover an answer, and partly by the nature of the literary work being discussed. Most literary essays, though, attempt to offer *readings* of works, to explain the meaning of texts by examining their parts. The reading is frequently associated with formalist criticism, but any approach may work through a literary text, explaining it in light of the writer's thesis or question. Whereas a formalist reading may demonstrate the way in which form develops meaning, possibly giving a line-by-line explication, a psychological reading may analyze the underlying patterns being developed in a work, and a feminist reading may follow the development of certain attitudes toward women.

Cleanth Brooks's "Keats's Sylvan Historian: History without Footnotes" is an almost classic example of a formalist reading, in this instance a reading of Keats's "Ode on a Grecian Urn." Before beginning the reading. Brooks indicates the difficulty many critics, especially formalist ones, have with the poem. For these critics, the last two lines of the poem—"Beauty is truth, truth, beauty, — that is all / Ye know on earth, and all ye need to know!"—are an unpoetic intrusion, a statement that raises philosophic questions about its truth or falsity rather than an organic part of the poem. Brooks then poses the questions he will investigate:"If we could demonstrate that the speech [of the urn in the last two lines] was 'in character,' was dramatically appropriate, was prepared for— then would not the lines have . . . justification . . .? (152)." The perceptive reader, of course, is likely to recognize this as less a question than a statement of thesis. Brooks's reading will attempt to establish the urn as a character and show the final lines as a statement appropriate to that character. At this point, Brooks begins his reading, starting with the first lines and moving stanza by stanza through the poem. Although it is impossible in a brief space to follow Brooks's complete reading, a few examples may suggest its nature and attention to detail.

He starts by demonstrating the first stanza's apparently paradoxical view of the urn and its manner of speech. On the one hand, urns are not expected to speak at all, and this urn is described as a "bride of quietness" and a "foster-child of silence." On the other hand, the urn is a "sylvan historian" that can "express a flowery tale," a "leaf-fring'd legend." Brooks puzzles over the expression "sylvan historian," noting that it could mean "a historian who is like the forest rustic, a woodlander" or "a historian who writes histories of the forest." He assumes "the urn is sylvan in both senses" (155). Brooks moves on through the poem, showing particularly how the paradox of the urn's "silent speech" is developed and the nature of the urn's character as a historian. He calls attention, for example, to the first lines of the second stanza—"Heard melodies are sweet, but those unheard / Are sweeter . . ."—and analyzes the way they continue the paradox. By the end of his stanza-by-stanza reading, Brooks has shown the poem to have developed the urn as a particular character with its own kind of silent speech. It should be no surprise, Brooks argues, that at the end of the poem the urn speaks in its own right. Given the character of the urn and the development of the poem, the lines "Beauty is truth . . ." are not a philosophic intrusion by the poet but a natural outgrowth of the poem.

Such line-by-line readings are nearly impossible when dealing with longer poems or works of prose fiction, although Roland Barthes's *S/Z,* discussed in the section on structuralist studies in Chapter 1, is an attempt to consider every word of a short story. Most readings of prose fiction, however, follow the development of certain elements chapter by chapter, usually focusing on scenes the writer believes to be especially crucial or particularly illustrative while summarizing and paraphrasing other parts of the work. The point of a reading of either poetry or prose is to work through the literary text and to show its lines of development in light of the writer's thesis or question.

Not all literary papers, of course, work through the whole of a text. Many concentrate on a single scene, character, or aspect. However, even these call for the writer to have a reading of the entire work, that is, to have in mind and usually to show or state, at least in general terms, the overall development of the literary work. The discussion of a single aspect of a work can hardly be fruitful without an understanding of how it fits in the whole. For example, C. F. Burgess's "Conrad's Pesky Russian," an article from *Nineteenth-Century Fiction,* explains a single minor character in Joseph Conrad's *Heart of Darkness,* a Russian trader, whom the narrator, Marlow, meets in his search for the enigmatic and fascinating Kurtz. Although often mistreated by Kurtz, the Russian has stood by him and gives Marlow and the reader necessary information about his actions. Citing descriptions of the Russian's dress, attitudes, and speech, Burgess argues that Conrad has cast the Russian in the role of a fool, not unlike the fool in *King Lear,* who is both loyal to his master and fearful of the master's treatment. This argument, though interesting, would have little significance did Burgess not place it in the context of a fuller reading of *Heart of Darkness.* He argues that it is through the fool and Kurtz's treatment of him that Marlow comes to his ultimate attitude toward Kurtz, an attitude of "fascinated revulsion" toward a man who could behave atrociously and yet command such steadfast devotion. The place of the Russian is thus located within the novel's central development of Marlow's gradual discovery of Kurtz's deeds and his own vision into the heart of darkness.

## Confirmation and Refutation

In addition to arguing for a certain reading of a literary work, the writer may decide to argue against other possible readings. A comparison with the structure of argumentative essays may again be helpful here. The body of an argumentative essay, according to Corbett, usually consists of two elements: the confirmation, in which the writer presents evidence and arguments in support of the thesis; and the refutation, in which the writer acknowledges and answers objections that have been or might be made to the thesis. The confirmation can be seen as parallel to the writer's own reading of a work: The writer presents a certain view of a work and then presents supporting evidence— from the text itself, from other writers whose views of the work are similar to or at any rate compatible with the view proposed, or from any other sources the writer's approach to criticism might suggest. The refutation may, as in some of the examples already cited, be a part of the introduction, a relatively brief expression of dissatisfaction with prevailing critical opinion. In other essays, the refutation is more extensive and is incorporated with the confirmation; in still other essays, the refutation follows the confirmation.

In the following paragraph from an essay on the role of fortune in Fielding's *Tom Jones,* a graduate student attempts to refute several critics' views before presenting her own. Immediately after her introductory paragraph, she first quotes these critics, then takes issue with them:

Unlike Arnold Kettle, Dorothy Van Ghent sees Fortune's ultimately benevolent role as the symbolic core of the novel:

> Not fatality but Fortune rules events in Tom Jones—that Chance
> which throws up event and counterevent in inexhaustible
> variety. Tom himself is a foundling, a child of chance. In the
> end, because he is blessed with good nature, he is blessed with
> good fortune as well. . . . Fortune, capricious as it is, has some
> occult, deeply hidden association with nature (in Fielding);
> therefore, in the long run, good nature does infallibly lead to
> good fortune, bad nature to bad fortune. (101)

Thus, Van Ghent sees all of the coincidences and accidents in the novel as eventually leading to the triumph of Tom and the defeat of Blifil, because Fortune, despite all her unpredictable tricks and reverses, ultimately favors those who are naturally good. In Tom's particular case, Fortune does indeed prove to be the servant of good. Fielding, however, explicitly rejects the idea that Fortune is always so obliging. "The idea that virtue is the certain road to happiness, and vice to misery, in this world," he says, is "a very wholesome and comfortable doctrine . . . to which we have but one objection, namely, that it is not true." The idea is not only unsound, according to Fielding, but also unchristian. If we expect earthly rewards for goodness, "one of the noblest arguments that reason alone can furnish for the belief of immortality" would be weakened (690).

Moreover, the plot itself provides strong evidence that bad nature does not always lead to bad fortune, good nature to good. Blifil, certainly the worst-natured character in the novel, does indeed lose Allworthy's estate, but he is not reduced to utter poverty and misery. Tom's generosity supplies him with a comfortable income, and there are strong indications that he will again rise in the world: He is planning to marry a "very rich" widow, and has saved enough money to buy a seat in "the next Parliament" (884). And Square, who truly reforms and who contributes to Allworthy's reconciliation with Tom, dies at a relatively young age. His goodness does not bring him happiness in this world, although we may assume that he finds it in the next: but that world is beyond the reach of Fortune. Fielding would reject Van Ghent's idea, both because it is religiously unsound and because, in the world of <u>Tom Jones</u> as well as in our own world, "it is not true."

By showing that Van Ghent's analysis seems inadequate, the student prepares the way for her own analysis: She anticipates the objections of readers who might hold views similar to Van Ghent's, leaving them curious about what other views might be possible. If Fortune does not consistently favor the virtuous and punish the wicked in *Tom Jones,* what role does it actually play? An effective refutation can thus help to persuade readers while also heightening their interest in the argument to be offered.

In "Milton's 'Satan' and the Theme of Damnation in Elizabethan Tragedy," Helen Gardner weaves together confirmation and refutation to advance her argument that Satan is comparable to such tragic figures as Macbeth and Faustus. Like these characters from Elizabethan tragedy, Gardner writes, Satan commits a sin against nature knowingly and willfully, finds himself unable to turn back or repent, and gradually deteriorates into something much less than he was when he first sinned. To confirm her interpretation of Satan's character, Gardner marshals evidence from the text of *Paradise Lost* and from the texts of the plays with which she compares it. She also builds on the arguments of other writers, both literary critics and theologians: She note with approval that Charles Williams and C. S. Lewis have "destroyed, one hopes for ever, the notion that Satan had grounds for his rebellion" (47); she cites John Donne and Thomas Aquinas to buttress her assertion that the damned and fallen angels are alike in that they cannot repent and therefore cannot be pardoned; and she quotes James Joyce's Stephen Dedalus to help explain her understanding of tragic awe and pity.

Later in the essay, Gardner replies to critics whose views of Satan conflict with her own, refuting both Percy Bysshe Shelley's contention that Satan is a heroic figure who deserves to be pitied and Lewis's contention that Satan is a contemptible creature who deserves only to be hated and scorned. Thus, while Gardner acknowledges what she sees as Lewis's contribution to a proper understanding of Satan's character, she does not hesitate to correct him when she thinks he carries his derision of Satan too far. Toward the end of her essay, Gardner refers to William Blake and, again, Charles Williams, agreeing with their perception that there is a dualism in *Paradise Lost,* a tension between Satan as "infernal Serpent" and Satan as "lost Archangel." Throughout her essay, Gardner combines her own reading of the works in question with her responses to other writers, confirming an interpretation she finds tenable and refuting those she considers lacking.

## Writing about Several Works

The readings discussed so far deal with individual literary texts, but many critical essays treat several works. The need remains the same: to show the overall development of the works in light of the thesis or question. Gorer, for example, must discuss all of Austen's major novels if he is to make a case for the underlying pattern he proposes. He handles the difficulty of working with several novels in a brief essay in two ways. First, he considers four of the novels together, demonstrating similarities of character and plot. He writes, for instance, "All four novels are about young women (Marianne, Elizabeth, Fanny, Emma) who are made love to by, but finally reject, the Charming but Worthless lover (Willoughby, Wickham, Crawford, Frank Churchill) and finally marry a man whom they esteem and admire rather than love passionately (Colonel Brandon, Darcy, Edmund Bertram, Mr. Knightley)" (198). After demonstrating the similarities of the novels, Gorer takes each novel separately and in chronological order to show the "working out" of Austen's attitudes. To take only one instance, Gorer shows the evolution of the attitude toward fathers by pointing out that in *Pride and Prejudice* the father is beloved; in *Mansfield Park* two father figures are unsympathetic; in *Emma* the father is senile and foolish; and finally in *Persuasion* the father is "hated, proud, silly and endlessly selfish" (203). Thus, working novel by novel, Gorer shows lines of development analogous to those that might be demonstrated in a line-by-line analysis of a single poem.

## The Conclusion

The concluding paragraphs of most literary essays, like those of most other argumentative essays, offer some sort of recapitulation: The writer reasserts the essay's thesis and perhaps refocuses the reader's attention on especially compelling supporting evidence. Generally, to be effective, a recapitulation must be brief. A long, elaborate summary of an essay one has just finished reading is wearying and distracting; a concise, vigorous reminder of a writer's most powerful arguments can overcome one's last bit of resistance. In "Old Critics and New: The Treatment of Chopin's *The Awakening*," Priscilla Allen uses her last paragraph to restate her argument that most critics have interpreted Kate Chopin's novel too narrowly, seeing it simply as a work "about sex" rather than as an account of a human being's struggle for freedom and fulfillment. Avoiding any unnecessary details that would dilute the force of her paragraph, Allen stresses her main ideas, driving them home one final time:

> Critics have said that Chopin's novel is about a woman's sexual awakening. Today, when we have so many female characters portrayed as natural experts in the bedroom, that is hardly a revolutionary theme. My quarrel with the critics is as much on what they fail to see and say as on what they define as the core and totality of the book (a bit as if, treating *Moby Dick,* they called it a book about the whaling industry). The heroism of Edna is that she is able to pursue her felt needs with so little guilt and that rather than settling for less than a chance to fulfill them she chooses instead to die. For so young a woman, she shows tremendous strength in discovering, defining, and following her natural human needs, despite all the societal pressures on her to conform to a set pattern. *The Awakening* is a far more revolutionary novel than any of the critics have realized. What gives it its shock effect today (for it still has that power) and its relevance is that it is a portrait of a woman determined to have full integrity, full personhood—or nothing. (237-238)

By quickly restating Allen's principal objections to most criticism of *The Awakening* and by reaffirming the essential elements of her own interpretation of the novel, this paragraph quickly reorients any readers who may have lost track of Allen's thesis during the course of her article.

The last sentences of the paragraph also do something more. Just as many literary essays begin by asserting the significance of their theses, many end by asserting the significance of the works they discuss. Presumably, one writes about a work because one finds it worthwhile and wants others to appreciate it more fully. The temptation to end an essay by praising the work is therefore both strong and natural, particularly when the work is not widely known or admired. When handled well, such praise does not seem either mechanical or self-indulgent. Allen's final comments on *The Awakening,* for example, are subtle and precise, and they seem a natural extension of the analysis she has just presented. Rather than insisting on the novel's potency and relevance, Allen seems to take these qualities for granted, concentrating instead on identifying their exact origin in the novel's "portrait of a woman determined to have full integrity, full personhood—or nothing." Allen's emphatic language and her use of repetition seem designed to leave the reader with a powerful last impression of the novel's meaning and importance.

Some writers use their last paragraphs to give the reader a fuller perspective on a work, placing it in the context of an author's career or a historical period. G. Robert Stange's "Expectations Well Lost: Dickens' Fable for His Time" ends with such a paragraph. During his essay, Stange discusses themes he considers central to *Great Expectations,* occasionally comparing it to novels by

Stendhal and Balzac. In his conclusion, however, he focuses on comparisons hinted at earlier in the essay:

> Profound and suggestive as is Dickens' treatment of guilt and expiation in this novel, to trace its remoter implications is to find something excessive and idio-syncratic. A few years after he wrote *Great Expectations* Dickens remarked to a friend that he felt always as if he were wanted by the police—"irretrievably tainted." Compared to most of the writers of his time the Dickens of the later novels seems to be obsessed with guilt. The way in which his development-novel differs from those of his French compeers emphasizes an important quality of Dickens' art. The young heroes of *Le Rouge et le Noir* and *Le Père Goriot* proceed from innocence, through suffering to learning. They are sur-rounded by evil, and they can be destroyed by it. But Stendhal, writing in a ra-tionalist tradition, and Balzac, displaying the worldliness that only a Catholic novelist can command, seem astonishingly cool, even callous, beside Dickens. *Great Expectations* is outside either Cartesian or Catholic rationalism; pro-found as only an elementally simple book can be, it finds its analogues not in the novels of Dickens' English or French contemporaries, but in the writings of that other irretrievably tainted artist, Fyodor Dostoevski. (17)

This conclusion invites the reader to consider several aspects of the novel: *Great Expectations* is not only interesting in itself but also important as a re-flection of Dickens's personal sense of guilt, as an example of the difference between his earlier novels and his later ones, and as an indication of his place in his century—his distance from Stendhal and Balzac and his kinship with Dostoevski. Since Stange is writing about a widely well-regarded novel, a con-cluding paragraph insisting on its merits would be superfluous. Still, his con-clusion is in some ways similar to Allen's last paragraph on *The Awakening*. Each critic uses the concluding paragraph to encourage readers to appreciate a work's significance more fully and precisely.

In one final example, a graduate student concludes an essay on Pope's youthful imitations of Chaucer by arguing that these poems, usually regarded as minor, are nevertheless significant enough to warrant careful study:

> A comparison of these works by Chaucer and Pope tends to accentuate the poets' differences and to reinforce old stereotypes: Chaucer is a genially tolerant humorist, Pope a sharp and often harsh satirist. Such a conclusion is not surprising, for there are indeed differences between the two poets, and both stereotypes have some truth to them. The comparison may work to Pope's disadvantage, for his portrait of the Wife of Bath seems flat and two-dimensional compared to Chaucer's. Still, what emerges most clearly from such a comparison is Pope's sure and remarkably early

sense of what he does well. His choice of <u>The Merchant's Tale</u> shows sound judgment, for this tale gives him many opportunities to display his developing talent for satire. In his version of <u>The Wife of Bath's Prologue</u>, Pope transforms Chaucer's Wife into a character he can portray well; and while we may be disappointed by some of the changes he makes, it would have been far more disappointing if he had tried to imitate Chaucer's Wife and failed. We might expect a poet of Pope's youth and relative inexperience to be completely awed by a figure such as Chaucer, unable to do anything but follow him slavishly; but Pope, even at sixteen, had too much independence and too much judgment to make such a mistake. While these two poems are surely not among Pope's greatest works, they are good enough to be studied and enjoyed for their own sakes. Moreover, translation and imitation are central to Pope's poetic achievement, and these two poems hold the promise of the fully accomplished translator and imitator he was to become. Even in these early works. Pope proves himself a poet with an impressive ability to shape the works he imitates to his own genius and his own ideas about what poetry should be, to capitalize as fully as possible on another poet's work and make it the foundation for a poem distinctively his own.

Unlike Stange, who is writing about a work almost universally regarded as excellent and important, this student is writing about poems usually regarded as deserving no more than a passing glance. Thus, she uses her concluding paragraph to make a final plea for the poems' significance. Careful not to overstate the poems' merits, she argues that they nevertheless provide valuable evidence about Pope's artistic character, about his particular strengths as a translator and imitator. By placing these minor poems into the context of Pope's career as a whole, the student provides a specific basis for the reader's appreciation.

Like any other part of a literary essay, the conclusion can be handled either gracefully or clumsily. It can seem either a natural outgrowth of the paper or an unnecessary and mechanical addition. The closing comment on a work's importance, for example, can easily degenerate into the enthusiastic insincerity of a grade-school book report's obligatory endorsement of a work as a masterpiece to be enjoyed by all. As is true of other elements discussed in this chapter, conclusions are written not to satisfy the requirements of a text on the literary essay but to communicate a point clearly and effectively. Those who attempt critical writing cannot expect success to come from a list of rules or prescriptions, but they can find some guidance in the successful practice of writers struggling with similar problems.

## THE LANGUAGE OF CRITICISM

Those who are fascinated by literature are almost inevitably fascinated by language as well. Even more than students of other disciplines, those who have devoted themselves to the study of literature have traditionally shared a love of and a concern for language, perhaps partly because most literary critics are also English professors who teach composition courses at least occasionally. It is natural for such people to see themselves as in some sense guardians of the English language, and in composition classrooms many perform that role. Most tell their freshmen that clarity and conciseness are essential characteristics of good writing; most endorse statements such as E. B. White's declaration, "The approach to style is by way of plainness, simplicity, orderliness, sincerity" (69); and many criticize the use of jargon and pretentious diction in political writing and in the social sciences. It would seem natural to expect, then, that the language of criticism itself would be distinguished by its lucidity and its freedom from jargon.

A sampling of the articles found in scholarly journals, however, would quickly convince most readers that such characteristics are not universal, that many literary critics write in styles very different from the ones they praise in their composition classrooms. The vocabulary of many critics is highly specialized, and their sentences are often convoluted. When charged with inconsistency, such critics may reply that the standards promoted in composition classes cannot properly be applied to literary criticism, that complicated ideas cannot always be expressed in nontechnical language or in straightforward sentences. Others may reply, as Altick does in *The Art of Literary Research*, "We, of all people, should know and do better. . . . There is no difference between a good, scholarly style and a good English style addressed to the intelligent layman. The hallmark of good scholarly prose is lucidity" (183).

## Jargon: The Ongoing Debate

An exchange in *PMLA* shows both sides of the controversy. In January of 1983, the journal printed a letter from Ellsworth Barnard, who objected to the language used in two articles published in the May 1982 issue. Barnard listed many examples of what he considered the "outlandish terminology" of the two essays, including such words as *sacramentality, liminal, parodic, autophagous, affect* (as noun), *narratological, problematizing,* and *transgressive;* he also quoted passages such as "the collision of the modes incipient in the words is converted to a presentational dramatization" and "to temporalize the spatiality of the dialogue." Professing a "bias in favor of plain English," Barnard argued that such language is indeed jargon, that it makes the reader's task unduly difficult, and that it is, moreover, avoidable: "If by taking a little trouble we can put our ideas into common words—which need not be colorless—is not the effort worthwhile?"

Peter Brooks, the author of one of the articles Barnard criticized, wrote a letter to defend his style. Specialized terminology is not jargon, Brooks contended, if rare but legitimate words and "well-formed" neologisms are "set in a context of exposition that makes their meaning clear and shows why these terms are important to the conduct of the argument." Moreover, by remaining too rigidly loyal to "plain English," critics may limit their ability to provide benefits offered by such fields as philosophy, linguistics, anthropology, and psychoanalysis. Refusing to accept "the challenge of new concepts and their vocabulary," Brooks argued, may amount to "a rejection of new ways of conceiving our subject." Finally, Brooks maintained that modern criticism, like modern poetry, sometimes should be difficult: Language that is difficult without being obscure can challenge the reader's assumptions (87–88).

Clearly, literary critics are divided on this issue; each writer must use careful, independent judgment in all decisions relating to style. No path is safe or universally approved: A style such as Brooks's is sure to alienate some readers, and the "plain English" Barnard advocates will probably fail to impress some others. Also, as both letters indicate, style is far from being a superficial matter. One's use of language reveals a great deal about one's approach to literary criticism and one's view of its purpose.

Certainly, not all technical language is jargon. Every discipline requires some specialized vocabulary, and no sensible person would begrudge the writer the use of long-established terms that make possible the concise discussion of meter, poetic forms, elements of fiction, and so forth. And many approaches to literary criticism necessarily involve borrowing some terms from other fields: A critic taking a psychological approach, for example, needs to be able to talk about the unconscious and the Oedipus complex. When terms are as widely understood as these, writers can use them without hesitation or explanation; writers using less familiar terms, however, generally believe courtesy to the reader obliges them to provide definitions.

## Contrived Terminology

The debate about style, though, involves much more than the occasional use of a new word to express a concept that cannot conveniently be stated in any other way. Many charge that some critics use technical language unnecessarily and ostentatiously, seeking out uncommon words where common ones would serve as well or better, and creating new terms for concepts that are neither interesting nor useful. Too frequently, it is charged, critics invent terminology in order to hide a simple idea behind complicated language. Perhaps it is kindest to use a fictional example to illustrate this fault. In *The Pooh Perplex: A Freshman Casebook*, Frederick C. Crews parodies the style of a Chicago critic attempting to establish the genre of *Winnie-the-Pooh:*

> We divide all emotions into mental pains, pleasures, and impulses instigated by opinion. From these categories we derive the following schemes of imitation in poetry: the serious and the comic. From these . . . further subdivisions are precipitated: the tragic and the punitive, the lout-comic and the rogue-comic. Between these extremes we have succeeded in isolating two other types, the sympathetic and the antipathetic, and various further categories as well; but for the moment it may be well to pause at this point and reintroduce *Winnie-the-Pooh*. Close examination of the text informs us that this book is of the lout-comic subdivision of the comic species, and, being of essentially pleasant subject matter, produces pleasure directly as opposed to the cathartic or purgative method. In short, *Winnie-the-Pooh* is funny. (94)

Similar charges might be leveled at those who use odd forms of common words; for example, is it really necessary to call an act "transgressive" when it might just as easily be termed "a transgression"?

Nearly everyone would agree it is false and pretentious to use technical terms and unusual forms merely to impress. Still, many feel tempted to use elaborate language in order to establish critical credentials—with professors, with journal editors, with readers in general. Critical prose would probably improve a great deal if all writers examined their stylistic options—and their motives—fully and honestly whenever they think of deviating from common language: Is my use of this word legitimate and unavoidable? Is there a more familiar word I might use? Am I using this word because I wish to express a difficult concept as precisely and economically as possible or because I wish to sound scholarly? The following remarks by Douglas Bush to a meeting of literary critics are instructive here:

> Since criticism is not a science and cannot be made one by any amount of theorizing, it should follow the world's great critics in the belief that the most precise and subtle ideas about literature can be expressed in ordinary language. . . . Jargon does not make simple ideas scientific and profound; it only inspires profound distraction of the user's aesthetic sensitivity. (704)

If an idea can possibly be expressed in simple, direct language, it probably should be.

## Reaching an Audience

Finally, reflecting on the purpose of literary criticism may also help the writer make decisions about style. This chapter opened by suggesting that literary criticism begins with the desire to communicate, to share with others one's ideas about a literary work. If one believes those ideas are valid and important, it seems sensible to want to communicate with as many other people as possible. Critics who use highly specialized language, especially those who use such a language without defining it, limit their audiences severely: They can be understood only by other literary critics and possibly only by literary critics who have in common particular assumptions, approaches, and training. Although it might be unrealistic to hope that either students' papers or articles in scholarly journals will interest the general public, it is not foolish to try to write in a style comprehensible to any intelligent person who happens to be interested in one's ideas. Wordsworth says in the "Preface" to *Lyrical Ballads* that poets should write in "a selection of the language really used by men"; if this selection is "made with true taste and feeling," Wordsworth says, the poet's language will be free of "the vulgarity and meanness" of everyday speech. Perhaps the principle Wordsworth recommends to poets could be a useful one for literary critics as well. The language of criticism is not identical to the language used on the street—it traditionally excludes contractions and colloquialisms, for example, and it demands a somewhat wider vocabulary and a more scrupulous attention to the exact meanings of words. If the language of criticism becomes too far removed from "the language really used by men" (and women), however, it can make criticism into a barren, pointless business of critics writing to impress other critics, rather than to communicate their insights and enthusiasms with all who share their love of literature and their sense of its importance.

## WORKS CITED AND RECOMMENDED

Allen, Priscilla. "Old Critics and New: The Treatment of Chopin's *The Awakening.*" *The Authority of Experience: Essays in Feminist Criticism.* Ed. Arlyn Diamond and Lee R. Edwards. Amherst: Massachusetts UP, 1977. 224-238.

Altick, Richard. *The Art of Literary Research.* 2nd ed. New York: Norton, 1975.

Barnard, Ellsworth. Letter. *PMLA* 98 (1983): 87.

Brooks, Cleanth. "Keats's Sylvan Historian: History without Footnotes." *The Well Wrought Urn.* New York: Harcourt, 1947. 151-166.

Brooks, Peter. Letter. *PMLA* 98 (1983): 87-88.

Burgess, C. F. "Conrad's Pesky Russian." *Nineteenth-Century Fiction* 18 (1963): 189-193.

Bush, Douglas. "Literary History and Literary Criticism." *Literary History and Literary Criticism: Acts of the Ninth Congress of the International Federation for Modern Languages and Literature, New York University, August 25-31, 1963.* Ed. W. J. Bate. New York: Harcourt, 1972. 698-706.

Corbett, Edward P. J. *Classical Rhetoric for the Modern Student.* 2nd ed. New York: Oxford UP, 1971.

Crews, Frederick C. *The Pooh Perplex: A Freshman Casebook.* New York: Dutton, 1965.

Fielding, Henry. *Tom Jones.* Ed. George Sherburn. New York: Random, 1950.

Gardner, Helen. "Milton's 'Satan' and the Theme of Damnation in Elizabethan Tragedy." *English Studies* ns 1 (1948): 46-66.

Gorer, Geoffrey. "Myth in Jane Austen." *American Imago* 2 (1941): 197-204.

Holland, Norman. *The Dynamics of Literary Response.* New York: Oxford UP, 1968.

———. *Poems in Persons: An Introduction to the Psychoanalysis of Literature.* New York: Norton, 1973.

Howe, Irving. *Politics and the Novel.* New York: Avon, 1970.

Marx, Leo. *The Machine in the Garden: Technology and the Pastoral Ideal.* London: Oxford UP, 1970.

Scott, Wilbur. *Five Approaches of Literary Criticism.* New York: Collier, 1962.

Smith, James. "As You Like It." *Scrutiny* 9 (1940-41): 9-32.

Stange, G. Robert. "Expectations Well Lost: Dickens' Fable for His Time." *College English* 16 (1954): 9-17.

Stein, William Bysshe. "The Lotus Posture and *Heart of Darkness.*" *Modern Fiction Studies* 2 (1956-57): 167-170.

Strunk, William, Jr., and E. B. White. *The Elements of Style.* 3rd ed. New York: Macmillan, 1979.

Todorov, Tzvetan. *The Fantastic: A Structural Approach to a Literary Genre.* Ithaca: Cornell UP, 1975.

Van Ghent, Dorothy. *The English Novel: Form and Function.* New York: Harper, 1953.

# *Chapter 5*

## METHODS OF LITERARY RESEARCH

Criticism and research are interdependent and often inseparable: Both are guided by a spirit of imaginative but careful inquiry, and both have as their ultimate purpose the fuller understanding and enjoyment of literature. For many people, however, early experiences with research are dispiriting, confusing, or both. For those whose object is simply to find the minimum number of outside sources required for a term paper, research too often seems a dry and mechanical business of sifting through reference books, squeezing information onto note cards, and copying down other people's ideas rather than developing their own; moreover, research can at first seem an intimidating task, for even a modest college library contains so many volumes that it is easy to feel overwhelmed. Studying the aims and methods of literary research, however, can transform the library from a treacherous maze to comfortable, familiar territory, clearly mapped out for the researcher's convenience. More important, it soon becomes clear that research itself is not an annoying requirement but a process that is both satisfying in itself and an essential part of the struggle with the text. The best research is illuminated by original critical thought, and the best criticism is informed by solid research.

Research is capable of affirming, challenging, or transforming ideas about literature. Almost everyone will readily grant the importance and usefulness of the research done by major scholars working with primary materials, but student researchers often doubt the significance of their own work, knowing that they are unlikely to find anywhere in their college libraries even a scrap of previously undiscovered material that will add to factual knowledge; it sometimes seems that the kind of research they can do will lead to nothing but the discouraging conclusion that everything they wanted to say has already been said many times before. It would be very wrong, however, to assume that new discoveries can be made only by people working with new materials, that research with secondary materials is doomed to be unoriginal. The researcher working with well-established facts may see connections among those facts that no one else has seen before; the researcher discussing a work that has already been analyzed by dozens or hundreds of critics may arrive at a new interpretation. And even when one does not discover something positively new, research is valuable as a means of understanding a text more fully, of teaching oneself about a literary work by seeing it examined from various points of view. Research broadens perspectives by inviting one to compare one's own ideas about a work with the ideas, responses, and insights of other readers.

Researchers who begin with fairly definite ideas of their own may find facts and opinions they can use to support their interpretations—not particularly exciting discoveries, perhaps, but solid and useful ones. Often, researchers may also discover ideas quite new to them, be challenged and persuaded, and modify their interpretations accordingly. Even reading books and articles that seem utterly mistaken can be valuable: In the process of deciding just why and to what extent other authors are mistaken, researchers can refine and sharpen their own ideas. It is undeniably exciting to sit alone in one's room, puzzling out a completely independent interpretation of a literary work; it can be just as exciting to test that idea in the library, knowing that it will become increasingly precise and substantial as research continues.

The first step toward successful literary research, then, is recognizing the many ways in which it can contribute to an understanding of literature. Learning how to use a number of reference materials is the next step: Although research is not impossibly difficult, it involves much more than casually browsing through the library catalogue and locating a few books with promising titles. Before plunging into research, one must plan a careful *search strategy*—a systematic method of locating material relevant to a topic. A good deal of this planning can be done even before going to the library; once at the library, the researcher must spend some time with bibliographies and other reference materials before looking for books and articles that might be cited in the paper. A thorough, successful search strategy includes at least four stages:

1. Planning
2. Preliminary reading
3. Working with reference materials
4. Locating secondary materials

The rest of this chapter is devoted to describing a method for researching a topic in literature, a method that is workable and should be adequate for many sorts of research papers. It is important to realize, however, that this method is not by any means the only one possible, nor is it appropriate for all projects. Research strategies are determined in part by the kinds of questions being asked and in part by the individual researcher's own interests, needs, and background. Particularly after acquiring some experience and confidence, researchers can find many valuable ways of adapting the process this chapter describes. Throughout the chapter, we will refer in passing to a number of reference works; many of these are described in more detail in Appendix A. Also included in this bibliography are a number of more detailed guides to research that one should consult before starting a major project such as a master's thesis or a doctoral dissertation.

## PLANNING

Before beginning, it is important to think carefully about the topic, about the thesis, and about the scope of the paper. The experienced researcher goes to the library with a tentative thesis in mind, with some clearly formulated ideas that will be tested through research. The familiar distinction between subject and thesis is crucial enough to be repeated here. A subject is simply a work or area to be studied; a thesis makes an assertion about a subject, an assertion that will be defended throughout the paper. "Dickens's view of childhood in *Oliver Twist* and *Great Expectations*" is a subject; "Dickens presents radically different views of childhood in *Oliver Twist* and *Great Expectations*" is a thesis. Those who do not have a thesis as well as a subject before beginning their research are in danger of being overwhelmed by the ideas they read about, and they may end up with a paper that is no more than a patchwork of other people's observations and opinions. Although one's thesis may well be modified during research, one's own ideas, however influenced by the reading one does and the insights one gains, should remain at the core of the paper.

During this planning stage, the researcher also considers the sorts of materials to be consulted and the probable extent of the research. For example, depending on one's critical approach, one might well decide to consult biographies or literary histories as well as critical essays about the work to be studied; a researcher planning to take a psychological approach might decide to look for works by Freud and for works discussing theories of psychological criticism. Other critical approaches might suggest background reading in fields ranging from sociology to religion to political theory. This is also the time to make realistic decisions about limiting research. External considerations may have some influence here: A researcher who has only two weeks to write a ten-page paper on the character of Satan in *Paradise Lost* clearly will not be able to find—and will not have any use for—all the material relevant to this topic. Searches that need not or cannot be exhaustive should be limited in some rational way. For example, one might limit oneself to books and articles published in the last twenty years or decide to try to identify the best or most influential criticism on the topic. On the other hand, a researcher who has a full semester to write a thirty-page paper on John Gardener's *Grendel* probably should try to track down every shred of relevant criticism, especially since relatively little has been written about this work. The professor may also have something to say about how extensive research should be; for example, it is important to know whether or not the professor expects students to go beyond the materials available in their own library.

Especially for one's first major research paper, a preliminary planning conference with a reference librarian can be very helpful. Professional librarians have a thorough knowledge of research tools and have done a great deal of research themselves. Most also have training and experience in at least one academic discipline: The staff of a college library may well include someone with an M.A. or Ph.D. in English as well as a degree in library science, and reference librarians with degrees in other fields can help those students working with interdisciplinary topics or approaches. Most reference librarians think of themselves primarily as teachers and are eager to help students plan their search strategies and to evaluate the materials they find.

## Four Stages of a Search Strategy

### 1. PLANNING

Through reading, analysis, and possibly consultation, the researcher determines the probable direction and scope of research. The researcher also studies primary materials carefully and formulates a tentative thesis.

### 2. PRELIMINARY READING

To find background information and gain a broader perspective on the topic or author, the researcher may read a general article in a literary history or an encyclopedia.

### 3. WORKING WITH REFERENCE MATERIALS

To find books and articles on the topic, the researcher consults bibliographies and other reference tools. The researcher may:

Consult major general bibliographies such as *The New Cambridge Bibliography of English Literature* or *Literary History of the United States*

Find specialized bibliographies by checking bibliographies of bibliographies and other sources

Use electronic resources to do subject or author searches

Find recent books and articles by checking serial bibliographies such as the *MLA Bibliography*

Consider using other reference tools to find book reviews, biographical information, and materials in microform collections

Check bibliographies and notes in texts and in books and articles on the topic

The researcher evaluates reference materials while using them.

### 4. LOCATING SECONDARY MATERIALS

To find secondary materials in the library, the researcher:

Consults the library catalogue to find books

Consults the library's serial record to find periodicals

To find materials the library does not have, the researcher:

Uses tools such as the Online Computer Library Center (OCLC) to see if other libraries have the materials needed

Visits nearby libraries or arranges an interlibrary loan

# PRELIMINARY READING

Librarians recommend moving from the general to the particular in a library search: Before beginning research on a particular topic, the researcher should read a general article in an encyclopedia or other reference work. Thus, a researcher planning a paper on Nathaniel Hawthorne's portrayal of female characters may find that reading a general article on Hawthorne is the best way to begin. Sometimes a researcher is so thoroughly familiar with a topic that it is safe to skip this stage; for example, someone who has already written three other research papers on Hawthorne might indeed be ready to begin researching a specific topic. In most cases, however, it is good to do some preliminary general reading before beginning research.

Here, literary histories can be very helpful. Reading the chapter on Hawthorne in Robert Spiller's *Literary History of the United States* would give the researcher a general account of Hawthorne's life, short discussions of his major works, and some insight into his place in the American literary tradition. It might also alert the researcher to some additional primary works that should be considered; for example, after reading Spiller's chapter, the researcher might decide to analyze *The House of the Seven Gables* as well as *The Scarlet Letter* and *The Blithedale Romance*. A researcher who is interested in writing a paper on Swift's political thought but who knows only a few of his works might find that the chapter on Swift in Albert C. Baugh's *A Literary History of England* will suggest a number of important works to consider. The footnotes in this chapter also identify good editions of Swift's works and letters, as well as a number of important books and articles about him. When literary histories prove insufficient for the researcher's needs—for example, when one is writing about an author discussed briefly or not at all in the literary histories available—it is often helpful to check more general sources, such as the *Encyclopaedia Britannica*. These often contain excellent essays on literary topics, essays that sometimes end with brief but helpful bibliographies.

## Taking Notes during Preliminary Reading

While using a literary history or encyclopedia that has some bibliographical listings, the researcher starts taking notes. Many researchers use index cards or slips of paper for note taking, for these can easily be alphabetized or reorganized at any time; taking notes in a pad or notebook allows less flexibility. Whatever the methods chosen, it is best to include in each note all the information that might eventually be needed in the paper's bibliography or list of works cited. For a book, this means including the author, full title, city and date of publication, and publisher, as well as the edition if it is not the first; for an article, one includes the author, tile of the article, name of the journal in which it was published, volume number, date of publication, and page numbers. The researcher checks this information carefully, making sure that it has been copied correctly. Also, it is a good idea to note the sources in which each book or article is cited. Thus, if *A Literary History of England* alerts the researcher to a book, *LHE* might be included in the note taken for that book. Most researchers also keep a running list of all the literary histories, bibliographies, and other reference works consulted.

Most researchers keep their notes in alphabetical order by authors' names as they do their research, so that they can check quickly to see if they already have notes for the books and articles they see cited later. When a book or article is cited in more than one source, that fact is recorded in the note. Thus, if a title first seen in *A Literary History of England* is also listed in the *New*

*Cambridge Bibliography of English Literature,* the researcher, might write *LHE, NCBEL* in the note. Making such notations is particularly helpful when the researcher is trying to identify the most important works written on a topic: A work that is cited in several selective bibliographies is probably generally regarded as important and should be one of the works read. Admittedly, such a system can at best suggest the bibliographers' opinions of these books and articles, not their true quality. Some fine works are inevitably neglected by even the best bibliographers, and some mediocre ones find their way into many bibliographies. If the researcher must find some way of deciding which books and articles to read, however, this system is better than nothing.

## WORKING WITH REFERENCE MATERIALS AND ELECTRONIC RESOURCES

Modern college libraries provide researchers with numerous research tools, both print and electronic. The electronic tools offer such speed and convenience that many researchers, especially those who are very skilled and confident with computers, may feel tempted to rely on such tools exclusively. To do a truly exhaustive search, however, one must learn to use print resources as well—for as of this writing much valuable bibliographic information has not yet been transferred to electronic databases. The first step toward a successful, responsible search is to learn as much as possible about the various tools available in one's home library, to become thoroughly familiar with what each offers and in what ways each is limited.

### Print Bibliographies

For many research projects, working with print bibliographies is still an appropriate way to begin. *Bibliography* is a broad term meaning, roughly, "writing about books"; it can refer to anything from a list of the sources consulted in writing a term paper to a book discussing the manuscript versions or various editions of a literary work. The bibliographies usually consulted at this stage in research are *enumerative bibliographies,* simple listings of books and articles about a particular work, author, or topic. A few bibliographies in the field of literary studies are *annotated*—that is, the compilers provide brief summaries or evaluations of the works they list—but most bibliographies list only titles, authors, and publication data. Most major research papers involve combing through various enumerative bibliographies, looking for titles that seem relevant to a topic.

The first step is finding bibliographies likely to lead to such titles. For many topics, it makes sense to begin with a major bibliography of English or American literature. A researcher working on a topic in English literature, for example, may start with Watson's *New Cambridge Bibliography of English Literature;* a researcher working on a topic in American literature might start with the bibliography volume of Spiller's *Literary History of the United States*. These bibliographies are easy to use and widely respected, and they can lead to a great deal of relevant information. A researcher working on a paper on Tennyson, for example, will find that the *New Cambridge Bibliography of English Literature* lists bibliographies on Tennyson, various editions of his works and letters, and twenty single-spaced columns of books and articles about him.

For most research papers assigned in advanced courses, however, the search probably cannot end with these two major bibliographies. Both bibliographies are *selective;* that is, they do not attempt to list everything published on a particular author or topic but only the works the compilers consider most important. Furthermore, the most recent edition of *Literary History of the United States* was published in 1974, the volumes of the *New Cambridge Bibliography of English Literature* in 1969–1977—so the researcher must look elsewhere for more recent scholarship. And some minor authors and many modern authors are not covered in these works at all; a researcher writing a paper on Kingsley Amis, for example, will find that the *New Cambridge Bibliography of English Literature* contains no listings on him.

To find more exhaustive listings, the researcher usually turns to more specialized bibliographies. For a paper on William Wordsworth, for example, the researcher could consult Frank Jordan's *The English Romantic Poets: A Review of Research* and James V. Logan's *Wordsworthian Criticism: A Guide and Bibliography.* Most libraries contain many specialized bibliographies on particular authors, periods, and genres, but finding them may take some time and ingenuity. Some specialized bibliographies are listed in the *New Cambridge Bibliography of English Literature* and in the *Literary History of the United States.* The researcher might also consult several other sources:

1.  *Bibliographies of bibliographies.* This sounds like an intimidating tool, but it can lead to very important reference works. In a search for specialized bibliographies, the researcher might check Trevor H. Howard-Hill's *Bibliography of British Literary Bibliographies* and Charles Nilon's *Bibliography of Bibliographies in American Literature.* Richard D. Altick and Andrew Wright's *Selective Bibliography for the Study of English and American Literature* can also be very helpful here: The chapter on "Bibliographies of Literature" lists bibliographies of bibliographies; general bibliographies in English and American literature; and a number of bibliographies focusing on particular topics, periods, and genres. For example, a researcher working on a paper on Ernest Hemingway would find that Altick and Wright list more specialized bibliographies, such as James T. Callow and Robert S. Reilly's *Guide to American Literature from Emily Dickinson to the Present* and James Woodress's *American Fiction 1900–1950.* For many topics, the researcher need not look beyond the listings Altick and Wright offer.

2. *The Bibliographic Index: A Cumulative Bibliography of Bibliographies.* Even bibliographies of bibliographies soon become outdated; to learn about recently published bibliographies, the researcher can use the *Bibliographic Index.* This index comes out three times a year, with bound volumes published each December. It lists by subject not only bibliographies published separately but also bibliographies appearing in books, pamphlets, and periodicals. It is important to remember that this bibliography lists only bibliographies published in a particular year.

## Computer Catalogues

Especially if one is interested in finding relatively recent sources, it often makes sense at this point to turn to the computer catalogues and other electronic resources available. These resources vary so much from library to library that it is impossible to generalize about them in any detail; and new electronic databases become available so frequently and are expanded so often that any attempt to describe them would quickly become dated. A conference with a reference librarian is the best way to learn about the various electronic resources one's particular library offers.

Even so, a few general guidelines can be offered. Most college libraries have computer catalogues listing all of the books in their own libraries; many libraries also have expanded electronic catalogues listing books held by nearby libraries willing to share their resources through interlibrary loan. Periodical articles are listed by resources such as InfoTrac. Usually, such resources indicate whether the periodicals mentioned are available at one's home library or would have to be obtained through interlibrary loan; sometimes, summaries of some or all of the articles are included. It is important to remember, however, that the listings provided by these convenient resources are not exhaustive. Most emphasize recent materials but may not give the researcher access to books and articles published in past decades—and at least in fields such as literature, one cannot assume that the most recently published works are the best or the most important. Many electronic resources survey only a relatively limited number of periodicals; some emphasize popular magazines rather than scholarly journals; some do not list such materials as book reviews or dissertations.

## The *MLA Bibliography*

Despite the recent proliferation of other resources, the *MLA International Bibliography of Books and Articles on the Modern Languages and Literatures*—usually referred to simply as the *MLA Bibliography*—remains the single most comprehensive and reliable bibliography in the field of literary studies. It is a *serial bibliography*—that is, new volumes are compiled annually, covering material published in that particular year. Before 1956, the *MLA Bibliography* listed only works published in the United States, but since then it has attempted to list all critical and scholarly works published in a given year, regardless of the author's nationality or the language in which the work was written. The *MLA Bibliography* lists books, doctoral dissertations, essays in *festschriften* (volumes of commemorative essays) and other anthologies, and articles from some three thousand periodicals. Learning to use the *MLA Bibliography* is absolutely crucial to doing serious research in literature. Although some find it somewhat confusing at first, it soon becomes a familiar and useful tool.

It is important to understand something about the history and organization of the *MLA Bibliography* before attempting to use it, for its format has changed several times over the years. Before 1970, the *MLA Bibliography* was printed in the June issue of the journal *PMLA (Publications of the Modern Language Association)*; most libraries have separate, bound volumes of the bibliographies for 1963 through 1969, but for bibliographies from earlier years one must look for the appropriate volume of the *PMLA*. More recent *MLA Bibliographies* have been printed separately from the *PMLA*. In 1981, the bibliography began to be published on CD-ROM, as well as on paper. Most college libraries now carry the CD-ROM version for 1981 to the present; many also have the bibliographies for the years between 1963 and 1981 on CD-ROM. To avoid duplication, some libraries have now stopped ordering print volumes for the current years. Ideally, one should learn how to use both the print and the electronic versions of the *MLA Bibliography*, so that one can use the earliest as well as the most recent volumes and adapt to the resources available at various libraries.

## THE *MLA BIBLIOGRAPHY:* PRINT

For the years from 1969 to 1981, each *MLA Bibliography* consists of three volumes, all bound together for library use and each covering a particular topic: Volume I, for example, covers English and American literature. For the years since 1981, each annual bibliography consists of two parts—a five-volume author index (English and American literature are still in Volume I) and a subject index. There have also been important changes in the table of contents, in the way items are organized, and in the information available in each item.

For example, suppose that a researcher is working on a paper on Kate Chopin's *The Awakening* and is using the 1980 *MLA Bibliography.* The table of contents for Volume I is organized by nationality and then by century, so the researcher starts by looking under the column headed "American Literature" and finding the subheading "Nineteenth Century." Across from this subheading in the number 10654. It is important to note that this number is an item number, *not* a page number: Each book, article, and other item in the *MLA Bibliography* is assigned its own number, and item 10654 begins the listings for works on nineteenth-century topics. The researcher flips pages quickly until reaching item 10654, which appears on page 205. The listings for the nineteenth century begin with several general topics—for example, Bibliography, Drama, Poetry, Themes—followed by listings on particular authors. The researcher might

skim the general listings—might anything listed under Prose Fiction be helpful?—before looking for Chopin in the alphabetical list of authors. The listings
for Chopin begin with item 10753 on page 207 and are ordered alphabetically
by author.

To understand and use these listings, one must decode the abbreviations.
For example, the researcher may decide that these items might be helpful:

> 10753. Butler, Henry Scott. "Sexuality in the Fiction of Kate Chopin." *DAI*
> 40:6277A.

> 10755. Paulsen, Anne-Lise Stomness. "The Masculine Dilemma in Kate
> Chopin's *The Awakening*." SoSt 18 (1979): 381-424.

> 10757. Stein, Allen F. "Kate Chopin's *The Awakening* and the Limits of Moral
> Judgment." [F 125] 159-69.

Item 10753 is a citation for a dissertation summarized in *Dissertation Abstracts International.* Item 10755 is a citation for a journal article, with the
title of the journal abbreviated. To find the full name of the journal in which
Paulsen's article appears, the researcher would consult the "Master List and
Table of Abbreviations," which follows the table of contents for Volume I. That
alphabetical list reveals that *SoSt* is the abbreviation for *Southern Studies: An
Interdisciplinary Journal of the South;* Paulsen's article appears on pages
381-424 of Volume 18. Stein's article appears not in a journal but in a
*festschrift,* as the bracketed number in the citation indicates. The list of
"*Festschriften* and Other Analyzed Collections," which follows the master list of
periodicals, indicates that collection 125 is *A Fair Day in the Affections: Literary Essays in Honor of Robert B. White, Jr.,* edited by Jack M. Durant and M.
Thomas Hester.

Beginning with the 1981 edition, the format of the *MLA Bibliography*
changed in several ways. The table of contents is no longer as detailed: The
headings for national literatures remain, but there are no subheadings for periods. To find the listings on Chopin, then, the researcher must flip through the
section on American literature until finding "American Literature/1800-1899"
and then look for Chopin in the alphabetical list of authors. Finding books and
articles about a particular work is now a little easier: Instead of simply listing
all works on an author alphabetically, the *MLA Bibliography* now groups these
works under subheadings such as "Novel / *The Awakening*" or "Short
Story/'Story of an Hour.'"

There have also been some changes in the type and amount of information
contained in each citation. For example, citations for articles in *festschriften*
and other collections now contain full bibliographical information, eliminating
the need for a master list. Here is a listing from the 1992 *MLA Bibliography* for
an article in a collection:

> [6814] Harrison, Antony H. "Swinburne and the Critique of Ideology in *The
> Awakening*." 185-203 in Harrison, Antony H., ed.; Taylor, Beverly, ed. *Gender
> and Discourse in Victorian Literature and Art.* Dekalb: Northern Illinois UP;

> 1992. xviii, 286 pp. [Treatment of desire. Sources in Swinburne, Algernon Charles. Marxist approach, feminist approach.]

The bracketed phrases at the end of this citation provide some information about the article's content and critical approach, and also refer to headings in the *MLA Bibliography*'s subject index.

Undoubtedly, this subject index is the most significant and helpful of all the changes in the bibliography's format. The subject index makes it much easier to use the bibliography to find books and articles not about particular authors but about topics. For example, a researcher looking for analyses of novels portraying Jewish immigrants might consult the 1987 bibliography and find this entry under "Jewish Immigrants—American literature. Prose 1900–1990."

> Antin, Mary. *The Promised Land.* Narrative technique. Treatment of JEWISH IMMIGRANTS; relationship to cultural assimilation. I:8267.

To locate further information, the researcher would turn to Volume I of the 1987 edition of the *MLA Bibliography*, look up item 8267 in the author index, and find the following entry:

> [8267] Rubin, Steven J. "Style and Meaning in Mary Antin's *The Promised Land*: A reevaluation." SAJL. 1986. 5:34–43. [Narrative technique. Treatment of Jewish immigrants; relationship to cultural assimilation.]

The final step would be consulting the master list of periodicals in Volume I and learning that SAJL is the abbreviation for *Studies in American Jewish Literature*. The researcher is now ready to find the article.

## THE *MLA BIBLIOGRAPHY:* CD-ROM

It is now possible to search the *MLA Bibliography* on CD-ROM (a personal computer connected to a CD player), using resources such as WILSONDISC and SilverPlatter. These resources permit the researcher to conduct author searches and two kinds of subject searches—by key words or by the descriptors used in the MLA subject index. When using SilverPlatter, for example, one could begin a search for sources on *The Awakening* by typing the command "chopin and awakening" and getting a list of entries such as this one:

> TI:  Art Is an Unnatural Act: Mademoiselle Reisz in The Awakening
>
> AU:  Seidel, -Kathryn
>
> SO:  Mississippi-Quarterly:-The-Journal-of-Southern-Culture, Mississippi State, MS (MissQ). 1993 Spring, 46:2, 199–214.
>
> LA:  English
>
> DE:  American-literature; 1880-1889; Chopin, -Kate; The Awakening-; novel-; treatment of women-artists; lesbianism-

Most of the items in this entry are self-explanatory: They give us the title of a journal article, its author, the source in which the article appeared, and the language in which the article is written. The item also includes a number of descriptors (DE), key words and phrases that can be used to do subject searches of materials of related interest.

The great advantage of doing a CD-ROM search is that it gives the researcher access to a list that covers many years—1963 to 1980, for example, or 1981 to the present. Using such lists is certainly quicker and more convenient than dragging down twenty or so volumes of the *MLA Bibliography* and flipping hundreds of pages until one has found the desired sections in each one. Also, with the full journal names printed in every item, one no longer has to refer continually to a master list of periodicals, and a printer attached to the CD-ROM frees one from the tedious business of copying information onto index cards. Once again, however, it is vital to determine how many years are covered by the electronic version of the *MLA Bibliography* available at one's library. A reference librarian is the best source of information about such matters.

## Other Serial Bibliographies

Although the *MLA Bibliography* is the most important serial bibliography in literary studies, other serial bibliographies can also be helpful. *The Year's Work in English Studies,* for example, contains bibliographical essays on scholarship in English and, to a much lesser extent, American literature. Although it is not nearly as comprehensive as the *MLA Bibliography,* it provides much more information about the works that it does discuss, commenting briefly on their content and sometimes on their importance. *American Literary Scholarship* is a comparable serial bibliography for American literature. The *Annual Bibliography of English Language and Literature*, a British bibliography, lists works on English and American literature and has an index that is especially helpful for finding works about a particular topic rather than a particular author. In addition, a number of journals publish serial bibliographies of research in particular fields. For example, *English Language Notes* now publishes an annual selective bibliography of research on the Romantic movement, *American Literature* publishes a quarterly bibliography of research on American literature, and *Southern Folklore Quarterly* publishes an annual bibliography of research on folklore. Altick and Wright list other specialized serial bibliographies under "Serial Bibliographies of Literature" in their *Selective Bibliography for the Study of English and American Literature.* Another helpful source is *A Guide to Serial Bibliographies for Modern Literature,* edited by William A. Wortman (New York: MLA, 1982).

For interdisciplinary studies, the *Essay and General Literature Index* and the *Humanities Index* can be very useful. The former lists essays and articles that appear in various sorts of anthologies, covering not only literature but also such fields as philosophy, religion, law, science, the arts, and history; the

*Humanities Index* lists periodical articles on a similar range of subjects. To find periodical articles on such subjects as anthropology, political science, psychology, and sociology, the researcher might begin by consulting the *Social Sciences and Humanities Index*. Reference librarians can suggest a number of more specialized bibliographies in other fields.

## Other Reference Tools—Print

Some topics and critical approaches require the use of other sorts of reference tools. Although we cannot give complete descriptions of all such tools here, it is important to know that they exist; reference librarians can give further guidance about their use. For example, although most of the bibliographies mentioned in this chapter do not list book reviews, several indices to book reviews are available in most libraries. The *Book Review Digest*, which began publication in 1905, surveys about 100 periodicals, citing reviews of books published in the United States and providing summaries of or brief excerpts from many of them. The *Book Review Index* is more comprehensive: It surveys more than two hundred periodicals and does not require, as the *Digest* does, that a book be reviewed at least twice before it is included. The *Book Review Index* does not provide any summaries or excerpts, however, and it began publication only in 1965. The *New York Times Book Review Index* cites reviews that appeared in the *New York Times* between 1986 and 1970.

Several reference tools can aid the researcher looking for biographical information. *Biography and Genealogy Master Index* is a guide to more than 350 works of collective biography such as *Who's Who; Biography Index* lists biographies that appear in books, periodicals, and the *New York Times* obituary columns. Several works of collective biography can be especially useful to the student of literature: *Contemporary Authors,* for example, provides concise biographical sketches and some bibliographical information about living and recently deceased authors in many fields from various countries. For fairly extensive information about deceased authors, the researcher might consult the *Dictionary of National Biography* (English authors) or the *Dictionary of American Biography* (American authors). The Gale Research Company is now putting out *The Dictionary of Literary Biography,* a series that will offer biographical information on authors—sketches for minor figures, full essays for major ones—including information about standard editions, bibliographies, biographies, and criticism; the first volume, *The American Renaissance in New England,* came out in 1978, and many other volumes have followed. *Contemporary Dramatists, Contemporary Novelists,* and *Contemporary Poets,* all edited by James Vinson, contain biographical and bibliographical information about many authors writing in English, along with some comments by the authors themselves.

Many libraries contain special microform, book, and pamphlet collections of interest to students of literature, and these collections often have their own reference tools; since the materials in these collections may not be adequately listed in the library catalogue, it is a good idea to ask for a list of the special collections your library owns. The *American Periodical Series,* for example, is a microfilm collection of eighteenth- and nineteenth-century American periodicals; the *Bell and Howell Black Culture Collection,* also on microfilm, includes some seven thousand books, pamphlets, periodicals, and other items on black history and culture. The *Library of American Civilization,* on ultrafiche, includes thousands of books, periodicals, and other items published before World War I; the *Library of English Literature,* another ultrafiche collection, includes both major and minor literary works dating from the Anglo-Saxon period to 1900. Many college libraries also have special collections of books from the libraries of alumni and other friends of the college. The materials in these collections, like those in the microform collections just mentioned, may not be fully represented in the library catalogue, but librarians can identify the special reference tools needed to gain access to them.

One other source of bibliographic citations should not be overlooked: the primary text itself. Many modern editions of literary works include brief, helpful bibliographies, usually found at the end of the volume. And as the researcher begins to work with secondary sources, it is important to watch for further bibliographic information in the books and articles read—what sources did the authors of these books and articles consult? Checking the bibliographies and notes in secondary sources often leads to some additional works directly relevant to the topic.

## Other Reference Tools—Electronic

At most college libraries, it is now possible to do electronic searches of various on-line resources such as DIALOG. Some of these resources are relatively inexpensive and available to all users of the library; for others, one may need special clearance or be asked to pay a fee. Reference librarians can provide further information about a particular library's resources and policies.

Researchers who have access to the Internet or the World Wide Web will find that they have still more resources at their command. Through the Internet, one can search the catalogues of most of the major libraries in the world. The Internet and Bitnet also give researchers access to a growing number of electronic mail discussion groups (listservs) that focus on particular genres, periods, authors, or topics. To list only a few examples, as of this writing there are listservs devoted to discussions of Chicano literature, of Jane Austen, of literature and science, of the electronic journal *Postmodern Culture,* of Mark Twain, of children's literature, and of more general topics such as American literature. Many of these listservs have well-known scholars among their participants, and many of these scholars are willing to respond to specific, well-focused questions—but not, of course, to provide complete bibliographies or to do other researchers' homework for them. Electronic journals such as *Postmodern Culture* and *RIF/T* offer reviews, commentaries, and often original poetry and fiction as well. Texts of literary works, conference proceedings, and other documents are available through such resources as Online Book Initiative and Alex. Librarians can help researchers find the electronic addresses for these resources.

## Examining and Evaluating Reference Materials

How do researchers know when they have consulted a sufficient number of bibliographies and other sources, and can be confident that they have found the titles of all the works relevant to their topics? Ideally, one should check every bibliography and other source that might possibly list a work that should be read; but perhaps it is better not to speculate about how often that ideal is met. At any rate, the researcher can be sure of being reasonably thorough only by evaluating every bibliography and other reference tool used. Taking a few moments for a preliminary evaluation of a reference tool can ultimately save the researcher a great deal of time and frustration. For example, it is crucial that the researcher notice the date of any print bibliography used and read the preface to notice when its coverage begins and ends. Generally, a print bibliography's coverage ends two or three years before it is published; to find more recent works, the researcher would need to consult other sources such as serial bibliographies. And when using a source such as the *Goldentree* bibliography on Milton, the researcher should read the preface and notice that this bibliography emphasizes scholarship published in the twentieth century; if also interested in earlier scholarship on Milton, the researcher must look elsewhere.

When reading a bibliography's preface, the researcher also pays close attention to any statements about the volume's limits and purposes. Is it exhaustive or selective? That is, does it attempt to list all the works published about an author or topic or only those works the compiler considers best or most important? Does it list only certain kinds of materials? Does it, for example, list only books and articles, or does it also include book reviews and dissertations? How many journals does it survey? The researcher also looks for information about the organization of the bibliography. When working with the bibliography to *Literary History of the United States,* for example, the researcher should know that the fourth edition consists of a bibliography and two supplements, all bound together, and that consequently one may have to check in two or three places to find all the listings on a particular author. It is more difficult, but just as important, to try to detect biases or inadequacies in a bibliography. It is helpful to know, for example, that *The Year's Work in English Studies,* published in England, stresses work by British scholars and sometimes neglects important work done by Americans. Ideally, the researcher should read reviews of all bibliographies used; when time constraints make such thoroughness impossible, asking librarians and professors for their opinions is a good shortcut. Reading the section called "On the Use of Scholarly Tools" in *Selective Bibliography for the Study of English and American Literature* is also helpful; here, Altick and Wright give more extensive advice about evaluating reference tools and, in the course of doing so, make some helpful comments about a number of bibliographies.

## LOCATING SECONDARY MATERIALS

The final stage of a library search can be either the easiest or the most frustrating. After working with literary histories, bibliographies, and other reference tools, the researcher will probably have built up quite a stack of index cards and accumulated several long computer printouts, all identifying works that seem relevant to the topic. When time permits, the researcher may try to locate and skim each of these works, for there is no other way of being completely sure of a work's quality or of the contribution it might make to the paper. When time is limited, however, and the stack of index cards seems huge and the computer printouts endless, the researcher must do some tentative sorting, looking for the titles that seem most relevant to the topic and the works that seem most likely to yield important information and insights.

Finding books and articles in the library is relatively easy. To find books, the researcher consults the library catalogue. Almost all college libraries now have computer catalogues that will not only list a book's call number but also indicate whether or not it is currently on the shelves. To find articles in periodicals, the researcher uses the library's serial record. In most libraries, the serial record is some sort of computer list of all the periodicals the library owns.

Problems arise when the library does not own the books and periodicals needed. With alarming suddenness, a thick stack of cards and a long list of sources can dwindle to a pitiful few as the researcher looks for titles in the library catalogue and the serial record, only to be continually disappointed. Discouragement is inevitable at such times, but despair is premature. The local public library may possibly have some of the materials needed, and nearby college libraries usually let a visiting student use their books and periodicals while on their premises. Further, almost all college libraries have some system that allows students to borrow books from other libraries; many libraries, for example, belong to associations that extend borrowing privileges to students from all member colleges. Although the researcher's task has become more complicated, it is by no means hopeless.

To obtain books from other libraries, the researcher should first talk to a reference librarian or, if the library has one, an interlibrary loan librarian. How can the researcher determine which other libraries have the materials needed? More than two thousand college libraries, for example, belong to the Online Computer Library Center (OCLC), which provides a computer catalogue of millions of books, periodicals, and other materials available at member libraries. After learning where to find the materials needed, the researcher decides on the best way of obtaining them. Basically, the researcher can either visit the library that has the materials wanted or, if time permits, arrange an interlibrary loan. If it is at all possible, visiting the library is preferable in several ways. It is quicker: It may take several days or several weeks to receive material through an interlibrary loan. It is also less expensive: Students may be charged for an interlibrary loan, and both the student's library and the library lending the material will spend money on postage, on paying the people who process the request, and possibly on photocopying. And it is surer: Until seeing the material, the researcher cannot be certain that it will actually be helpful, and it seems a shame to put two libraries to the trouble and expense of an interlibrary loan for material that will not be used. If the researcher does decide to ask for an interlibrary loan, it should be done without delay. These loans can take quite a while to complete, and few experiences are more frustrating than receiving materials the day after turning in a paper. By cooperating with the library's staff, the researcher should soon be able to obtain all or most of the materials needed. The library search is then complete.

## Evaluating Secondary Sources

The task of evaluating the works located still lies ahead. In many ways, research has become quicker and easier in recent years; evaluation, however, remains time-consuming and difficult. Ann Smith, chief reference librarian at Augustana College's library, offers this reminder:

> It is important to realize that research, even now, still takes time and is still a very personal process. If anything, all the electronic tools now available make research an even more difficult task, placing even greater demands on the researcher's judgment. Not so long ago, finding sources was the greatest challenge the researcher faced, and for most sorts of papers the researcher could not reasonably be expected to go very far beyond the books and periodicals held by his or her own library. Now, electronic tools and interlibrary loan make it easy for one to identify and gain access to a vast number of sources—far more than one can actually use. Now, the researcher can spend less time finding sources but must spend far more time evaluating them. Which sources should actually be pursued and used, and which can safely be set aside? Electronic resources force the researcher to work and think harder, in a different way. Making careful individual judgments about the relative importance of the hundreds of resources available has become the researcher's most crucial responsibility. (Personal interview. 21 March 1995.)

As they read secondary sources, researchers constantly measure the books and articles they read against their own ideas, deciding which views deserve to be incorporated into their papers and whether or not their original ideas should be modified in light of what they have read. Researchers are very much on their own when making such decisions; no computer can do it for them.

A researcher may well find, for example, that some books and articles offer conflicting views of a work, author, or period, and may yearn for a simple way to determine which view is authoritative. Some quick research about secondary sources may help. If uncertain about the value of a scholarly book, the researcher might use the book review and biographical indices described on pages 150–151 to find out something about how the book was received and about the author's credentials. When reading a journal article, it is often helpful to check the letters in the next issue of the journal to see how readers responded to the article. Although such information is often helpful, however, it is never conclusive. A mediocre book may be praised by reviewers, and an excellent one attacked or neglected—there is no reason to assume that reviewers' opinions are more reliable than authors' opinions—and a distinguished scholar may write an undistinguished article far inferior to one written by someone who is not prominent enough to be listed in any biographical index. Nor should the researcher attach a great deal of weight to the reputation of the institution with which an author is affiliated or the journal in which the article is published, for an article written by a Harvard professor and published in *PMLA* may prove less valuable than one with much humbler origins. Ultimately, nothing can take the place of the researcher's own careful reading of a work and independent judgment of its merits.

While reading, researchers evaluate not only the secondary sources found but also the ideas with which the researchers began, trying to be open-minded but not overwhelmed. Research has little value for those who go to the library with opinions so fixed and inflexible that they ignore any evidence that might undermine their theses and automatically discount any authors who disagree with their conclusions. On the other hand, those who are easily awed by what they read may encounter different problems: They may surrender too quickly to opposing arguments, lose track of their own theses, and end up writing not a research paper but an anthology of other people's views. Researchers gain most by trying to consider everything they read both seriously and skeptically, keeping their original ideas in mind and thinking about the ways in which the new information, opinions, and perspectives they are encountering might add to their understanding. A researcher's thesis may well be transformed by research, but it should not be lost altogether. A researcher whose ideas are completely unscathed by research is probably being too stubborn and narrow; a researcher whose ideas change radically with every book or article read is probably being too compliant.

A frequent and unsettling experience during research is the discovery of a book or article that seems to make exactly the argument one plans to make oneself. Finding such a work sometimes tempts researchers to abandon all their ideas as hopelessly unoriginal and to begin a last-minute search for a completely new topic. Such a desperate response is seldom necessary. A calm, critical rereading of the book or article will probably reveal something that is truly original about the researcher's own ideas or perspective; at the least, the researcher will almost certainly find some points that could be developed more fully. Few if any articles or books are so perfect that they cannot be improved on in any way, and few if any views of a literary work are so searching and comprehensive that nothing can be added. If reading a book or article that seems to preempt much of what one wanted to say leads to reexamining insights, to drawing subtler distinctions, or to seeking the further implications of a thesis, so much the better. An independent and flexible thinker is in no danger of being drowned by research.

Completing a literary research project is a significant and satisfying accomplishment. Although it is natural to feel daunted by the magnitude and complexity of the task at first, even one successful search is usually enough to make a researcher feel much more at home in the library and much more familiar with a number of reference tools. And a researcher who has indeed located the material most relevant to a topic can feel more confident about being able to write a well-informed paper and more hopeful about making a truly original contribution to the study of literature. When undertaken in the proper spirit, research is perhaps the most independent and illuminating way of teaching oneself about a work of literature. One is no longer limited only to one's own ideas or only to the ideas the professor presents in class; rather, one is invited to enter into a dialogue with all the other thinkers who have written about the work being studied. One is challenged to see the literary work from various points of view, to reexamine and refine one's own ideas. Research is thus an invaluable part of the creative process of criticism.

# *Appendix A*

# LITERARY RESEARCH:
# SOME BASIC RESOURCES

## WORKS ON LITERARY RESEARCH

Altick, Richard D. *The Art of Literary Research*. Rev. John J. Fenstermaker. 4th ed. New York: Norton, 1992.

Altick's highly readable and often inspiring book is an extremely helpful guide to research. The opening chapters discuss the spirit, pleasures, and varieties of scholarship; later chapters guide the aspiring researcher through the steps of choosing a topic, finding materials, making notes, and composing the paper.

———. *The Scholar Adventurers*. Columbus: Ohio State UP, 1987.

*The Scholar Adventurers* complements *The Art of Literary Research;* here Altick chronicles the labors and discoveries of a number of modern literary researchers. He reveals the fascinations of literary research by reporting the exploits of such scholars as those who discovered Boswell's "lost" papers and those who untangled the facts from the legends about Marlowe's death. Reading a few chapters would be instructive and encouraging for someone about to undertake a project in literary research.

Baker, Nancy L. *Research Guide for Undergraduate Students: English and American Literature*. 3rd ed. New York: MLA, 1989.

Baker introduces the reader to almost a hundred reference tools, stressing approximately thirty that are especially likely to be helpful to the undergraduate student and also explains basic research strategy. Pages from a number of reference books are reproduced so that the reader can follow Baker's explanations more easily.

Bateson, F. W., and Harrison T. Meserole. *A Guide to English and American Literature*. 3rd ed. New York: Longman, 1976.

This work is both bibliography and a literary history. It combines both elements through chapters of five major periods of English literature (medieval, Renaissance, Augustan, Romantic, and modern) and "interchapters" listing works that people wishing to investigate a period should consult. Also helpful are the chapters on general works on English literature, American literature, and literary scholarship.

Doyle, Paul A. *Guide to Basic Information Sources in English Literature.* New York: Wiley, 1976.

> Doyle provides brief, helpful descriptions of many important works in literary research: general, specialized, and serial bibliographies; guides to book reviews and biographical information; literary histories; style manuals; some journals; and a number of other sorts of works. Although Doyle concentrates on English and American literature, he does also provide some information about reference works to Irish, Australian, and Canadian literature.

Kehler, Dorothea. *Problems in Literary Research: A Guide to Selected Reference Works.* 3rd ed. Metuchen: Scarecrow, 1987.

> Both a reference guide and a text book, *Problems in Literary Research* identifies a number of reference works researchers will find extremely helpful; Kehler starts with a basic core of eight essential works and gradually builds to a list of 36 main works and 161 supplementary ones. Her book is designed primarily for classroom use, but someone working independently would certainly benefit from the descriptions of reference works and should have no trouble finding a librarian or professor happy to help with the exercises.

Patterson, Margaret C. *Literary Research Guide.* 2nd ed. New York: MLA, 1983.

> Patterson describes her work as an "evaluative, annotated bibliography of important reference books and periodicals on American and English literature, of the most useful sources for research in other national literatures, and of more than 300 reference books in literature-related areas." She covers some areas most of the other works listed here do not—for example, Irish, Scottish, Welsh, Commonwealth, continental, comparative, and world literature. Also, in the reference section near the end of the book Patterson lists works helpful to researchers in such areas as film, paleography, and interdisciplinary studies; she also answers questions about everything from tracking down a quotation to tracking down a former professor's new address.

Sheehy, Eugene P. *Guide to Reference Books.* 10th ed. Chicago: ALA, 1986.

> Sheehy lists and briefly describes reference books in many fields. In literature, he covers such works as dictionaries, handbooks, biographies, and bibliographies. This book might be especially helpful to those who are working on interdisciplinary topics and need to find reference works in such fields as history, psychology, and sociology. A supplement is now available.

## LITERARY HISTORIES: GENERAL

Baugh, Albert C., et al. *A Literary History of England.* 2nd ed. New York: Appleton, 1967.

> This one-volume history covers English literature from its beginnings to "the nineteenth century and after" (1939). Chapters are devoted to genres, to literary trends and movements, and to major figures. The essays provide background information;

footnotes identify standard editions, biographies, and some important critical works. It is important to check the Bibliographical Supplement at the back of the book for additional listings.

Daiches, David. *A Critical History of English Literature.* New York: Ronald, 1970.

This is the most serious one-person attempt at a comprehensive history of English literature. Daiches says his work "is not meant to be looked up, but to be read"; it is indeed readable and offers criticism as well as history.

Spiller, Robert E., et al. *A Literary History of the United States.* 4th ed., revised. New York: Macmillan, 1974.

This valuable work consists of two volumes, a history and a bibliography; the bibliography is described on page 161. The history contains essays on periods, genres, movements, and some major figures, tracing American literature from colonial times to the middle of the twentieth century.

Wilson, F. P., and B. Dobree, eds. *The Oxford History of English Literature.* Oxford: Clarendon, 1945-   .

Fifteen volumes have been published so far. Each volume covers a particular period (e.g., *English Literature at the Close of the Middle Ages; English Literature 1789-1815*) and is written by a scholar with expertise in that field. Many reviewers have said that the volumes vary greatly in quality: Some, for example, think that C. S. Lewis's volume on the sixteenth century is the most perceptive and original, whereas others find Douglas Bush's volume on the early seventeenth century much more substantial. Many volumes contain helpful bibliographies.

## LITERARY HISTORIES: SPECIALIZED

Many valuable literary histories focus on a particular period, genre, or topic. Altick and Wright list many of these literary histories in the chapters titled "English Literature" and "American Literature" in *Selective Bibliography for the Study of English and American Literature.*

## BIBLIOGRAPHIES OF BIBLIOGRAPHIES

Altick, Richard D., and Andrew Wright. *Selective Bibliography for the Study of English and American Literature.* 6th ed. New York: Macmillan, 1979.

This convenient guide lists bibliographies; literary histories; other aids to historical, critical, and biographical research (e.g., encyclopedias, dictionaries, periodicals, guides to libraries); bibliographical handbooks and guides to research; and a number of books "which every student of literature should not merely refer to, but read." Altick and Wright provide some annotations and a useful introductory section on the use of scholarly tools. Those committed to the study of literature should seriously consider purchasing this invaluable guide.

*Bibliographic Index: A Cumulative Bibliography of Bibliographies.* New York: Wilson, 1937– .

This international index lists by subject bibliographies "published separately or appearing as part of books, pamphlets, and periodicals." Any bibliography containing at least fifty items may be included. This index comes out in April and August and cumulates in December.

Howard-Hill, Trevor H. *Bibliography of British Literary Bibliographies.* 2nd ed. Oxford: Clarendon, 1987.

In the first volume of this work, Howard-Hill records "all publications in English which list the printed works of British writers" from 1475 to the present. Included are general, period, regional, genre, subject, and author bibliographies. The second volumes, *Shakespearean Bibliography and Textual Criticism,* is devoted entirely to Shakespeare, who is accordingly excluded from Volume I.

Nilon, Charles H. *Bibliography of Bibliographies in American Literature.* New York: Bowker, 1970.

Most of this work is devoted to listing author bibliographies. Included are authors from the seventeenth through the twentieth centuries, ranging from Cotton Mather to Gore Vidal. Nilon also lists other bibliographies of American literature and a number of genre bibliographies (literary history and criticism, drama, fiction, and poetry). An ancillary section lists some bibliographies for such areas as children's literature, folklore, Indian language and literature, and music.

## BIBLIOGRAPHIES

Gohdes, Clarence, and Sanford E. Marovitz. *Bibliographical Guide to the Study of the Literature of the U.S.A.* 5th ed., revised and enlarged. Durham: Duke UP, 1984.

This guide offers brief descriptions of selected reference tools, bibliographies, both general and specialized literary histories, critical books and articles, and other sources relevant to the study of American literature and culture. Included are lists of works on such areas as religion, women's studies, theater and film, minorities, the American language, and folklore. Although this guide is intended primarily for teachers, librarians, and graduate students, undergraduates may also find it helpful.

*Goldentree Bibliographies in Language and Literature.* New York: Appleton, 1966– .

More than twenty of these selective bibliographies have appeared so far, focusing on topics such as *Chaucer, The British Novel through Jane Austen, Afro-American Writers,* and *Literary Criticism: Plato through Johnson.* These bibliographies, especially designed for graduate and advanced undergraduate students, are not exhaustive, but they attempt to give a balanced, representative listing of texts, more exhaustive bibliographies, and important criticism and scholarship. The *Goldentree Bibliographies* emphasize scholarship and criticism published in the twentieth century.

Leary, Lewis. *American Literature: A Study and Research Guide*. New York: St. Martin's, 1976.

This volume contains bibliographical essays on genres and major writers; lists literary histories and important periodicals; and contains chapters on such other topics as "Foreign Influences and Influences Abroad," "Types and Schools of Criticism," and "The Research Paper."

————. *Articles on American Literature, 1900-1950*. Durham: Duke U, 1954.

Leary has compiled "a listing of articles on America written in English and appearing in periodicals from 1900 through 1950." He defines "articles" broadly enough to include some reviews and review articles. Most of the volume is devoted to bibliographies on individual authors, arranged alphabetically; other sections list articles in such areas as bibliography, humor, literary criticism, regionalism, and religion. Leary has since published two similar works: *Articles on American Literature, 1950-1967,* prepared with the assistance of Carolyn Bartholet and Catharine Roth, which appeared in 1970; and *Articles on American Literature, 1968-1975,* prepared with the assistance of John Auchard, which appeared in 1979. All three works are published by Duke University Press and are similar in organization and scope. Some different areas are covered.

Ljungquist, Kent P., and Judith S. Baughman. *Bibliography of American Fiction through 1865; Bibliography of American Fiction, 1866-1918; Bibliography of American Fiction, 1919-1988*. New York: Facts on File, 1990-1993.

These three volumes list writings by and about American writers, including primary works, concordances, biographies, critical studies, and bibliographies. The listings are selective: The editors, contrasting their volumes with the long list of unevaluated sources one can obtain from computer searches, point out that the entries in these bibliographies "are compiled by scholar-specialists who have read the works they select and include them because of their significance."

Spiller, Robert E., et al. *A Literary History of the United States*. 4th ed., revised. New York: Macmillan, 1974.

The bibliography volume to this work provides selective listings on periods, genres, movements, and major authors and can help the researcher to find information about texts, editions, biographies, histories, and critical works. The organization is somewhat confusing: The fourth edition consists of a bibliography and two supplements, all bound together, so one may have to check in two or three places to find all the listings on a particular topic.

Watson, George, et al. *The New Cambridge Bibliography of English Literature*. 5 vols. Cambridge: Cambridge UP, 1969-1977.

This revision of Bateson's *Cambridge Bibliography of English Literature* lists specialized bibliographies, texts and editions of original works, collections of letters, biographies, literary histories, critical books and articles, and other secondary materials. It does not list unpublished dissertations, encyclopedia articles, reviews, and "ephemeral journalism." The bibliography consists of four volumes (600–1660, 1660–1800, 1800–1900, 1900–1950) and an index.

Bateson's *Cambridge Bibliography of English Literature* is still occasionally useful, particularly because it includes some sections that Watson decided to leave out (e.g., Political and Social Background, Classical and Oriental Scholarship).

## SERIAL BIBLIOGRAPHIES

*Annual Bibliography of English Language and Literature.* Cambridge: Modern Humanities, 1920–  .

This bibliography lists books, pamphlets, reviews, dissertations, and periodical articles written in English and published in Great Britain, the United States, and more than twenty other countries. It is similar to the *MLA Bibliography,* but its organization is less complicated. Although the *ABELL* is generally less comprehensive than the *MLA*, it does list some works the *MLA* does not (notably book reviews); it is worthwhile to check both sources if one is engaged in an ambitious research project.

*Essay and General Literature Index.* New York: Wilson, 1934–  .

This index, which comes out annually, is useful for finding articles and essays printed in books (not periodicals). In addition to literature and literary criticism, this index surveys many other subjects in the humanities and social sciences.

*Humanities Index.* New York: Wilson, 1974–  .

This index surveys English-language periodicals and includes many author and subject entries. It covers not only literature but also such fields as archaeology and classical studies, history, performing arts, philosophy, and religion. For earlier years, one can consult the *Social Sciences and Humanities Index* (1965–1974) and the *International Index to Periodicals* (1907–1965).

*Modern Language Association International Bibliography of Books and Articles on the Modern Languages and Literatures.* New York: MLA, 1921–  .

The *MLA Bibliography,* the most comprehensive serial bibliography of research in literature and linguistics, lists books, articles in periodicals and anthologies, and dissertations. Before 1956, it listed only works by American scholars; since then, it has been international. There is a fuller description of the *MLA Bibliography* in Chapter 5.

Woodress, James L. *American Literary Scholarship.* Durham: Duke UP, 1955–  .

This bibliography is similar to *The Year's Work in English Studies* except, of course, that it deals with American rather than English literature. It contains bibliographical essays on periods, genres, and some major figures, commenting on editions, biographies, and major critical works.

*The Year's Work in English Studies.* London: English Assn., 1919–    .

> This work contains bibliographical essays on scholarship in English and, to a much lesser extent, American literature. It is not nearly as comprehensive as the *MLA Bibliography,* but it is a convenient way to find major books and articles published in a particular year, and it can help the researcher spot critical trends.

## OTHER HELPFUL BOOKS

Abrams, M. H. *A Glossary of Literary Terms.* 6th ed. New York: Harcourt, 1993.

> This is a convenient, inexpensive guide to important terms used in literary criticism, from *aestheticism* to *epiphany* to *New Criticism* to *wit.* Abrams's book is not nearly as exhaustive as Holman's, but his selection of terms is excellent, his explanations are perceptive and often fairly detailed, and he refers the reader to other works that treat the subject more fully. For example, after an explanation of "meter," Abrams lists about a dozen books and articles on prosody. A section called "Modern Theories of Literature and Criticism" contains brief essays describing "the innovative critical views and procedures of the last half-century," such as archetypal criticism, feminist criticism, and structuralism.

Buck, Claire, ed. *The Bloomsbury Guide to Women's Literature.* New York: Prentice, 1992.

> This guide attempts to introduce readers to "the true global and historical dimensions" of women's literature. More than thirty short essays are devoted to the women's literature of various countries and periods; the rest of the volume is devoted to bibliographical listings.

Davidson, Cathy N., and Linda Wagner-Martin, eds. *The Oxford Companion to Women's Writing in the United States.* New York: Oxford UP, 1995.

> The editors describe their work as an attempt to "redefine U.S. literary history from a diversity of female and feminist perspectives by questioning traditional literary historiography: categories, genres, theories, periods, and canons." Entries and short essays focus on authors, periods, genres, themes, and issues, as well as topics such as sexual harassment and birth control.

Drabble, Margaret, ed. *Oxford Companion to English Literature.* 6th ed. New York: Oxford UP, 1987.

> This volume contains entries on English authors, literary works, and literary societies. It is an extremely useful tool when one needs to identify a character, find a publication date, or do other sorts of quick research.

Gibaldi, Joseph. *MLA Handbook for Writers of Research Papers.* 4th ed. New York: MLA, 1995.

> This handbook contains some information on the earlier stages of research—using the library, taking notes, and so forth—but becomes indispensable when one is

ready to document sources, compile the list of works cited, and prepare the manuscript. The *MLA Handbook* is the accepted authority on such matters in English departments and in scholarly journals in the humanities.

Hart, James D. *Oxford Companion to American Literature.* 5th ed. New York: Oxford UP, 1983.

This volume contains brief biographies and bibliographies on American authors; summaries of more than one thousand literary works; and entries on such subjects as literary movements, scholarly organizations, and printers. An abridged version of this work, called *The Concise Oxford Companion to American Literature,* came out in 1986.

Holman, C. Hugh, and William Harmon. *A Handbook to Literature.* 6th ed. New York: Macmillan, 1991.

Holman and Harmon explain more than thirteen hundred words and phrases one might encounter while studying English and American literature—e.g., terms associated with literary criticism, literary movements, and some common allusions. The explanations are brief, but can be helpful for quick reference or as a starting point for more thorough investigation. Unlike the Oxford and Cambridge companions, this handbook does not list names of authors, works, or characters.

Magill, Frank. *Critical Survey of Long Fiction.* 8 vols. Englewood Cliffs: Salem, 1983.

This series covers 272 authors of novels and novellas, providing a critical assessment of and limited bibliographical listings for each. Also included are twenty essays on the novel, the short story, and classifications such as the Gothic novel and the realistic novel.

———. *Critical Survey of Short Fiction.* 7 vols. Englewood Cliffs: Salem, 1981.

The first two volumes in this series contain essays that offer critical and historical commentaries on the short story. The other five volumes provide essays on 261 writers "who contributed to the genre or who exerted an inescapable influence" on it.

Simpson, J. A., and Edmund S. Weiner. *Oxford English Dictionary (New English Dictionary).* 2nd ed. Oxford: Clarendon, 1989.

The *OED* is unquestionably the most authoritative and exhaustive dictionary of the English language. It is of special interest to students of literature because it attempts, to quote the preface to the first volume, "to furnish an adequate account of the meaning, origin, and history of English words now in general use, or known to have been in use at any time during the last 700 years." It provides a very convenient way of finding out how words and their meanings have changed over the centuries. Perhaps the most distinctive feature of the *OED* is its practice of supplying quotations to show these changes.

Stapleton, Michael. *Cambridge Guide to English Literature*. New York: Cambridge UP, 1983.

> Stapleton defines "English literature" as "the literature of the English-speaking world" and thus includes entries not only on British literature but also on the literature of the United States, Canada, Australia, New Zealand, South Africa, the West Indies, and Nigeria. He briefly describes works, authors, characters, and "relevant historical events" from earliest times to the present and also defines such basic literary terms as "sonnet." Believing that "a guide who never makes a comment makes a dull companion," Stapleton often offers his opinions of the works and authors he discusses. His guide is all the livelier and more readable as a result.

## JOURNALS

Each year, the opening pages of the *MLA Bibliography* include an alphabetical list of periodicals that publish articles relevant to the study of literature. Further information about these periodicals can be found in the *MLA Directory of Periodicals: A Guide to Journals and Series in Languages and Literatures,* compiled by Kathleen L. Kent. This biannual guide is available in two versions: a clothbound volume, covering all of the more than three thousand periodicals on the *MLA Bibliography*'s master list; and a paperbound volume, limited to about one thousand periodicals published in the United States and Canada. Both versions of the *Guide* include basic information about such matters as the periodical's address, sponsoring organization, and frequency of publication as well as a brief description of the sorts of articles it includes.

The following list of journals is obviously not comprehensive. Nor does it attempt to identify the most important or most highly regarded journals. It is intended only to offer the student a preliminary sense of the various sorts of journals that might be consulted during a research project. Journals range in scope from the *PMLA*, which publishes articles about literature written in any of the modern languages, to journals focusing on a particular period, genre, or author. Some journals have come to be associated with certain critical approaches—*Critical Inquiry,* for example, often includes psychological, structuralist, and deconstructionist studies. Several of the journals listed here are interdisciplinary: For example, the *Afro-Hispanic Review* publishes articles on sociological and anthropological issues, original poetry, translations, and book reviews, as well as works of literary criticism. A few hours of browsing in the current issues section of a college library is probably the most efficient and pleasant way of becoming better acquainted with the orientations of these and other journals.

*Afro-Hispanic Review.* (1982–   )

*Amerasia Journal.* (1971–   )

*American Literary Realism, 1870–1910.* (1967–   )

*American Literature.* (1929/30–   )

*Biography.* (1978–   ).

*Black American Literature Forum.* (1969/70–   )

*The Chaucer Review: A Journal of Medieval Studies and Literary Criticism.* (1966–   )

*Critical Inquiry.* (1974/75–   )

*Criticism.* (1959–   )

*Diacritics.* (1971–   )

*English Language Notes.* (1963–   )

*Feminist Review.* (1979–   )

*Keats-Shelley Journal.* (1952–   )

*Melus: The Journal of the Society for the Study of Multi-Ethnic Literature in the United States.* (1968–   )

*New Literary History: A Journal of Theory and Interpretation.* (1969–   )

*Novel: A Forum on Fiction.* (1967–   )

*Philological Quarterly.* (1922–   )

*PMLA: Publications of the Modern Language Association of America.* (1884/85–   )

*Representations.* (1983–   )

*Shakespeare Quarterly.* (1950–   )

*Signs: Journal of Women in Culture and Society.* (1975/76–   )

*Twentieth Century Literature: A Scholarly and Critical Journal.* (1955)

# *Appendix B*

# SOME ADVICE ON FORM

## QUOTATIONS

Using quotations in a paper about literature may seem as simple as it is inevitable. In fact, however, using quotations well is a delicate and often difficult business, and using them poorly is one of the surest ways of seriously damaging a paper. Far more than technical correctness is at stake: Although clumsily handled quotations can indeed fill a paper with dozens of annoying mechanical errors, they can also harm a paper in larger, more substantial ways. If quotations are not selected carefully and explained adequately, they can weaken a paper's argument by distracting, confusing, or simply failing to persuade readers; if they are not introduced gracefully, they can make a paper almost unbearably awkward. The use of quotations is thus an important element of the art of writing papers about literature, requiring careful consideration of content and style as well as close attention to mechanics. It is an element that challenges both the beginning writer and the experienced one.

### Selecting Quotations

Use quotations when they will support or clarify an argument. Do not pad papers with unnecessary quotations: Resist the temptation to use quotations simply to add to the beauty of a paper, to show the extent of your research, or to summarize something you do not intend to analyze. Also, keep quotations short; often, quoting a sentence will do as well as quoting a paragraph, and quoting a phrase or a word will do as well as quoting an entire sentence. In the following passage, the quotation is much longer than it needs to be:

> In Hawthorne's "The Gentle Boy," public intolerance makes
> individuals bigoted and cruel. Even the children are affected. In one
> scene, "the children of the neighborhood had assembled in the little
> forest-crowned amphitheater behind the meeting house. . . . But it
> happened that an unexpected addition was made to the heavenly
> little band. It was Ibrahim, who came towards the children. . . . In

an instant, he was the center of a brood of baby-fiends, who lifted

sticks against him, pelted him with stones, and displayed an instinct

of destruction, far more loathsome than the bloodthirstiness of

manhood" (904). The children are imitating their parents when they

persecute this Quaker child.

Unless the writer intends to analyze this scene closely, relating the entire incident can only slow down the paper and distract the reader. The writer should reexamine the quotation, looking for phrases that will quickly and vividly make clear the effects of public intolerance:

In Hawthorne's "The Gentle Boy," public intolerance makes

individuals bigoted and cruel. Even the children are affected: In one

scene, a group of children is transformed from a "heavenly little

band" into "a brood of baby-fiends" when they see a chance to

imitate their parents by persecuting a Quaker child (904).

Here, paring down the quotation helps the reader to focus on the writer's central point.

## Commenting on Quotations

Quotations should be accompanied by explanations that show how they are relevant to the point being made. If such explanations are lacking, the reader may be confused or skeptical:

Although the speaker in Marvell's "To His Coy Mistress" speaks of

death, his manner and tone indicate that he is not frightened or

desperate himself and is not trying to frighten the lady: "The

grave's a fine and private place, / But none, I think, do there

embrace." He reminds her of mortality to emphasize the folly of

infinite delay, but he does not try to terrify her into submission.

Although the relationship between the assertion and the quotation may seem self-evident to the writer of this paper, the reader may need some commentary in order to be convinced:

Although the speaker in Marvell's "To His Coy Mistress" speaks of

death, his manner and tone indicate that he is not frightened or desperate himself and is not trying to frighten the lady: "The grave's a fine and private place, / But none, I think, do there embrace." The ironic understatement of the speaker's description of the grave and the silliness of his pretended uncertainty about embracing seem designed to amuse the lady, to temper unpleasant facts with wit. He reminds her of mortality to emphasize the folly of infinite delay, but he does not try to terrify her into submission.

Here a single sentence does a great deal to help the reader understand the writer's assertion about Marvell's manner and tone, making the relationship between assertion and quotation clear.

Similarly, quotations from critics must be explained and supported. Do not assume that readers will accept a critic's pronouncements without question; the mere fact that a critic has made a statement proves nothing. An argument has a weak foundation when it is built on critical judgments presented as facts:

As Dorothy Van Ghent points out, Fielding's conception of comedy calls not for "self-discovery" but for "a various ornament of 'self-exposures' on the part of many men" (86). In Austen's novels, however, self-discovery is far more important, and comic complications are resolved as the heroine comes to a gradual awareness of her own character and emotions.

Many readers will not accept the comparison with Austen unless they see the basis of Van Ghent's statement about Fielding:

As Dorothy Van Ghent points out, Fielding's conception of comedy calls not for "self-discovery" but for "a various ornament of 'self-exposures' on the part of many men" (86). Tom is discovered in the bushes with Molly, and Square is found in Molly's closet; Black George is exposed as a thief, Thwackum as a hypocrite, and Blifil as a villain. In Austen's novels, however, self-discovery is far more important, and comic complications are resolved as the heroine comes to a gradual awareness of her own character and emotions.

After quoting a critic, briefly explain the basis of that critic's argument or provide some new supporting evidence of your own. Quotations, from either primary or secondary sources, often provide support for arguments, but they do not take the place of arguments or relieve you of the responsibility of explaining and defending all the assertions you want the reader to accept.

## Integrating Quotations into a Text

When introducing quotations into your text, avoid wordy and overly obtrusive formulas:

> Just as Andrea fails to make a convincing defense of his art, he fails to win Lucrezia's love—or even her attention. Robert Langbaum explains the reasons for his failure in a passage that reads as follows: "he is talking far too much about himself for successful love-making" (143).

Look for subtler, more concise ways of smoothly integrating quotations into your text:

> Just as Andrea fails to make a convincing defense of this art, he fails to win Lucrezia's love—or even her attention. As Robert Langbaum says, Andrea "is talking far too much about himself for successful love-making" (143).

Phrases such as "as Langbaum says," "according to Langbaum," and "Langbaum notes that" can help introduce quotations without fanfare.

Interrupting one of your own sentences with a long quotation is often awkward and distracting, for the reader may be forced to reread the first half of your sentence in order to understand the second half:

> Gulliver's antipathy for all human beings, best expressed when he declares that "I could not endure my wife or children in my presence; the very smell of them was intolerable, much less could I suffer them to eat in the same room," is so extreme that one must term him mad, especially considering that his family and Don Pedro have treated him kindly and gently.

Here, replacing one convoluted sentence with two shorter ones greatly simplifies the reader's task.:

> Gulliver's antipathy for all human beings is best expressed when he declares that "I could not endure my wife or children in my

presence; the very smell of them was intolerable, much less could I suffer them to eat in the same room." His revulsion is so extreme that one must term him mad, especially considering that his family and Don Pedro have treated him kindly and gently.

A number of small changes such as this one can greatly enhance the clarity and grace of a paper.

## Spacing and Punctuating Quotations

Various conventions govern the spacing and punctuating of quotations:

1. *Short direct quotations:* Short quotations, whether of verse or of prose, are enclosed in double quotation marks and incorporated into the text:

   In "The Vanity of Human Wishes," Johnson declares that the poor traveler "walks the wild heath, and sings his toil away."

   In Idler 73, Johnson seems almost to praise the pursuit of wealth, since it temporarily "secures us from weariness of ourselves."

   When quoting two or three lines of verse, incorporate them into the text but separate them with a slash, leaving a space on each side of the slash:

   In "The Vanity of Human Wishes," Johnson declares that "the needy traveller, serene and gay, / Walks the wild heath, and sings his toil away."

2. *Longer direct quotations:* Longer quotations—more than three lines of verse or four lines of prose—are separated from the text and indented. Do not enclose indented quotations in quotation marks. Do not single-space indented quotations: Double-space them, leaving an extra line of space before and after the quotation.
   a. For *long verse quotations,* indent ten spaces from the left margin and reproduce the punctuation, spacing, and indentation of the lines accurately:

      While not exaggerating Levet's good qualities, Johnson insists upon their importance:

His virtues walk'd their narrow round,

Nor made a pause, nor left a void;

And sure th' Eternal Master found

The single talent well employ'd.

In this passage, as in many others, Johnson's praise for Levet is both ardent and measured.

**b.** For *long prose quotations,* indent ten spaces from the left margin. Do not center the quotation by indenting from the right margin as well:

Johnson's conclusion that wealth cannot buy happiness is hardly original, but his reasons for finding wealth insufficient—and his manner of stating his reasons—are worth noting:

Of riches, as of everything else, the hope is more than the enjoyment; while we consider them as the means to be used, at some future time, for the attainment of felicity, we press on our pursuit ardently and vigorously, and that ardor secures us from the weariness of ourselves; but no sooner do we sit down to enjoy our acquisitions, than we find them insufficient to fill up the vacuities of life.

Almost casually, Johnson extends his statement about riches to include all human desires, maintaining that everything we wish for and obtain will disappoint us.

**3.** *Quotations within quotations:* Enclose quotations within quotations in single quotation marks.

W. J. Bate sees Johnson as a fierce advocate for free will and reason: "The 'laying open' and 'confuting' of all determinism . . . is carried through every aspect of Johnson's writing on human life, on literature, and on everything else. . . ." (145).

In a longer, indented quotation (not enclosed in double quotation marks) a quotation within a quotation is enclosed in double, not single, quotation marks.

**4.** *Introducing quotations:* When introducing a quotation with a complete sentence, use a colon before the quotation:

> Friendship, Johnson says in <u>Rambler</u> 160, should be both
>
> pleasant and obtainable: "Every man might . . . find some
>
> kindred mind with which he could unite in confidence and
>
> friendship."

When introducing a quotation with a phrase such as "he says," use a comma before the quotation:

> In <u>Rambler</u> 160 Johnson says, "Every man might . . . find some
>
> kindred mind with which he could unite in confidence and
>
> friendship."

When a phrase such as "he says" is used in the middle of a quotation, the phrase is preceded and followed by commas:

> "Every man," Johnson says in <u>Rambler</u> 160, "might . . . find
>
> some kindred mind with which he could unite in confidence and
>
> friendship."

Often, quotations can be worked into the text without any introductory punctuation:

> But in fact, Johnson says, our inclinations often lead us to
>
> extend friendship to the unworthy and to deny it to the
>
> deserving, with the result that "we see many straggling single
>
> about the world, unhappy for want of an associate, and pining
>
> with the necessity of confining their sentiments to their own
>
> bosoms."

**5.** *Changes in quotations:* Generally speaking, you should copy quotations exactly. In some situations, however, you may make slight changes in a quotation if you mark the changes correctly.

a. If you *leave out* a part of a passage you quote, use an ellipsis (a series of three spaced periods) to show the omission. Be sure not to alter the meaning of the passage by omitting part of it. If you leave out words in the *middle* of a sentence, use three spaced periods to show the omission.

**ORIGINAL**

Affliction is inseparable from our present state; it adheres to all the inhabitants of this world, in different proportions indeed, but with an allotment that seems very little regulated by our own conduct.

**ELLIPSIS IN MIDDLE**

In <u>Adventurer</u> 120, Johnson declares that virtue will not protect us from the troubles all human beings experience: "Affliction . . . adheres to all the inhabitants of this world, in different proportions indeed, but with an allotment that seems very little regulated by our own conduct."

If you leave out words at the *end* of a sentence, use a period immediately after the quotation (i.e., do not leave a space before this period), followed by three spaced periods:

**ELLIPSIS AT END**

In <u>Adventurer</u> 120, Johnson declares that no human being can escape unhappiness: "Affliction is inseparable from our present state; it adheres to all the inhabitants of this world. . . ."

Do not use an ellipsis at the beginning of a quotation, even if you have omitted the opening words of a sentence:

Johnson considers unhappiness "inseparable from our present state."

**b.** If you have to *change or add* a word for the sake of clarity or grammatical consistency, use square brackets (*not* parentheses) to indicate the change:

**ORIGINAL**

His habitual ways of meeting threat or pressure of any kind involve the courage of direct encounter, and the attempt to bring a fuller knowledge to bear.

**QUOTED WITH BRACKETS**

Bate says that "[Johnson's] habitual ways of meeting threat or pressure of any kind involve the courage of direct encounter, and the attempt to bring a fuller knowledge to bear."

Often, you can avoid the need for brackets simply by beginning the quotation at a later point:

Bate says that Johnson's "habitual ways of meeting threat or pressure of any kind involve the courage of direct encounter, and the attempt to bring a fuller knowledge to bear."

**c.** If you want to *emphasize* part of a quotation, underline it and indicate parenthetically that you have done so:

Idler 73 may seem a conventional essay about the unhappiness that often accompanies wealth, but it soon becomes apparent that Johnson is commenting not only on wealth but on all human desires: "Of riches, as of everything else, the hope is more than the enjoyment . . ." (emphasis added).

**6.** *Quotation marks with other punctuation marks:*
   **a.** Commas and periods are always placed *inside* quotation marks, whether or not they are part of the quotation:

Declaring that "wit, as well as valor, must be content to share its honors with fortune," Johnson points to the large role that chance plays in human life.

Pointing to the large role that chance inevitably plays in human life, Johnson declares that "wit, as well as valor, must be content to share its honors with fortune."

**b.** Semicolons and colons are always placed *outside* quotation marks, whether or not they are part of the quotation:

Johnson declares that "wit, as well as valor, must be content to share its honors with fortune"; thus, he points to the large role chance inevitably plays in human life.

**c.** Dashes, question marks, and exclamation points are placed *inside* quotation marks when they are part of the quotation and *outside* when they are not:

Inviting us to examine the history of past ages, Johnson asks, "what do they offer to our meditation but crimes and calamities?"

What, we may ask, is Johnson implying when he declares that "wit, as well as valor, must be content to share its honors with fortune"?

## TITLES

**1.** *Short works:* Titles of short works—essays, short stories, short poems, articles, songs, chapters, and any parts of a longer work—are enclosed in quotation marks. Titles of *unpublished works* are also enclosed in quotation marks, regardless of the work's length:

"A Modest Proposal" (essay)

"Araby" (short story)

"The Satiric Adversary" (article)

"The Second Coming" (poem)

"A Long Day in London" (chapter)

"Three Love Problems" (section of novel)

"Wordsworth's Debt to Milton" (unpublished book-length dissertation)

2. *Long works:* Titles of works long enough to be published separately— books, plays, long poems, movies, and newspapers and other periodicals—are italicized (underlined):

The Warden (book)

Antigone (play)

Paradise Lost (long poem)

All That Jazz (movie)

Chronicle of Higher Education (newspaper)

The Kenyon Review (journal)

3. *Sacred works:* The titles of sacred works are neither enclosed in quotation marks nor underlined; they are simply capitalized.

the Bible

Genesis

the Koran

the Talmud

4. *Your titles:* Your own titles should not be enclosed in quotation marks or underlined. Think of them as titles of sacred works:

An Analysis of Hardy's Early Poetry

5. *Capitalization:* Capitalize the first and last words of a title and all other words except articles, conjunctions, and prepositions (no matter how many letters):

The Jew in the Literature of England

A Portrait of the Artist as a Young Man

"Love among the Ruins"

6. *Titles within titles:* If an underlined title contains a title enclosed in quotation marks, the quotation marks are kept; similarly, if a title in quotation marks contains an underlined title, the underlining is kept:

Milton's "Lycidas": The Tradition and the Poem

"The Buried Letter: Feminism and Romanticism in Villette"

However, if a title enclosed in quotation marks contains another title that would normally be enclosed in quotation marks, the title within the title should be enclosed in single quotation marks:

"Aesthetic-Theological Thoughts on 'The Windhover'"

If an underlined title contains another title that would normally be underlined, the title within the title is not underlined:

Assessing Great Expectations

7. *Shortened titles:* The first time a title is mentioned in a paper, it should be given in full—*Adventures of Huckleberry Finn,* not *Huck Finn.* If the title is used frequently, however, and if the full title is so long as to be cumbersome, a shortened title may be used in later references. Be sure not to shorten a title so much that the reader might not recognize it: *Critics and Criticism* would be an acceptable short title for *Critics and Criticism Ancient and Modern,* but *Critics* might be confused with another title.

8. *Punctuating titles:* Enclose a title in commas *only* if it is being used as a nonrestrictive appositive—that is, only if it could be omitted without changing the sentence's meaning:

Stephen Crane's famous Civil War novel, The Red Badge of Courage, is widely regarded as an early classic of realism.

Since Crane wrote only one famous Civil War novel, the title itself is a nonrestrictive appositive and should be enclosed in commas; even if the title was omitted, the sentence would have to be about *The Red Badge of Courage.*

Stephen Crane's novel The Red Badge of Courage is widely regarded as an early classic of realism.

Since Crane wrote more than one novel, the title is restrictive and should not be enclosed in commas; if the title was omitted in the example just above, "Crane's novel" could refer either to *The Red Badge of Courage* or to *Maggie: A Girl of the Streets.*

9. *Labeling titles:* Do not feel compelled to label every work you mention by identifying its genre. It seems almost silly to refer to "Melville's novel *Moby-Dick*"; how many readers need to be told that *Moby-Dick* is a novel?

## AUTHORS' NAMES

1. *Last names:* Generally, refer to authors and critics by their full names the first time you mention them, unless the author is so famous that using a first name seems unnecessary. Thereafter, refer to authors and critics by their last names. Do not use titles such as *Mr., Dr.,* or *Professor.*

George Orwell's "Shooting an Elephant" shows how imperialism enslaves the oppressor as well as the oppressed. Orwell uses an incident from his own past to illustrate this point.

Some writers refer to Samuel Johnson as "Dr. Johnson" and to Byron as "Lord Byron," but these practices are fading.

2. *Women's names:* When reading criticism, you may occasionally see a woman author or critic referred by her first name or by a title and her last name: For example, Jane Austen becomes "Jane" or Elizabeth Barrett Browning becomes "Mrs. Browning." Most people now recognize such practices as patronizing.

3. *Pseudonyms:* Usually, authors who have made their pseudonyms famous are referred to by those pseudonyms, not by their given names. Thus, most writers will refer to Mark Twain, not Samuel Clemens, and to George Eliot, not Mary Ann Evans; but it would be odd to refer to Emily Brontë as Ellis Bell.

## TENSE

1. *Present tense:* Most writers use the present tense to describe events in poetry, fiction, or drama:

In East of Eden, Adam Trask tries to create a paradise for his wife and is utterly crushed when she proves unworthy.

Most writers also use the present tense to describe the statements authors make in their works:

In The Grapes of Wrath, Steinbeck portrays the suffering of the Okies and condemns the banks and corporations responsible for their misery.

2. *Past tense:* The past tense, however, is used to describe events in an author's life:

Steinbeck <u>wrote</u> <u>The Winter of Our Discontent</u> toward the end of his career.

## FIRST-PERSON PRONOUN

Using the first-person pronoun is becoming more common and acceptable in formal critical writing. Saying "I will argue" certainly seems simpler and more direct than saying "The author will argue" or "This paper will argue." You should not overuse the first-person pronoun, however, by continually prefacing statements with "I think," "I feel," or "It is my belief." If you simply state your opinions, readers will assume they are yours.

## MANUSCRIPT FORM

Professors' requirements for manuscript form vary. If your professors' requirements differ from the guidelines presented here, you should of course follow your professor's directions, not ours.

1. *Paper:* Most professors prefer 8½-by-11-inch white bond paper. Erasable or onionskin paper tends to smudge. If your professor accepts handwritten papers, use full-size, good-quality paper; do not use paper torn out of a spiral notebook. Whether typing or writing, use only one side of the paper.
2. *Typing:* Most professors prefer regular, plain type to "script" or other unusual prints; all professors appreciate clean type and a fresh ribbon. If you use a word processor, be sure that the print is clear and dark. Double-space throughout the paper, including the list of works cited (or the notes and bibliography). If your professor accepts handwritten papers, write legibly and use dark ink, not pencil.
3. *Copies:* Always keep copies of your papers for your files, and do not throw them away or delete them until your papers are returned. Professors are scrupulously careful not to lose or damage student papers, but accidents can always happen.
4. *Margins:* Margins should be at least 1 inch on all four sides of the page; many professors prefer margins of 1½ inches at the top and the left.
5. *Indenting:* Indent five spaces for paragraphs, ten spaces for indented quotations.
6. *Titles:* Although separate title pages are necessary for theses and dissertations, most professors do not require them for research appears. Instead, put your name, your professor's name, the date, and any other

information the professor may require in the upper right-hand corner of the first page of your paper. Then center your title at the top of the page; do not underline it or put it in quotation marks. Double-space twice, indent, and begin typing your paper.

7. *Page numbers:* Place page numbers in the upper right-hand corner; do not add periods, hyphens, or other marks. Usually, the first pages of the text and of the list of works cited (or the endnotes and bibliography) are not numbered, although they are counted.

8. *Corrections and insertions:* Whenever it is possible, type corrections. Some professors allow students to make small corrections or additions in ink; these should be made above the typed line in which the error appears, not below it or in the margins. If you need to delete a word, cross it out; do not put it in parentheses. Use a caret (^) to indicate an insertion, a slash (/) to indicate that two words have inadvertently been run together.

9. *Binders:* Binders, folders, and staples are generally nuisances; most professors prefer a paper clip in the upper left-hand corner of the paper.

# *Appendix C*

# SOME GUIDELINES ON DOCUMENTATION

Almost any paper about literature requires some documentation: Even if you do not consult any secondary sources while preparing a paper, you will at least need to specify which edition of a literary work you used and to identify all quotations correctly. In a research paper, obviously, documentation becomes much more extensive and complicated. Documentation has two basic purposes: to aid readers who may wish to check any of your sources, either because they doubt your accuracy or because they wish to learn more about the subject; and to acknowledge your indebtedness to all the people from whom you have borrowed words or ideas. For the most part, documentation is governed by considerations of convention, courtesy, and honesty. To aid readers, scholars in an academic field generally agree to use the same format for documentation; and scholars in all academic fields agree about the seriousness of any failure to document sources honestly. Mastering documentation, then, requires careful attention to our discipline's conventions about format; even more, it requires determination and vigilance to ensure that all debts are acknowledged fully and clearly.

## PROPER AND IMPROPER USES OF SOURCES: PLAGIARISM

Full, honest documentation requires you to tell your readers exactly what sources you used in writing your paper and exactly how you used them. Mention every source that contributed to your paper, and make the nature of the contribution clear. Did you borrow an idea from the source? Did you borrow any words as well? You do not need to document bits of common knowledge found in many sources (e.g., *Lyrical Ballads* was published in 1798"), but you do need to document almost everything else—not only direct quotations but also any facts, ideas, or insights you gained from a particular source. The failure to document sources fully and precisely constitutes plagiarism.

Plagiarism involves misinforming or misleading the reader: The reader is led to believe that a writer's words or ideas are original, when in fact they are borrowed from other sources. Some plagiarism is intentional—a writer copies down all or part of a journal article or a chapter from a book, making no mention of the original work or its author anywhere in the paper. Much plagiarism, however, is at least partly unintentional—the writer is ignorant of or confused about the proper way to document sources or simply becomes careless while taking notes and forgets to identify a direct quotation as such. Good intentions, however, do not constitute an adequate excuse for plagiarism or a convincing defense when plagiarism is detected. Most professors agree that students have an obligation to learn about and abide by the conventions of documentation and must accept full responsibility for any failure to do so. Moreover, most professors do not feel capable of judging a student's intentions: A plagiarized paper is a fact, but any person's motivations are, ultimately, a matter about which one can only speculate. Those who plagiarize unintentionally are therefore usually punished just as severely as those who plagiarize intentionally. Since plagiarism is a dishonorable offense, and because the penalties for it may range from failure in a course to expulsion to professional disgrace, all writers should take all precautions to ensure that no plagiarism, intentional or unintentional, mars their writing.

You may summarize, paraphrase, or quote directly from outside sources, but you must be sure to do two things: Give the reader full information about each source, and make the extent of your indebtedness clear. Do not, for example, let the reader mistake a direct quotation for a summary or a paraphrase. Suppose that you wish to use in your paper this passage from David Perkins's *The Quest for Permanence: The Symbolism of Wordsworth, Shelley, and Keats* (Cambridge: Harvard UP, 1959):

**ORIGINAL PASSAGE**

> Death itself is not an obsession with Wordsworth, nor does his quest primarily involve an attempt to find some reconciliation to the fact of death (as does that of Shelley, Keats, Yeats, or, for that matter, the Shakespeare of the sonnets). The great lines in the closing sonnet of *The River Duddon*—"We men, whom in our morn of youth defied / The elements, must vanish—be it so."—are not bravado. They are a real acceptance, even though that acceptance is not placid or joyous. But what is not accepted, and is a constant "trouble" to his "dreams," is man's isolation from nature while he lives. The quest for permanence, in so far as Wordsworth is concerned, should be regarded as a quest for a certain kind of stability and reassurance while we are alive. (35–36)

It would, of course, be plagiarism to quote this passage word for word without identifying it as Perkins's. It would also be plagiarism to express Perkins's ideas in your own words without acknowledgment:

**PLAGIARISM (*IDEAS BORROWED WITHOUT ACKNOWLEDGMENT*)**

Wordsworth, unlike Shelley and Keats, is not principally concerned
with finding a way to accept the fact of human mortality. He is able

to reconcile himself, genuinely and sincerely, to death; but he cannot reconcile himself to humanity's estrangement from nature.

The difference between plagiarism and legitimate summary is the frank acknowledgment of indebtedness:

## LEGITIMATE SUMMARY

As David Perkins points out in The Quest for Permanence, Wordsworth, unlike Shelley and Keats, is not principally concerned with finding a way to accept the fact of human mortality. He is able to reconcile himself, genuinely and sincerely, to death; but he cannot reconcile himself to humanity's estrangement from nature (35–36).

If you use any of Perkins's words, however, simply identifying the source is not enough: You must also enclose the quoted words in quotation marks. If you mention an author's name but do not use quotation marks, the reader will assume that you have borrowed some ideas but that all the words you are using are your own. Misleading the reader in this way is another form of plagiarism:

## PLAGIARISM (*DIRECT QUOTATION PRESENTED AS SUMMARY*)

As David Perkins points out in The Quest for Permanence, death itself is not an obsession with Wordsworth, nor does his quest primarily involve an attempt to find some reconciliation to the fact of death. Wordsworth is able to accept mortality, but what he cannot accept is man's isolation from nature while he lives (35–36).

If you borrow even a single phrase from another author, do not mislead your reader. Enclose all quoted words in quotation marks.

## LEGITIMATE USE OF DIRECT QUOTATION

As David Perkins points out in The Quest for Permanence, "death itself is not an obsession for Wordsworth, nor does his quest primarily involve an attempt to find some reconciliation to the fact of death." Wordsworth cannot, however, accept "man's isolation from nature while he lives" (35–36).

Very close paraphrasing is another form of plagiarism. Many students believe that paraphrase involves no more than "switching some words around"; some have been told that "if you change some of the words in a passage, it's yours." Both of these notions are mistaken. Legitimate paraphrasing involves expressing an idea *entirely* in your own words. Even if you change all the words but follow the author's sentence pattern very closely, the paraphrase will not be legitimate. And, of course, all paraphrases must be acknowledged, just as all summaries and direct quotations must be:

## ORIGINAL SENTENCE

The quest for permanence, in so far as Wordsworth is concerned, should be regarded as a quest for a certain kind of stability and reassurance while we are alive.

## LEGITIMATE PARAPHRASE

According to Perkins, Wordsworth believes that it is in this life that human beings must seek "a certain kind of stability and reassurance" (36).

The sentence is completely recast; the one phrase quoted directly is enclosed in quotation marks.

## PLAGIARISM (*ILLEGITIMATE PARAPHRASE— TOO CLOSE TO ORIGINAL*)

According to Perkins, the quest for permanence, for Wordsworth, must be seen as the search for a particular sort of security and confidence during one's lifetime.

The writer in the example above has preserved the rhythm of Perkins's sentence and has simply replaced some words with synonyms and near-synonyms; the sentence is still essentially Perkins's and should not be presented as summary or paraphrase. In matters of documentation, being too cautious is far preferable to not being cautious enough. If you are ever in doubt about whether or not to acknowledge something, acknowledge it—or, if there is time, ask your professor for advice.

Whoever quotes his source brings deliverance to the world
Talmud

# THE MECHANICS OF DOCUMENTATION

In literary studies, the *MLA Handbook for Writers of Research Papers,* edited by Joseph Gibaldi, is the authority on documentation, as well as on other matters such as mechanics and manuscript preparation. This handbook is absolutely essential for anyone writing a research paper. In the few pages available to us here, we can try only to explain something about the logic of documentation and to give a few examples of ways to handle some of the most common situations. These pages can in no sense be a substitute for the *MLA Handbook.* You will need the handbook for full explanations of the matters we touch on here and for direction about documenting types of sources we will not even mention—dissertations, for example, and nonprint sources such as recordings and films.

For many years, the *MLA Handbook* recommended the use of footnotes or endnotes and a bibliography; now, it recommends parenthetical documentation and a list of works cited. Since the handbook continues to explain both methods of documentation, however, and since not everyone accepts the parenthetical method, it would be wise to ask professors which method they prefer. Here, we will first give some information about the list of works cited, which is used with both methods; then, we will briefly describe both the parenthetical and the traditional methods of documentation.

# THE LIST OF WORKS CITED

The list of works cited is placed at the end of your research paper and provides full information about all the works to which you have referred. If you also wish to include works that you have consulted but not cited, "Works Cited and Consulted" or "Selected Bibliography" would be a better title than "Works Cited." The entries in a list of works cited are arranged alphabetically by authors' last names. The entire list should be double-spaced, both within and between entries.

It is helpful to think of an entry in a list of works cited as consisting of three principal sentences—an author sentence, a title sentence, and a publication data sentence. The exact format of the entry will depend on the type of work being cited and the amount of information that must be included.

## Book Entries

Here is an entry for a book with a single author:

McGuire, Richard. <u>Passionate Attention: An Introduction to Literary</u>
<u>Study</u>. New York: Norton, 1973.

Notice that the author's last name is given first, followed by a comma and his first name, followed by a period. The full title of the book is given, including its subtitle, and is underlined with a continuous line. The period at the end of the title is not underlined. The city in which the book was published is given next, followed by a colon, the publisher (only "Norton," not "W. W. Norton & Company, Inc."), a comma, the date of publication, and a period. Notice also that the first line of the entry begins at the margin and that the second line (and any other lines) is indented one-half inch (five spaces if using a typewriter). This sketch may make it easier to remember the basic elements in an entry for a book:

Last name, First name. <u>Full Title and Subtitle.</u> City: Publisher, Date.

An entry becomes more complicated when more information must be included and more sentences added, as in the following sample book entries.


**A BOOK WITH AN EDITOR AND A TRANSLATOR:**

Kristeva, Julia. <u>Desire in Language: A Semiotic Approach to Literature and Art</u>. Ed. Leon S. Roudiez. Trans. Thomas Gore, Alice Jardine, and Leon S. Roudiez. New York: Columbia UP, 1980.

(Notice that a new sentence is added for each new item of information.)


**A BOOK BY TWO OR MORE AUTHORS:**

Bardes, Barbara, and Suzanne Gossett. <u>Declarations of Independence: Women and Political Power in Nineteenth-Century American Fiction</u>. New Brunswick: Rutgers UP, 1990.

(Notice that the first author's name is reversed, but the second author's name is presented in the usual order.)


**AN ANTHOLOGY:**

Ruoff, A. LaVonne Brown, and Jerry W. Ward, Jr., eds. <u>Redefining American Literary History</u>. New York: MLA, 1990.

**AN ESSAY IN AN ANTHOLOGY:**

> Bruce-Nuova, Juan. "Canonical and Noncanonical Texts: A Chicano
> Case Study." <u>Redefining American Literary History</u>. Ed. A
> Lavonne Brown Ruoff and Jerry W. Ward, Jr. New York:
> MLA, 1990.

(Notice that separate sentences are given to the titles of the essay and of the anthology.)

**A MULTIVOLUME WORK:**

> Magill, Frank A., ed. <u>Critical Survey of Long Fiction: English
> Language Series</u>. 8 vols. Englewood Cliffs: Salem, 1983.

(A new sentence is added after the title to indicate the number of volumes.)

## Entries for Periodical Articles

Entries for articles in periodicals differ from those for books, but again there are three principal sentences: author, title, and publication data. The publication data needed, however, are different: Include the title of the periodical, the volume number, the year of publication, and the page numbers of the entire article (*not* just the pages to which you refer):

> Unrue, Darlene Harbour. "Katherine Anne Porter, Politics, and
> Another Reading of 'Theft.'" <u>Studies in Short Fiction</u> 30
> (1993): 119–126.

Again, a sketch may make it easier to remember the basic elements in an entry for a journal article:

> Last name, First name. "Title of Article." <u>Title of Journal</u>. Volume
> number (year of publication): page numbers for article.

Here are some other sample entries for articles in periodicals.

**AN ARTICLE IN A JOURNAL WITH CONTINUOUS PAGINATION:**

> Chay, Deborah G. "Rereading Barbara Smith: Black Feminist
> Criticism and the Category of Experience." <u>New Literary
> History</u> 24 (1993): 635–653.

(Because the journal pages continuously throughout a volume, the issue number and month need not be included in the citation.)

**AN ARTICLE IN A JOURNAL THAT PAGES EACH ISSUE SEPARATELY:**

Fernandes, Joyce. "Sex into Sexuality: A Feminist Agenda for the

'90s." Art Journal 50.2 (1991): 35–39.

(Because the journal pages each issue separately, the citation indicates the issue number [2] as well as the volume number [50].)

**AN ARTICLE FROM A NEWSPAPER:**

Kernan, Alvin. "Radical Literary Criticism May Represent the Last

Phases of an Old Order Collapsing." Chronicle of Higher

Education 19 Sept. 1990: B1–2.

(Include the complete date—day, month, year—but not the volume or issue number. Also note that the month—except for May, June, and July—is abbreviated. )

**AN ARTICLE FROM A MAGAZINE:**

Goldstein, Rebecca. "Looking Back at Lot's Wife." Commentary Sept.

1992: 37–41.

(When citing an article from a monthly magazine intended for a general audience rather than a scholarly one, include the month but not the volume or issue number.)

## Entries for Material from Electronic Sources

CD-ROMS and on-line databases offer the researcher new ways of gaining access to material in periodicals. When citing such sources, the researcher must include information both about the periodical in which the material first appeared and about the electronic medium used to gain access to it. For example, here is a citation for an article made available on a CD-ROM:

Fuller, Patty. "The Censorship Debate Erupts Again." Alberta Report

21 Mar. 1994: 26–27. Academic Abstracts Fulltext. CD-ROM.

1995.

The first items in this entry provide information about the article as it originally appeared in print: author, title, name of newspaper, date of original publication, page numbers. The entry then continues to provide information about the title of the database (Academic Abstracts Fulltext, underlined), the publication medium (CD-ROM), and the date of electronic publication (1995).

Citations for material available through an on-line database follow a similar format:

> Noddings, Nel. "A Morally Defensible Mission for Schools in the 21st
>
> Century." <u>Phi Delta Kappa</u> Jan. 1995: 365–370. <u>Magazine</u>
>
> <u>ASAP</u>. Online. DIALOG. 15 Mar. 1995.

Again, the entry begins with information about the article as originally printed: author, title, publication, date, pages. Data about the electronic publication of the article follows: database (Magazine ASAP, underlined), publication medium (Online), computer service (DIALOG), and date the researcher accessed the article.

The fourth edition of the *MLA Handbook* offers the researcher detailed information about the formats used to cite material from many other sorts of databases—for example, nonperiodical publications on CD-ROM, publications on diskette, and material accessed through a computer network or an electronic journal—as well as information about citing other sorts of print sources. The researcher should definitely consult the *MLA Handbook* before preparing a final list of works cited.

## PARENTHETICAL DOCUMENTATION

The method of documentation recommended in the most recent editions of the *MLA Handbook* is similar to those used in most of the natural and social sciences. This method uses no footnotes or endnotes; instead, sources are acknowledged parenthetically in the text:

> Literary criticism may be defined as "the activity that seeks
>
> continually to demonstrate the significance and profundity of the
>
> work in such a way that it is there for all people to see and take
>
> delight in" (McGuire 6).

Only the author's name and the page number are included in the parenthetical citation; all other information about the source—title, publisher, and so on—will be provided at the end of the paper in the list of works cited. In fact, if you mention the author's name in the text of your paper, only the page number must go into the parentheses:

McGuire defines literary criticism as "the activity that seeks
continually to demonstrate the significance and profundity of the
work in such a way that it is there for all people to see and take
delight in" (6).

If, however, you include more than one work by a particular author in your list
of works cited, you must include the work's title—or a shortened version of
it—in the parentheses; otherwise, the reader might not know to which of the
author's works you are referring. Suppose, for example, that you include both
I. A. Richards's *Principles of Literary Criticism* and his *Practical Criticism* in
your list of works cited:

Criticism has also been defined as "the endeavor to discriminate

between experiences and to evaluate them" (Richards, Principles 2).

Essentially, the parenthetical method seeks to make citations as brief as
possible but to give the reader all necessary information. Information that can
readily be found in the text or in the list of works cited is not repeated in the
parenthetical citation, but information is included if leaving it out might possibly confuse the reader.

It is also important to notice how these citations are punctuated. There is
no comma in a citation including only the author's name and a page number
or only the title and a page number:

(McGuire 6)

(Principles 2)

In a citation including author, title, and page number, there is a comma
between the author's name and the title but none between the title and the
page number:

(Richards, Principles 2)

The *MLA Handbook* explains these points more fully and provides
many examples.


## TRADITIONAL DOCUMENTATION

The traditional method of documentation also calls for a list of works cited
(often titled "Bibliography"). Instead of relying on parenthetical references to
sources, however, it uses footnotes (placed at the foot or bottom of the page
on which the reference occurs) or endnotes (placed on a separate page at the

end of the paper). Note that numbers are typed as superscripts, slightly above the line in the text:

> Literary criticism has been defined as "the activity that seeks continually to demonstrate the significance and profundity of the work in such a way that it is there for all people to see and take delight in."[1]

The note itself generally contains the same information contained in an entry in the list of works cited, plus a page number. The information is presented somewhat differently, however. Whereas a "Works Cited" entry consists of three main sentences, a note consists of just one sentence. The first example shows the note form; the second shows the "Works Cited" form:

> [1]Richard L. McGuire, <u>Passionate Attention: An Introduction to Literary Study</u> (New York: Norton, 1973) 6.

> McGuire, Richard L. <u>Passionate Attention: An Introduction to Literary Study</u>. New York: Norton, 1973.

In the note, the author's first name is given first, followed by the last name and a comma. The title is next. The publication data—city, publisher, date—are now enclosed in parentheses: Notice that there is no punctuation before or after the parentheses. The page number is the last item of information included, followed by the only period the note contains. Also notice that the first line of the note is indented five spaces and that the second line is even with the margin. This sketch shows the basic elements in a note for a book:

> [number]Author's first and last names. <u>Full Title and Subtitle</u> (City: Publisher, date) page.

A note for an article in a periodical is similar in format:

> [2]Darlene Harbour Unrue, "Katherine Anne Porter, Politics, and Another Reading of 'Theft,'" <u>Studies in Short Fiction</u> 30 (1993): 119.

The *MLA Handbook* recommends using a colon, not a comma, before the page number. This sketch shows the basic format of a note for an article in a periodical:

> [number]Author's first and last names, "Title of Article," <u>Title of Journal</u> volume number (year of publication): page number.

If you cite a source more than once, you should not repeat all this information in each note. Instead, simply give the author's name and a page number in subsequent references:

³ McGuire 18.

The *MLA Handbook* does not recommend using a comma between the author's name and the page number in subsequent references. If you cite more than one book by a particular author, subsequent references should also include a short title:

⁴ Richards, <u>Principles</u> 35.

⁵ Richards, <u>Practical</u> 87.

Again, the *MLA Handbook* contains much more information, including sample notes for many sorts of sources, both print and nonprint.

# A Glossary of Critical Terms

This brief glossary includes both critical terms used in this book and some that students may encounter in reading contemporary criticism.

**affective fallacy**  A term used particularly by the New Critics to denote what they viewed as the fallacy of evaluating or analyzing a literary text according to its effect on the reader. (See page 13.)

**anti-fiction**  Fiction that abandons the traditional conventions of fiction. Because such conventions as plot and the illusion of reality have frequently been used to define fiction or story, fictions without these conventions may appear to be the antitheses of fiction, or anti-fictions.

**ambiguity**  In literary criticism, a term that usually refers to the deliberate use of literary language to produce multiple meanings.

**anxiety of influence**  A term used by Harold Bloom to characterize the relationship of any poet to a previous or "precursor" poet. The anxiety of influence describes the poet's feeling that no original work remains to be done. Thus, new poems become "misreadings" of precursor poems as the poet attempts to write "against" the older poem and stake out new ground. (See page 109.)

**archetype**  In the psychology of Carl Jung, a term for the specific universal images that have resided in the human mind since the remotest times. Some critics use the term more generally to refer to images that recur frequently enough in literary

texts to be identified, in Northrop Frye's words, "as an element of one's literary experience as a whole." (See pages 100–105.)

**bildungsroman**  A novel that traces the youthful development of a central character. Because the typical examples so frequently portray male characters (Joyce's *A Portrait of the Artist as a Young Man,* Dickens's *David Copperfield*, Goethe's *Sorrows of Young Werther,* etc.), some critics use the term *female bildungsroman* to signify novels following the growth of a female character. (See also *künstlerroman.*)

**canon**  A body of texts held to be worthy of recognition and study. Much recent debate has been concerned with the ideology of canon formation and with attempts to change, enlarge, or eliminate the traditional literary canon, which is perceived as based in a male, Eurocentric view of the world.

**carnivalesque**  A term used by Mikhail Bakhtin in reference to texts in which no single, authoritative voice prevails. Bakhtin saw the polyphonic or dialogic style as having its roots in the carnival, a tradition in which hierarchies and authorities are always questioned, subverted, and, ultimately, de-privileged.

**codes**  Used both in linguistics and in the study of culture and literature, a term referring to those conventions that allow meaning to be shared or communicated. Traffic signals operate within a code: A red light communicates one meaning and a green light communicates another. Language itself is coded insofar as different conventions (sentence order, for example) communicate different meanings. (See page 36.)

**contextual criticism**   A formalist critical approach that examines the literary text as an artistic object without reference to the exterior world. The term is associated with the work of Eliseo Vivas and Murray Krieger.

**conventions**   Long used to refer to specific, customary literary practices (such as the use of the soliloquy in Renaissance drama), a term now generally used to denote all the practices that allow meaning to be communicated in both literary and nonliterary texts. Many linguists argue that language can communicate only because of the arbitrary but public conventions of the language. (See page 38.)

**deconstruction**   A critical approach or orientation that denies the possibility of coherence in language generally. Unlike the New Critics, who attempted to demonstrate the unity and coherence of literary texts, deconstructionists show the ways in which texts are incoherent and open to contradictory meanings and are, thus, always in the process of deconstructing themselves. (See pages 39–44.)

**defamiliarization**   A term referring to the way in which artistic texts force viewers and readers to see the world anew. A text, according to the Russian critic Viktor Shklovsky, must defamiliarize or "make strange" a phenomenon in order for readers to get beyond their automatic responses and stereotypical ways of seeing.

**diegesis**   A term used by some narratologists to distinguish between two levels of narrative discourse. The diegetic level is the story proper, the series of events being narrated. The term *extradiegetic* refers to the level of narration itself.

**différance**   A term coined by Jacques Derrida from the French word *différer* (to differ and to defer) to refer to two characteristics of language that, in his view, prevent the possibility of a single, fixed meaning: first, that linguistic signs or words have meaning only in their difference from other signs; and second, that meaning is never completed but always deferred to future utterances. (See page 39.)

**discourse**   In contemporary criticism, a term most frequently used to refer to kinds of writing having their own conventions and assumptions. For example, the discourse of politics might have a different set of conventions and assume a different audience than the discourse of criticism.

**dystopia**   Term used to refer to a kind of book depicting a world corrupted by the culmination of present political or technological trends; antithesis of *utopia,* which portrays a perfect society (usually removed in time or place). Orwell's *Nineteen Eighty-Four* and Huxley's *Brave New World* are examples.

**écriture**   The French word for *writing,* used mainly in criticism that conceives of writing as a social institution; that is, both writer and reader are understood to be participating in an already established system of conventions and codes. According to Hélène Cixous, *écriture féminine,* or women's writing, is a mode of writing, or *écriture,* the conventions of which differ from those of patriarchal writing. (See page 90.)

**epistemology**   The study of the nature, methods, and validity of knowledge. As criticism and theory have become increasingly concerned with their own premises and methods, epistemology has become more significant in literary studies.

**explication**   A detailed analysis or explanation of a text. Explications frequently offer line-by-line analyses of all aspects of a literary text or passage.

**feminist criticism**   An approach to literary criticism generally concerned with the question of sexual difference within texts and within the cultures from which they come. The many methods and purposes of feminist criticism probably make it more accurate to speak of *feminisms.*

**formalist criticism**   A term describing the critical approaches that concentrate on the forms and structures of literary texts, often to the exclusion of attention to any exterior context. More specifically, the term refers to the orientation of the Russian formalists of the early twentieth century. Central to Russian formalism was its distinction between literary and nonliterary or scientific language. (See pages 10–18.)

**gender**   In contemporary literary studies, a term referring to the cultural attributes assigned to male and female; usually differentiated from *sex*, which is a biological term denoting female or male. There is an increasing recognition of the way in which both literary and critical texts have participated in the construction of male and female roles in society.

**gynocritics**   A term, associated particularly with the work of Elaine Showalter, that refers to the study of all aspects of women as writers and the writing of women. (See page 86.)

**hermeneutics**   Traditionally associated with biblical interpretation, a term that has come to refer as well to the theory or science of the interpretation of literary texts. The term *hermeneutic circle* refers to the logical problem of circularity in interpretation. One must interpret the parts of a literary text in order to interpret the whole, yet one cannot interpret the parts without a prior interpretation of the whole.

**heuristic**   In literary criticism, a system or paradigm for the study or interpretation of literary texts, or a set of procedures that lead to a discovery about a literary text.

**hypertext**   Electronic or computerized text that contains within it links to other text. A hypertext document allows a reader to "click on" a specific piece of text (a line from *Paradise Lost,* for example) and be presented with another text (the book of Genesis, a biography of Milton, etc.).

**ideology**   A term traditionally used in literary criticism to refer to an explicit body of political ideas. In this usage, ideological fiction would be viewed as built upon and probably promulgating a specific political doctrine. More recently, critics have come to see ideology as inescapable and all literary texts as ideological insofar as they offer a view of the world and the individual's place within it.

**indeterminacy**   A term used in much contemporary criticism to refer to the lack of a final or fixed meaning in any utterance. Literary texts are perceived as indeterminate insofar as no single meaning or interpretation can be certain.

**intentional fallacy**   A term used particularly by the New Critics to denote what they viewed as the fallacy of evaluating or analyzing a literary text according to the intention of its author.

**intertextuality**   The understanding and study of texts in their relation to other texts. Some critics suggest that all texts are formed from other texts and that they are read and understood only in reference to other texts.

**kūnstlerroman**   A novel that traces the youthful development of an artist, such as Mann's *Death in Venice* and Joyce's *Portrait of the Artist as a Young Man.*

*langue* **and** *parole*   Terms used in the linguistic theory of Ferdinand de Saussure. *Langue* refers to the underlying conventions and rules that govern a language (its grammar, for example) and *parole* refers to individual utterances in the language (a single phrase or sentence). Some structuralist critics use the terms in an analogous way to discuss literary texts, speaking of the underlying conventions or structure of, for example, the romance novel as the *langue* and individual romance novels as *parole.* (See page 33.)

**lexie**   A term used by some structuralist critics to denote a section of text that has a function different from surrounding sections of text. (See page 35.)

**literary competence**   A term used by some critics to refer to the ability to respond appropriately to various signs and conventions in literary texts. Derived from the term *competence,* as used by the linguist Noam Chomsky to denote the unconscious human knowledge of language that allows us to speak and write without direct reference to linguistic or grammatical rules or forms.

**Marxist criticism**   A critical approach that examines the relationship of literary texts to the historic class struggle envisioned in the theories of Karl Marx. According to Marxist critics, all literary productions bear the marks of the history from which they came. In this sense, ideology is inescapable, even in determining the forms literature takes and in the matter of what

counts as literature. (See pages 75-77.)

**metacriticism**   Criticism dealing with the theory of criticism or interpretation. Metacriticism examines the principles and methods of critical inquiry.

**metafiction**   Fiction about fiction. Metafictional novels and short stories recognize themselves as literary constructs and may be about their own creation.

**mimetic**   A term that refers to imitation (*mimesis* in the Greek). Mimetic criticism assumes a literary or artistic text to be an imitation or representation of reality. Thus, a mimetic critic would study, and perhaps ultimately evaluate, a text according to its accuracy in representing the exterior world.

**multivalence**   Used in chemistry to indicate the capacity of an element to combine with another to form molecules, a term appropriated by literary critics to refer to multiple meanings within a text. Some linguists and critics argue that language by its very nature is multivalent.

**myth**   A term, traditionally referring to a hereditary story that explained some phenomenon, now sometimes used for recurring patterns in literature. Northrop Frye, for instance, uses the term *mythos* to characterize each of the four narrative patterns by which he classifies all literary texts. (See page 102.)

**narratology**   The study of the conventions and structures of narrative texts. Narratology attempts to determine the underlying "grammar" or "rules" that govern the structure of narrative.

**New Criticism**   A formalist critical approach, particularly influential in America from the 1940s through the 1960s. The New Criticism, in part a reaction to the historical and biographical criticism of the time, is characterized by close reading and by its view of the literary text as a self-sufficient artistic object. (See page 10.)

**new historicism**  An orientation toward the historical study and interpretation of literary texts beginning in the 1970s and 1980s. The new historicism contrasts with traditional historical study partly by its emphasis on the role of the community or society in the production of literary texts, rather than a concentration on the role of the individual writer. (See pages 51-55.)

**orientalism**  A term, deriving from Edward Said's book *Orientalism* (1978), referring to the conception of the Orient as it exists in the mind of Westerners. Through an immense number of texts dating from the Renaissance to the present, those in the West have created a vision of the Orient that Said terms a "textual universe."

**patriarchy**  A social unit governed by a male, especially a father or father figure. *Patriarchal* refers in general to male dominance.

**phallogocentric**  A term referring to cultures and languages that are centered on men. (See page 90.)

**plurisignation**  A term referring to language with multiple meanings. It is frequently used in modern criticism in place of *ambiguity*.

**poetics**  The study of the nature of poetry or of literary texts generally. For example, Aristotle's *Poetics* is his statement or theory of the principles and elements of literature.

**polyphonic; dialogic**  Terms, usually attributed to the Russian critic Mikhail Bakhtin, referring to a style of writing in which there seems to be a blend of voices rather than a single voice. A dialogic or polyphonic style contrasts with a monological style; it reflects a dialogue or speech taking place within a context rather than a monologue.

**postmodernism**  A reference to certain cultural trends since World War II that indicate a loss of traditional beliefs in coherence and meaning and in the forms that convey those beliefs. In literature, postmodernism is frequently associated with antifiction, parody, and pastiche; in criticism, the term often refers to poststructuralist approaches. The terms *Po Mo* and *posties* are sometimes used of the movement and those who embrace it.

**poststructuralism**  Term generally referring to forms of critical theory and practice that reacted to and denied structuralist claims of coherence and scientific validity. Whereas structuralists were striving for a comprehensive description of the deep structures of literary texts, poststructuralists emphasized the contradictions, openness, and indeterminacies of texts.

**psychobiography**  Biography, often based on psychoanalytic theory, that emphasizes the psychology of the subject in order to explain the person's life and behavior. (See page 59.)

**reader response**  A critical orientation concerned with the effects of a text on its readers and on the interaction between texts and readers. Far from believing that such critical activity exemplifies an affective fallacy, reader-response critics frequently suggest that literature comes into existence only when it is read. (See pages 25-30.)

**representation**  Strictly speaking, the substitution of one thing for another. From at least the time of Plato, artistic productions have been viewed as representational; for example, blue paint on a canvas may represent (or stand for) the ocean, or a particular set of descriptive words in a text may stand for a human being who exists in the world outside the text. Increasingly, however, critics have come to scrutinize and question the understanding of representation as a one-to-one relationship between the sign in the text and the object it supposedly stands for.

**semiotics; semiology**    Terms that refer to the study of signs—that is, the conventions of communication that produce meaning. *Semiotics* is the term used by C. S. Peirce, while *semiology* is preferred by Ferdinand de Saussure. Semiotics is not restricted to a study of language or literary texts but considers the conventions or sign systems that function in all human activity. (See page 34.)

**sign**    In linguistics, a basic unit of meaning—the word, for example. The term has come to be used outside linguistics as well, to refer to the basic unit of meaning in any cultural phenomenon. Fashion, for instance, may be seen as a system of signs that produces meaning. (See page 33.)

**structuralism**    In literary criticism, the study of the underlying conventions and structures of literary texts. The goal, at least of many early structuralists, was to be able to describe the deep patterns of literary texts as linguists can describe the grammar of sentences. (See pages 33–39.)

**synchronic; diachronic**    Words used to describe investigations of phenomena as they relate to time. Specifically, a synchronic study examines a phenomenon as it exists at a given time, while a diachronic study examines its historical change over time. Ferdinand de Saussure and other early twentieth-century linguists turned the study of language from the historical or diachronic interests of the nineteenth century to an analysis of language as it existed at that particular time.

**text**    Traditionally, a term for the words on the page, as opposed to a reader's interpretation or understanding of them. More recently, many critics use the distinction developed by Roland Barthes to contrast *text* with *literature* or *work*—in which *text* suggests writing as an open-ended process, while *literature* indicates a view of writing as a closed, representational product. The term has also come to be used of any written work and, by extension, to any communicative act. Thus, a painting is a visual text.

# INDEX

This index includes the names of almost all the writers mentioned in the text itself; it excludes the names of writers mentioned in the bibliographies only. The titles of several major reference works are included; most other titles are excluded. Terms mentioned only in Appendix D, "Glossary of Critical Terms," are also excluded.

Aaron, Daniel, 61
Abel, Elizabeth, 91
Abrams, M. H., 25, 54, 65, 163
Adams, Richard P., 63
Aeschylus, 75
Aggeler, Geoffrey, 50
Allen, Priscilla, 130
Altick, Richard, 121, 133, 157
*American Literary Scholarship,* 149, 162
*Annual Bibliography of English Language and Literature,* 149, 162
Antin, Mary, 148
archetypal studies, 30, 100–105
Aristotle, 19–20, 25, 31, 69, 106, 122
Arnold, Matthew, 67, 69, 70, 82
Astro, Richard, 65
Atkins, G. Douglas, 41–42
Austen, Jane, 26, 87, 108, 109, 118–119, 120, 122, 124, 129
authors' names, 179

Babbitt, Irving, 69–70
Bacon, Francis, 65
Bailey, Brigitte, 60
Baird, James, 104
Baker, Houston, 96
Baker, Nancy L., 157
Baldwin, James, 98
Balzac, Honoré, 24, 36–37, 77, 131
Barnard, Ellsworth, 133–134
Barnes, Annette, 83
Barricelli, Jean-Pierre, 81
Barthes, Roland, 60, 126
Bateson, F. W., 157
Baugh, Albert C., 142, 158–159
Baughman, Judith S., 161
Baym, Nina, 86
Beardsley, Monroe, 56

Bell, Bernard W., 97
Bell, Quentin, 58
Bellow, Saul, 117
Belsey, Catherine, 42–44
bibliographies, 143, 160–162
    *See also* documentation
    of bibliographies, 144–145, 159–160
    in research papers, 186–190
    serial, 145–150, 162–163
Birtha, Becky, 87
Blackmur, R. P., 18
Blake, William, 38–39, 129
Bloom, Allan, 80–81
Bloom, Harold, 30, 109–110
*Bloomsbury Guide to Women's Literature,* 163
Blotner, Joseph, 80
Bodkin, Maud, 101–102, 104
*Book Review Digest,* 150
*Book Review Index,* 150
Booth, Wayne, 6, 26
Boswell, James, 57
Bowra, C. M., 75
brackets, 175
Brontë, Emily, 15, 86, 88
Brooks, Cleanth, 12, 13–14, 16, 17, 125
Brooks, Gwendolyn, 95
Brooks, Peter, 134
Bruce-Nuova, Juan, 93
Buck, Claire, 163
Burgess, Anthony, 50
Burgess, C. F., 126
Burke, Kenneth, 32
Bush, Douglas, 135
Butler, Samuel, 65

Calinescu, Matei, 81
*Cambridge Guide to English Literature,* 165

Camus, Albert, 65, 103
Cather, Willa, 77
Caudwell, Christopher, 76
Chace, William, 79
Charvat, William, 79
Chaucer, Geoffrey, 131-132
Cheung, King-Kok, 97
Chicago school, 16, 20
Chopin, Kate, 87, 130, 146-147, 148
Christian, Barbara, 98
Cioffi, Frank, 56
Cixous, Hélène, 90
Clark, Priscilla B., 77-78, 81
Clausen, Christopher, 71-72
Clifford, James, 61
Cody, John, 59
Cohen, Ralph, 51
Coleridge, Samuel, 60, 101-102, 104
concluding paragraphs, 129-133
Conrad, Joseph, 3, 103, 122, 126
Cooper, James Fenimore, 103
Corbett, Edward P. J., 32, 119, 121, 126
Cornford, F. M., 104
Courtivron, Isabelle de, 91
Crane, R. S., 6, 16, 20, 55
Crews, Frederick C., 135
*Critical Survey of Long Fiction,* 164
*Critical Survey of Short Fiction,* 164
Crossman, Inge, 32
Culler, Jonathan, 22, 33, 38

Daiches, David, 17, 159
Dante, 75
Davidson, Cathy N., 163
Davis, Charles T., 95
Davis, Robert Con, 110
deconstruction, 39-44
Defoe, Daniel, 15, 78, 85
Derrida, Jacques, 39-40, 42, 44
Diamond, Arlyn, 83-84, 91
Dickens, Charles, 70, 130-131, 140
Dickinson, Emily, 59, 77
documentation, 182-193
    bibliography, 186-190, 191
    endnotes, 191-193
    footnotes, 191-193
    parenthetical, 190-191
    plagiarism, 182-185
    works cited, 186-190
Donne, John, 14, 17, 63-64, 71-72, 95, 128
Dos Passos, John, 76
Dostoevski, Fyodor, 131
Douglass, Frederick, 94
Doyle, Arthur Conan, 43-44

Doyle, Paul A., 158
Drabble, Margaret, 163
Dryden, John, 41-42
DuBois, Ellen Carol, 87, 89

*écriture féminine,* 90
Edwards, Lee R., 83-84, 91
electronic sources, documenting, 189-190
Eliot, George, 87
Eliot, T. S., 61-62, 79
ellipsis, 171
Ellison, Ralph, 98
Emerson, Ralph Waldo, 76-77
Empson, William, 18
endnotes, 191-193
*Essay and General Literature Index,*
        149-150, 162
ethnic and minority literature, 93-99
evaluating materials (research), 152, 154-155
Evans, Robert O., 122

Fairchild, Hoxie Neale, 73
Faulker, William, 37
feminist criticism, 68, 82-93
Ferguson, Francis, 103, 104
*festschriften,* 147
Feydeau, Ernest, 31
Fiedler, Leslie, 103
Fielding, Henry, 28-29, 127-128
first-person pronoun, 180
Fish, Stanley, 27-28
Fisher, Dexter, 94
Fitzgerald, F. Scott, 63
Flaubert, Gustave, 31
Folkenflik, Robert, 57
footnotes, 191-193
Ford, Nick Aaron, 94
formalist studies, 10-18
Foucault, Michel, 53
Frazer, Sir James, 100, 104, 117
Freud, Sigmund, 67, 106-108, 110
Friedson, Anthony, 61
Frost, Robert, 77
Frye, Northrup, 22-23, 102-103
Fryer, Judith, 85
Fuller, Edmund, 70, 73

Gardner, Helen, 72-73, 128-129
Gardner, John, 140
Garza, Rudolph O. de la, 97
Gass, William, 116-117
Gates, Henry Louis Jr., 96
Genet, Jean, 85

Genette, Gerard, 33
genre studies, 19-25
Gibaldi, Joseph, 81
Gilbert, Sandra M., 88, 89
Gilman, Charlotte Perkins, 87
Gindin, James, 58
Giovanni, Nikki, 98
Gittings, Robert, 51, 57, 58-59
Glaspell, Susan, 87
*Glossary of Literary Terms,* 163
Gohdes, Clarence, 160
*Goldentree Bibliographies,* 160
Gonne, Maud, 14
Gorer, Geoffrey, 108, 120-121, 123, 129
gothic novel, 23
Graff, Gerald, 16
Gray, Thomas, 31
Greenblatt, Stephen, 52-53
Greimas, A. J., 36
Gubar, Susan, 88, 89
Gunn, Giles, 72
gynocritics, 86-87

*Handbook to Literature,* 164
Hanford, James, 62-63
Harbage, Alfred, 78
Hardy, Thomas, 51, 58-59
Harmon, William, 164
Harrison, James, 104
Hart, James D., 164
Hawke, Terrence, 44
Hawthorne, Nathaniel, 86, 107, 141-142
Heidigger, Martin, 39-40
Heilbrun, Carolyn G., 89
Heilman, Robert, 17
Herbert, George, 27-28, 72
Hernardi, Paul, 24
Herring, Henry, 110
Hicks, Granville, 76-77
Highet, Gilbert, 64-65
Hill, John, 110
Himes, Chester, 98
Hirsch, E. D., Jr., 16, 24, 61
Holland, Norman, 29-30, 108-109, 110, 118,
    122, 124
Holman, C. Hugh, 164
Hopper, Stanley Romaine, 73
Horace, 25, 69
Horney, Karen, 110
Howard-Hill, Trevor, 160
Howe, Irving, 75, 122
*Humanities Index,* 149-150, 162
Hurston, Zora Neale, 87
Hyman, Stanley Edgar, 1, 104

Ingarden, Roman, 28
intentional fallacy, 12, 16, 56
interlibrary loans, 153-154
Internet, 151
intrinsic approaches, 9
introductory paragraphs, 120-122
Irigaray, Luce, 90
Iser, Wolfgang, 28-29

James, Henry, 77
Jameson, Frederic, 5, 6
Jauss, Hans Robert, 31
Johnson, Samuel, 21, 26, 57, 171-176
Jones, Ernest, 107-108
Jones, W. Powell, 31
Jordan, Frank, Jr., 144
journals, 165-166
Joseph, Sister Miriam, 30
Joyce, James, 128
Jung, Carl, 101, 104, 117
Jurkevich, Gayana, 103-104

Kaes, Anton, 52, 53, 55
Kafka, Franz, 103
Keats, John, 110, 125
Kehler, Dorothea, 158
Kent, Kathleen L., 165
Kettle, Arnold, 127
*Kenyon Review,* 18
Kolodny, Annette, 84
Kristeva, Julia, 90-91

Lacan, Jacques, 110
language of criticism, 133-136
*langue* and *parole,* 33-34
Latimer, Hugh, 52-53
Lauter, Paul, 95
Lawrence, D. H., 85, 89
Leary, Lewis, 161
Leitch, Vincent, 44
Lentricchia, Frank, 44
Lerenbaum, Miriam, 85
Lesser, Simon, 107-108
Lessing, Doris, 87
Lewis, C. S., 128
Lewis, Gregory, 23
lexie, 35-36
Lincoln, Kenneth, 96-97
Lipking, Lawrence, 71
listservs, 151
*A Literary History of England,* 142, 158-159
*A Literary History of the United States,* 142,
    144, 152, 159

Ljungquist, Kent P., 161
Logan, James V., 144
Longfellow, Henry Wadsworth, 79
Longinus, 106
Lovejoy, Arthur O., 48–49
Lowe, John Livingston, 60
Lowell, James Russell, 76
Lukacs, Georg, 77
Lynn, Steven, 39, 40, 41

Mack, Maynard, 15
Magill, Frank, 164
Mailer, Norman, 85, 89
Malin, Irving, 23
manuscript form, 180–181
Marks, Elaine, 91
Marovitz, Sanford E., 160
Marshall, Paule, 98
Martz, Louis, 61, 64
Marvell, Andrew, 64
Marx, Leo, 63, 116
Marxist criticism, 68, 75–77
Maslow, Abraham, 110
Mather, Cotton, 93
Mathew, Gervase, 51
McKean, Keith F., 73
Melville, Herman, 103, 104
Meserole, Harrison T., 157
Miller, Henry, 85, 89
Miller, J. Hillis, 41
Millett, Kate, 85, 89
Milton, John, 2, 6, 27, 48, 62–63, 76, 88,
    128–129, 140
Mitchell, Juliet, 110
MLA Bibliography, 145–149, 162, 165
MLA Directory of Periodicals, 165
MLA Handbook for Writers of Research
    Papers, 163–164
Moi, Toril, 89
Monk, Samuel Holt, 49–50
moral and religious studies, 69–74
More, Paul Elmer, 70
More, Thomas, 57, 65
Morris, Wesley, 52
Morrison, Toni, 98
Murdock, Kenneth B., 72
Murfin, Ross, 39, 53–54
Murray, Gilbert, 100–101, 102
Myers, Carol Fairbanks, 91
myth criticism, 100

Nagel, James, 65
Natoli, Joseph, 110

New Cambridge Bibliography of English
    Literature, 142–143, 144, 161–162
new criticism, 10–18, 71–72
new historicism, 52–55
Nietzsche, Friedrich, 39
Nilon, Charles, 160
Norris, Christopher, 44

O'Connor, Flannery, 23
Oedipus complex, 67, 102, 107–108, 109, 134
Ohmann, Carol, 86
Olson, Elder, 20–21
Online Computer Library Center (OCLC), 153
Orestes, 100
Ortiz, Simon, 96–97
Orwell, George, 75
Oxford Companion to American Literature,
    164
Oxford Companion to English Literature, 163
Oxford Companion to Women's Writing in
    the United States, 163
Oxford English Dictionary, 164

paraphrasing, 185
parenthetical documentation, 190–191
Paris, Bernard, 110
pastoral, 62–63
Patterson, Margaret C., 158
Perkins, David, 183–185
plagiarism, 182–185
Plato, 65, 67, 69, 106, 123
political and sociological studies, 74–82
Polletta, Gregory, 61
Pope, Alexander, 48–49, 131–132
Pound, Ezra, 79
Pratt, Annis, 84, 85, 86
preliminary reading (research), 141–143
Propp, Vladimir, 34–36
psychological criticism, 30, 106–112

quotations, 167–176
    commenting on, 168–170
    integrating, 170–171
    selecting, 167–168
    spacing and punctuating, 171–176
quotation marks, 171–177
    changes in quotations, 173–175
    introducing quotations, 173
    long quotations, 171–172
    with other punctuation, 175–176
    quotations within quotations, 172–173
    short quotations, 171
    titles, 176–177

Radcliffe, Ann, 23
Raina, M. L., 81
Ransom, John Crowe, 11-12, 13, 18
reader-response criticism, 26-30
refutation, 126-129
Register, Cheri, 91
rhetorical studies, 25-32
Richards, I. A., 13, 108
Richardson, Robert, 105
Richardson, Samuel, 78
Rickman, John, 110
Rivera, Rowena, 97
Robertson, D. W., Jr., 55
Rosenblatt, Louise, 27, 32
Ruoff, A. LaVonne Brown, 98

Sacks, Sheldon, 21
Sammons, Jeffrey, 77
Saussure, Ferdinand, 33-34, 37
Scholes, Robert, 44
Schorer, Mark, 15-16
Schreiner, Olive, 87
Scott, Nathan A., Jr., 73
Scott, Wilbur, 116
Selective Bibliography for the Study of
    English and American Literature,
    149, 152
semiology, 34
serial bibliographies, 145-150, 162-163
Shakespeare, William, 78, 80-81
    Antony and Cleopatra, 49
    As You Like It, 19, 120, 121
    Comedy of Errors, 52
    Coriolanus, 21
    Hamlet, 15, 21, 49, 52, 62, 67, 73, 100, 107,
        120-121
    Julius Caesar, 80
    King Lear, 19, 20-21, 49, 103, 126
    Macbeth, 21
    Measure for Measure, 52
    Othello, 19, 21, 49, 52
    Winter's Tale, 52
Sheehy, Eugene P., 158
Shelley, Mary, 88
Shelley, Percy Bysshe, 75, 80, 129
Shor, Ira, 75-76
Showalter, Elaine, 84, 86-87, 91
Sidney, Sir Phillip, 25
Siebers, Tobin, 71
Simpson, J. A., 164
Smith, Ann, 154
Smith, Barbara, 87
Smith, Frederik, 24
Smith, James, 120-121, 123

sociological and political studies, 74-82
Sophocles, 107
Spacks, Patricia Meyer, 89
Spenser, Edmund, 63
Spiller, Robert, 46, 48, 142, 159, 161
Stange, G. Robert, 130-131
Stapleton, Michael, 165
Starling, Marion Wilson, 94
statement of fact, 121-122
Stein, William Bysshe, 122
Stendahl, 131
Stevenson, Anne, 89
Strachey, Lytton, 57-58
structuralism, 33-39
studies of the literary tradition, 61-66
Sulieman, Susan, 32
Swift, Jonathan, 1, 21, 24, 50, 142

Taine, Hippolyte, 47
Tate, Allen, 13
Taylor, Edward, 72
Tennyson, Alfred, 76, 110
tense, 179
thesis, 140
Thomas, Brook, 54-55
Thoreau, Henry David, 76-77, 117
Tillyard, E. M. W., 49
titles, 176-179
Todorov, Tzvetan, 22, 24, 124
Tompkins, Jane, 32, 40
tragedy, 19-20
Trilling, Lionel, 47, 55
Twain, Mark, 103

Unamuno, Miguel de, 103-104

Van Ghent, Dorothy, 124, 127-128
Van Laun, H., 47
Vaughn, Henry, 64
Vinson, James, 150
Virgil, 62, 75
Vizenor, Gerald, 95

Wagner-Martin, Linda, 163
Walker, Alice, 87
Walpole, Horace, 23
Walton, Izaak, 57
Ward, Jerry W., Jr., 98
Warren, Austin, 24
Warren, Robert Penn, 12, 14, 17
Wasson, Richard, 75
Watson, George, 161
Watt, Ian, 78

Webster, Grant, 17
Weimann, Robert, 52
Weiner, Edmund S., 164
Wellek, René, 24
Weston, Jessie, 104
White, E. B., 133
White, John J., 104
Whitman, Walt, 76
Williams, Aubrey, 61
Williams, Charles, 128-129
Williamson, George, 63-64
Wilson, F. P., 159
Wimsatt, W. K., 13, 56
Winters, Yvor, 73

Woodhouse, A. S. P., 55
Woodress, James, 162
Woodring, Carl, 68-69, 79-80
Woolf, Virginia, 58, 87, 88-89, 91
Wordsworth, William, 80, 116, 122-123, 136
World Wide Web, 151
works cited, list of, 186-190
Wright, Andrew, 144, 149, 152, 159
Wright, Richard, 98

*Year's Work in English Studies,* 149, 152, 163
Yeats, W. B., 13-14
Young, R. V., 17